in **DETAIL** Building Skins

in **DETAIL**

Building Skins

New enlarged edition

Christian Schittich (Ed.)

with essays contributed by
Christian Schittich
Werner Lang
Roland Krippner

Edition DETAIL – Institut für internationale
Architektur-Dokumentation GmbH
München

Birkhäuser – Publishers for Architecture
Basel · Boston · Berlin

Editor: Christian Schittich
Co-Editor: Andrea Wiegelmann
Editorial services: Alexander Felix,
Michaela Linder, Melanie Schmid, Cosima Strobl, Miryam Thomann

Translation German/English:
Peter Green
Ingrid Taylor

Drawings: Kathrin Draeger, Norbert Graeser, Marion Griese, Silvia Hollmann,
Claudia Hupfloher, Nicola Kollmann, Elisabeth Krammer,
Sabine Nowak, Andrea Saiko

DTP: Peter Gensmantel, Andrea Linke, Roswitha Siegler, Simone Soesters

A specialist publication from Redaktion DETAIL
This book is a cooperation between
DETAIL – Review of Architecture and
Birkhäuser – Publishers for Architecture

A CIP catalogue record for this book is available
from the Library of Congress, Washington D.C., USA

Bibliographic information published by Die Deutsche Bibliothek
The Deutsche Bibliothek lists this publication in the Deutsche
Nationalbibliografie; detailed bibliographic data is available on the Internet at
<http://dnb.ddb.de>.

This book is also available in a German language edition
(ISBN 10: 3-7643-7633-3, ISBN 13: 978-3-7643-7633-8).

© 2006 Institut für internationale Architektur-Dokumentation GmbH & Co. KG,
P.O. Box 33 06 60, D-80066 München, Germany and
Birkhäuser – Publishers for Architecture, P.O. Box 133, CH-4010 Basel,
Switzerland

Printed on acid-free paper produced from chlorine-free pulp (TCF ∞)

Printed in Germany
Reproduction:
Martin Härtl OHG, München
Printing and binding:
Kösel GmbH & Co. KG, Altusried-Krugzell

ISBN 10: 3-7643-7640-6
ISBN 13: 978-3-7643-7640-6

9 8 7 6 5 4 3 2 1

Contents

Shell, Skin, Materials
Christian Schittich   8

Is it all "just" a facade?
The functional, energetic and structural
aspects of the building skin
Werner Lang   28

The Building Skin as Heat- and
Power Generator
Roland Krippner   48

Materials in the building skin –
from material to construction   60

Documentation Centre in Hinzert
Wandel Hoefer Lorch + Hirsch, Saarbrücken   70

Museum Liner in Appenzell
Gigon/Guyer, Zurich   74

House in Dornbirn
Oskar Leo Kaufmann + Albert Rüf, Dornbirn   76

Administration Building in Heilbronn
Dominik Dreiner, Gaggenau   80

Cycling Stadium in Berlin
Dominique Perrault, Paris
Reichert, Pranschke, Maluche, Munich
Schmidt-Schicketanz und Partner, Munich   86

Glasgow Science Centre
Building Design Partnership, Glasgow   92

Service Centre in Munich
Staab Architects, Berlin   94

Pavilion in Amsterdam
Steven Holl Architects, New York   98

Micro-Compact Home in Munich
Horden, Cherry, Lee Architects, London
Lydia Haack + John Höpfner Architekten,
Munich   102

Selfridges Department Store in Birmingham
Future Systems, London   104

A Summer Space
Johl, Jozwiak, Ruppel, Berlin   110

Eden Project near St. Austell
Nicholas Grimshaw & Partners, London   112

Allianz Arena in Munich
Herzog & de Meuron, Basel   114

Japanese Pavilion in Hanover
Shigeru Ban Architects, Tokyo   120

Factory Hall in Bobingen
Florian Nagler Architekten, Munich   126

House in Zurndorf
PPAG Architekten, Vienna   132

House near Tokyo
Shigeru Ban Architects, Tokyo   134

Prada Flagship Store in Tokyo
Herzog & de Meuron, Basel   138

Church in Munich
Allmann Sattler Wappner Architekten,
Munich   142

Administration Building in Kronberg
Schneider + Schumacher, Frankfurt/Main   150

Trade-Fair Tower in Hanover
Architects: Herzog + Partner, Munich   158

Administration Building in Wiesbaden
Herzog + Partner, Munich   164

Federal Environment Agency in Dessau
sauerbruch hutton, Berlin   168

Museum of Hiroshige Ando in Batoh
Kengo Kuma and Associates, Tokyo   174

Passenger Shipping Terminal in Yokohama
Foreign Office Architects, London
Farshid Moussavi, Alejandro Zaera Polo   178

Library in Delft
mecanoo architecten, Delft   182

Extension of Villa Garbald in Castasegna
Miller & Maranta, Basle   186

Academy of Music in Santiago de Compostela
Antón García-Abril, Madrid   190

The architects   194
Authors   197
Illustration credits   198

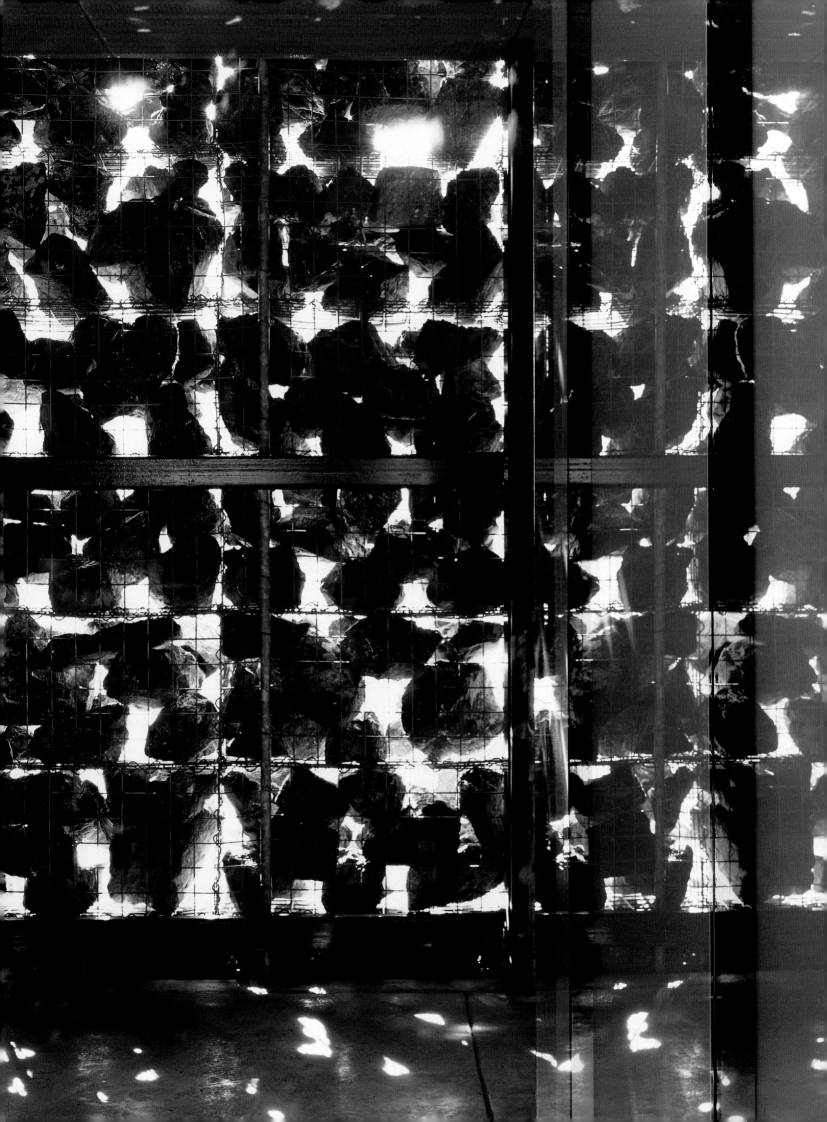

Shell, Skin, Materials

Christian Schittich

All eyes on the building skin

A large sculptural volume covered with air-filled "cushions" that light up at night for added dramatic effect, interwoven strips of gleaming stainless steel as a building skin, and transportable micro homes clad in aluminium panels covered with plastic sheeting – since the first edition of "In DETAIL Building Skins" was published, many more new and exciting examples of innovative architecture have emerged. Everywhere there is an upsurge in experimentation, boundaries are being tested and visual conventions called into question. More than ever attention is focusing on new materials and concepts.
As a transition between inside and outside – between the building and the urban space – the building skin plays an especially important role. First and foremost it provides protection from the elements, demarcates private property and creates privacy. But its aesthetic and cultural function is just as important. The building skin – and especially the facade – is the calling card of a building and its designer. Set into context, it characterizes the face of a city. No wonder that it draws more attention than any other building component.
The ideas established by Modernism stipulate that the external appearance of a building should reflect its internal life. Harmony should reign between form and function, inside and outside. Recently, this demand has been questioned with growing intensity. For as the building skin was separated from the load-bearing structure, it became a curtain, pure skin. To begin with this was expressed in the smooth, frequently sterile curtain walls, which defined our urban environments for so long. Most recently, however, the surface – and hence its material – has become the central focus of investigation. But the emphasis on the surface goes hand in hand with the risk of superficiality. The building skin may inadvertently become no more than attention-seeking packaging.
It isn't always easy to draw the line between a useful skin and ornamental packaging. Even in the heyday of Modernism, the demands for honesty and truthfulness to the material were difficult to fulfil. Today, as technical requirements grow ever more complex and challenging and insulation guidelines increasingly rigorous, nearly every external skin becomes a multi-layered system (whose surfaces rarely give us any insight into the interior life of the building). At any rate, how does one maintain the postulate of reflecting uses on the outside, when these uses change several times over the life cycle of a modern building? Or when, as is more and more frequently the case, the brief demands flexible spaces for different uses from the very beginning (to satisfy the needs of the investor)?

In the fast-paced information age, our perception has also changed, marked by a flood of flickering, colourful images. It is fascinating to observe how vastly different the reactions of individual architects are to this particular aspect. Some adapt to these new perceptions and react with equally colourful, serigraphed images on brittle glass. Or with flickering media facades and illuminated screens. Others, however, look back to the quality of ancient building materials – massive natural stone or exposed concrete, untreated timber and brick masonry, to demonstrate the solid physical presence of a building in an increasingly virtual world. Between these extremes, lies a third, equally contemporary path: the building skin as a responsive skin, as one component of a sustainable low-energy concept. This begins with simple folding and sliding shutters or with the popular moveable louvres and culminates in multi-layered glass facades equipped with a multitude of devices for shading and glare protection, light deflection, heat and energy gain. Newly developed materials are being tested, materials with improved properties and a performance that is capable of reacting flexibly to the external conditions. The term smart or intelligent materials is becoming the architects' mantra.
In a time when we are faced with diminishing stocks of raw materials and growing CO_2 emissions, this third approach is increasingly important. It seems to offer the best of both worlds: contemporary facade design without running the risk of superficial ornamentation (although, admittedly, these boundaries are not clearly drawn).
Given all these possibilities, the topic of "building skins" is as fascinating today as it has rarely been in the history of architecture. Wherever we look, we encounter unbounded joy in experimentation: testing boundaries, querying traditional perceptions, searching for new materials and concepts.

This present publication is dedicated to presenting a wide spectrum of the latest examples of external skins, from innovative climate facades to new materials. In addition to aesthetic qualities, we shall highlight the structural and constructional details in context. "True" skins were deliberately included – that is, buildings where roof and wall are one continuous element without visible transition.
For this current second edition, we have completely revised the first volume of "Building Skins" and added many new examples. The success of the first edition, which was sold worldwide in many different languages, prompted the publisher and the editorial team to do justice to this very popular and topical theme by bringing out a new edition.

From roofed shelter to curtain wall – A short history of the external skin

The cladding principle
Man builds a house as shelter from the elements, wind and rain, cold or excessive heat. He wants to draw a line around his property, create his own private sphere. But what came first: the roof or the wall? Did the original building skin serve primarily as a ceiling enclosure to provide weather protection or as a lateral enclosure to keep roaming wild animals at bay? This debate originated mostly with Gottfried Semper, who held that the animal pen, a fence woven from branches and twigs, was the origin of the wall, and hence of architectural space. In his seminal work "The Style"[1] in the mid 19th century, Semper refers to the common origin of cladding and spatial art. Semper divides architecture into load-bearing structure and cladding – a theory that would have a far-reaching influence on Modernism (through Otto Wagner, among others) and which is as pertinent today as it was then.
A more developed, but equally ancient form of construction in the Semperian sense are the round tents of some nomadic tribes, such as the Jurts among the Turkish tribes or the ancient Mongolian tribes (Fig. 1.2).
These typologies have survived to this day in the steppes of Central Asia and are distinguished, like others, by their rigorous separation of load-bearing structure and shell. Since time immemorial, however, people have also erected load-bearing external walls. The determining factor in the evolution of different building methods was the availability of local building materials, as well as the lifestyle in response to the local environment, thus the lifestyle of cattle-raising nomads or settled farmers.

At first building skins were entirely oriented towards fulfilling specific functions. It didn't take long, however, before people began to decorate the building skin as lovingly as they did their own clothing. To begin with this applied to simple homes, and especially to the monuments of different eras and cultures, equally true for elaborately frescoed Greek and Chinese temples or Islamic palaces and mosques. The European Antiquity transformed the facade (from lat. facies / face) into a unique showcase with which public buildings presented themselves to the urban space. In the Renaissance, especially, facades began to separate from the house; that is, they are placed in front of an old church or palace as a new "cloak" (Fig. 1.5). They fulfil a primarily aesthetic purpose: attractive packaging, not infrequently in connection with communicating messages. The design of facades in the classic sense, their proportion, fenestration, division by means of architraves, columns and rusticated ashlar stones, has been the main focus of architecture for many centuries in addition to interior design.

The external envelope opens up
The relation of window to wall – of open and closed surface – is one of the principle themes of the external skin and architecture. To begin with, it would seem, our ancestors had a true love of the dark, the mystic. Small openings in the wall were not only determined by construction methods in many traditional building styles – for in principle it is difficult to puncture the wall with large window openings in a massive stone or sunbaked clay structure – but also out of a desire for protection and shelter. Man yearns for his cave.

Moreover, in times when glass was still a rarity, openings were the primary source of energy loss, and this alone dictated that they should be as small as possible. As architecture was increasingly liberated from the constraints of the load-bearing wall, coupled with advances in glass manufacture and technology, appreciation for light in interior spaces increased as well. The original, instinctual preference for secretive, dark spaces gradually gave way to a desire for illumination.

Sacred buildings in the Gothic demonstrate the first attempts to create generous openings in the stone-faced shells. The formerly compact volumes of cathedrals and churches are dissolved into a skeleton of load-bearing and supporting elements. The building skin evolves into a structure composed of ribs and vaults, masonry surfaces, flying buttresses and pillars. Large sections of the external wall are liberated from their load-bearing function and freed for the insertion of huge windows covered in tracery: architectural space opens towards the light. Translucent, coloured glass which allows light to penetrate but obscures vision becomes a filter between inside and outside, but also a giant image carrier lit from behind.
But in housing windows would remain small for a long time to come (with the exception of the early bands of windows in framework construction, where larger openings are possible by linking many smaller formats due to the post-and-beam structure). Their existential significance as a link between inside and outside is expressed in the attentive treatment and special emphasis with coloured or structural frames. From the Middle Ages onwards, most windows are glazed, although the material remains a luxury until the Industrial Age. Hence, the glazed areas and formats are still moderate in size. The necessary muntins serve as operating elements and also create a lively pattern of light and shadow. In combination with the inhomogeneous glass panes they form a translucent element in the skin – a phenomenon that is once again current.

1.2

The traditional window is rarely a plain hole in the wall. It is nearly always one component in a spatially layered transitional zone. Curtains, blinds, folding shutters, window sills and flower boxes each fulfil a different task and create a "gentle" threshold from the outside to the interior. This threshold was treated in a unique manner in the traditional Japanese house (Fig. 1.3). Large sections of the external wall consist of paper-faced, light-permeable sliding doors with timber frames. When opened, they create a fluid transition from the garden into the living space. Wide roof edges and a veranda around the entire periphery of the house enlarge this transitional zone.

Iron and glass – new materials revolutionize the building skin
In the 19th century, the Industrial Revolution changed the world. New materials and production methods opened up entirely new opportunities – iron and glass conquered architecture. The process of dissolving the building skin – its de-materialization – is directly linked to the progressive independence from its load-bearing function. Important impulses are provided by the builders of greenhouses, by gardeners and engineers. The history of the greenhouse is an important chapter in the history of European architecture, even though many were created without the participation of architects. The pioneers of glass and iron architecture, John Claudius Loudon, for example, or Joseph Paxton, designed their daring structures primarily in accordance with purely functional aspects. To achieve a maximum amount of incident sunlight, they try to reduce the massive wall components to a minimum. Ornamentation, a common feature in the architecture of their day, is almost entirely absent in these structures. Often they utilize the glass panes to provide the necessary bracing for the construction, which leads to a filigree structure. Thus in the palm house, which the brothers Bailey erected in around 1830, probably with the help of Loudon, in Bicton Gardens in Devon, England (Fig. 1.7). The bent glass skin is very much like a membrane in this building, so thin and smooth is its execution. The highlight of transparent buildings was no doubt Paxton's Crystal Palace, constructed for the World Fair in London in 1851 (Fig. 1.6). Every aspect of this groundbreaking structure was developed in accordance with the requirements of the task, the conditions imposed by scale and span, the costs, prefabrication and assembly times. Only a "non-architect" like Paxton could be as innocent in his design for this particular task. Only a gardener, as he was, could so casually negate the formal canon. London's Crystal Palace fascinated everyone in Europe and precipitated a trend for glass exhibition buildings in other cities. Other building tasks, too, were soon after realized in transparent structures composed of iron and glass, such as train station terminals or large shopping arcades. Once again many of the daring, even visionary designs were created by engineers and designers, while the architects themselves seemed content with decorating facades and entrance structures with traditional styles, with ornamentation that ignores the changes that time has long since ushered in.

1.3

1.4

1.1   Dominus Winery in California, 1998; Herzog & de Meuron
1.2   Kirghiz yurt, the Pamirs
1.3   Traditional house, Japan
1.4   Traditional wood window in Bhaktapur, Nepal

11

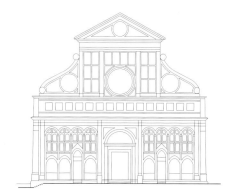

1.5

The transparent facade

Functional and commercial demands influenced the increasing openness in urban facades. In the middle of the 19th century, the first tall buildings with iron load-bearing structures were erected in the United States at a time when open interior spaces, supported only by piers, were very much in vogue. Skeleton construction made it possible to simultaneously open up the external walls with large windows in metal frames. To begin with, this approach is predominantly chosen for warehouses, factories and other purpose buildings, where architecture doesn't play such an important role.

Soon after, the breakthrough occurred in Chicago. Two major conflagrations (in 1871 and in 1874), which happened to coincide with a time of accelerated economic growth, unleashed a building boom. Real estate values in the downtown area skyrocketed, and this, together with the development of the necessary building technology (steel skeleton construction and elevators), led to the creation of the first high-rises. But the traditional massive external walls proved to be uneconomical and also offered few opportunities for advantageous lighting. The logical next step was to use iron and glass in ever more generous expanses on the facades of the new representative office buildings. Admittedly: the early high-rises in Chicago betray how difficult it was for architects to relinquish traditional principles of design, the new building tasks notwithstanding. Thus Henry H. Richardson's natural stone facade on the Marshall Field Store (1885–87) is still very much reminiscent of Roman Antiquity and reveals little with regard to the steel structure that lies hidden behind it (Fig. 1.9). Daniel Hudson Burnham's facades on the Reliance Building (1894) are far more transparent by comparison and also already divided into horizontal sections in correspondence with the floor slabs. This is a design principle which is also applied in the Schlesinger and Mayer Store (later: Carson, Pirie Scott, 1899–1906) designed by Louis H. Sullivan (Fig. 1.10). The impressive effect of this building is the result of the clean division by means of horizontal lines, which make the construction of the load-bearing structure visible on the facade. Here, Sullivan demonstrates his leitmotif, namely that the exterior of a building must be an expression of its internal structure and function, that is, there must be a correspondence between content and external form ("form follows function"). Yet Sullivan is equally convinced of the necessity of ornamentation. He is intent on enriching the building in its details, adding to the strength of its expression. But in doing so, his ornamentation is never superficial: it is always an integral component of the whole.

The rise and fall of the curtain wall

The growing independence of the external skin from its structural function leads of necessity to its complete separation from the load-bearing structure. The roots of this developed are found in the Chicago of the 19th century, even though the facades of its early high-rises are still realized on the level of load-bearing structures, that is, the glazing is set into fields delimited by the floor slabs and the pillars. Similar to the early metal facades, the first skins that are fully freed from the load-bearing structure (later called curtain wall) were realized in

1.6

1.5 Santa Maria Novella in Florence, facade, 1470; Leon Battista Alberti
1.6 Crystal Palace in London, 1851; Joseph Paxton
1.7 Palm house in Bicton Gardens in Devon, England

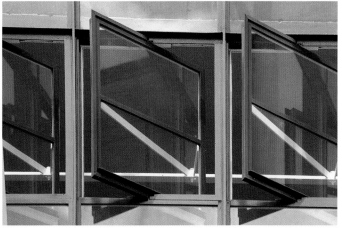

1.8

1.9

1.10

industrial buildings created without any obvious participation of trained architects. Once again, function drives the agenda: to achieve a maximum of light, the external walls are glazed as much as possible. One of the earliest examples is the east facade of the Steiff factory building in Giengen in southern Germany – a design that was most likely initiated by Richard Steiff, the grandson of the company founder. The external layer of the double-layered facade composed of translucent glass panels is suspended in front of the structure and stretches across three storeys and around the corners as a smooth skin, divided into even sections. The internal skin lies between the supporting pillars.

In the building for the shoe last factory in Alfeld on the Leine River (Fagus Works, 1911–19) Walter Gropius succeeds in collaboration with Adolf Meyer in suspending a curtain wall in front of an industrial hall as a filigree, transparent skin, a skin that no longer has any load-bearing function and clearly announces this freedom. Gropius demonstrates the principle of the "curtain wall" by dispensing with corner piers, achieving a fully glazed corner across three floors.

In 1918, Willis Jefferson Polk is the first to suspend a glass curtain wall in front of an inner-city office building (Fig. 1.13), although here, too, functional reasons were probably paramount. This building does not succeed in emphasizing the principle of the "curtain wall" as Gropius did in the Fagus Works, which were created in the same period, or in the structurally open corners of the Bauhaus (Fig. 1.8). The most daring execution of a glass facade in this period is Mies van der Rohe's design for a high-rise in Berlin (1922), which would, however, remain an abstract vision.

Nearly 30 years would then pass before Mies was able to realize his first high-rise on Lake Shore Drive in Chicago (1951) although much of the transparency and lightness of the designs from the 1920s is lost by then. In his American high-rise facades, Mies re-interpreted the curtain wall and imposed his own aesthetics. Unabashedly, he would go so far as to suspend profiles that had no structural function in front of the facades, like the "double-T" sections on Lake Shore Drive Apartments to emphasize the notion of "reaching for the sky" – the verticality of the building (Fig. 1.12). For the Seagram Building in New York (1958) he no longer used mass-produced components (the sectioning profiles are now integrated into the glass level), but expensive customized components in bronze, which enabled him to influence the cross section. All glass panes are tinted golden brown through the addition of iron oxide and selenium. The result is that the volume no longer appears transparent and light, but almost opaque: he seems to have abandoned the transparency he strove for in the 1920s.

A few years earlier, the architects Skidmore, Owings and Merrill (SOM) had created the prototype for a light curtain wall on a high-rise in the Lever Building (1952) diagonally across from the Seagram Building on New York's Park Avenue (Fig. 1.11). A delicate, regular network of polished stainless steel profiles, infilled with semi-reflective glazing with an iridescent blue-green sheen, clothes the facade, which appears completely detached from the load-bearing structure and is only linked by discrete point fixings to transfer the wind loads. The radically minimized profiles lend an air of lightness that can only be achieved with fixed single glazing. The result is a building that is hermetically closed on all sides without any operable windows, fully reliant upon artificial ventilation and air-conditioning.

As different as these two solutions are, they contributed in equal measure to the rapid proliferation of the curtain wall. Mies, in particular, the megastar obsessed with perfecting specific formal aspects yet responding with his language of forms neither to the location nor to the building task, contributes with this attitude to worldwide plagiarism of his architecture. This mass-production, however, culminates not only in a loss of originality but also in the loss of the love of detail. Until the early 1970s, glass curtain wall buildings spread around the world under the influence of the International Style with unprecedented speed. The office building has become an important building task and the glass facade with its grid has become its primary symbol. Moreover, the smooth, uniform curtain wall is promoted by the proliferation of anonymous investment architecture. Facade creations that began as creative, elegant solutions degenerate into monotonous surfaces.

From the mid-sixties onwards, the new method emerging in the US of fixing external glazing by means of load-bearing silicon and other innovative fixing techniques contribute to these changes. For they make it possible to clad the entire building shell – roof and facades – in the same smooth skin. All conceivable geometric forms could now be enclosed with unswerving regularity. A seductive idea at a time when the never-ending, identical angular cubes were increasingly criticized and semantics began to gain new importance in architecture. The formal eclecticism that followed seemed to respond to the investors' and the clients' demands for unique, image-building structures; however, it too became a subject of criticism. Critical voices were raised even more as awareness of energy efficiency increased in the wake of the oil crises of the 1970s, for the smooth, sealed glass containers were generally just that: encased in glass without operable windows and reliant upon artificial air-conditioning. The curtain wall in its original sense had inevitably reached its limitations.

A variety of architectural styles followed the International Style. Each reacted in a different way: Post-Modernism looked back to historic examples; Constructivism questioned traditional orders; and the proponents of High-Tech Design responded with structural components. But all share one common goal; to once again give the building skin a face.

1.11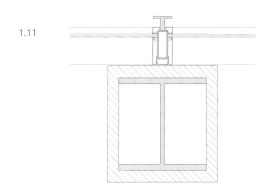

1.12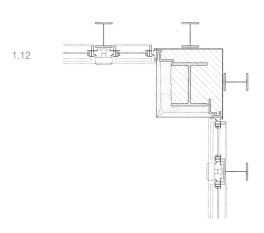

1.13

1.8   Bauhaus in Dessau, 1926; Walter Gropius
1.9   Marshall Field Store in Chicago, 1887; Henry H. Richardson
1.10 Schlesinger and Mayer Store (later Carson Pirie Scott Building)
        in Chicago, 1904; Louis H. Sullivan
1.11 Lever Building in New York, facade detail,1952;
        Skidmore, Owings & Merrill
1.12 Lake Shore Drive Apartments in Chicago, corner detail, 1951;
        Ludwig Mies van der Rohe
1.13 Halladie Building in San Francisco, 1918; Willis J. Polk

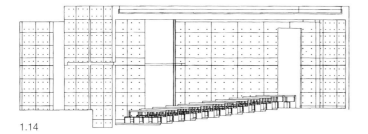

1.14

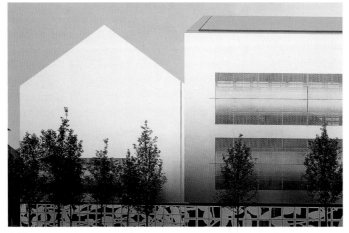

1.15

1.16

Material aesthetic and ornamentation

Material as concept

With their matt-shimmering skin of bead-blasted stainless steel the three Südwestmetall buildings (Fig. 1.15) blend into the urban surroundings of Reutlingen in terms of volume and proportions. The smooth expanse of this exquisite surface material, fitted with barely visible joints, reflects the colours of the sky and the environment – it is an outer skin with no tangible depth, a skin that seems to defy the eye. Designed by Allmann Sattler Wappner, the buildings respond in scale to their location, but play a subtle game of perception with the observer. Gleaming metal was also used in another project for the same client in Heilbronn (Fig. 1.16 and p. 80ff.) by Dominik Dreiner. This time it was a new type of mesh woven from narrow strips of stainless steel wrapped seamlessly around the building volume to produce changing light and colour moods. Both examples show a comprehensive approach to the building skin that is becoming more and more common. Namely one in which the roof and the wall have the same surface and blend into each another. Above all, however, these examples are illustrative of an approach to the use of materials that is both original and contemporary, one in which the surface quality and the characteristics of the material become the focus of architectural observation. The material itself, it seems, is often the concept.

With the increasing focus on the material, the issue is no longer the material truthfulness which Modernism dictated (and which never truly existed at any rate) but also the desired appearance of material, aesthetic and tactile qualities, the effect of colour and texture. Everywhere the aura of traditional building materials such as natural stone, brick and wood is being rediscovered and celebrated. Materials are being left untreated and uncoated, and thereby permitted to show their true character. This applies to visual concrete as much as to rough, "rusty" Cor-Ten steel and split stone. In our increasingly virtual and fast-living world, there seems to be a real need for the tangible, the real, for structure, and for spaces that have emotional quality.

Alongside this recourse to "naturalness", industrial building products such as plywood, fibre cement, plastic panels and expanded metal mesh are emerging from the shadows to which they had been condemned for years and rising to the surface even on grander or public buildings, moving into the limelight of visual perception. Placed in a hitherto unfamiliar context, they are being accorded new meaning. Parallels to this sensual use of humble materials can be found in the visual arts, one need only think of Arte Povera, for example, or the oeuvre of Josef Beuys. Furthermore, products from other industrial sectors, hitherto unused in construction, are being embraced by architecture. The joy in experimentation finds expression in countless innovations. However, the material use isn't always successfully integrated into the overall concept. Too often, what results is mere decoration of skins that are separated from the building, more empty shell than skin.

Concrete with character, sensory stone

Contemporary architecture is indeed no stranger to deliberate and considered material treatment. Tadao Ando, to name but one example, has been using authentic and substantial building materials for nearly thirty years, materials like untreated wood or (in the tradition of Le Corbusier or Louis I. Kahn) the raw power of fair-faced concrete (Fig. 1.14). Tadao Ando himself insists that he is less interested in expressing the nature of the material than in using it to create architectural space, to set moods.[2] Many of his best buildings feature surfaces that aren't entirely plane or level, but slightly curved or undulating within the individual formwork panels, which produces a sophisticated liveliness in the surfaces through the play of shadow and light on these subtle gradations.

With his buildings at the end of the 1980s, Ando contributed to a Renaissance of visual concrete. Initially the concepts that seem to inspire world-wide followers for years to come are generally found in his increasingly large-scale projects: totally smooth surfaces, divided rigorously according to the grid of the formwork panels and perforated by a uniform pattern of true and sometimes "feigned" tie holes. In parallel with this, however, diverse protagonists are experimenting with the material and looking for contemporary, specific forms of expression. As part of a new consciousness about material, concrete is increasingly featured in the full range of its visual forms. By using coarse shuttering boards, fluting or hammering it acquires a highly effective, rough charm, adding colouring pigments or certain aggregates generates a special material quality. In their "Schaulager", a kind of art warehouse and showroom (Fig. 1.17) in Basle, Herzog and de Meuron had the external walls beaten with a hammer to retain a mud-brick-like character. And Basle-based architects Morger, Degelo, Kerez made the concrete on the Art Museum in Liechtenstein (Fig. 1.19) look like marble by mixing green and black basalt chippings, pebbles and black pigments into the material, and then carefully polishing the surfaces.

"Real" stone, by contrast, is seen nowadays almost exclusively in the surface, in the form of thin-cut slabs, or even as millimetre-thin veneers stuck onto aluminium panels, of the kind that we see on countless facades and foyers of banks and insurance companies. Peter Zumthor (like Tadao Ando, a virtuoso in dealing with material) is not content with this. His buildings derive their impressive strength from the deliberate use of a few, largely untreated building materials: stone, timber or concrete. Zumthor aims to bare the "true nature of these materials, beyond any cultural connotations" and allow "materials to sing and glow in the architecture".[3] In works such as the stone thermal baths in Vals (Fig. 1.18) or the chapel at Sumvitg, he chooses his materials on the basis of local traditions, rooting the building in its environment. His thermal baths in Vals, for example, looks like a monolith rising up out of the mountain, whereby the stone – in the form of solid walls of local quartzite or lining the floor and sides of pools in the same material – leads inside and out to many aesthetic and sensory experiences. Jacques Herzog and Pierre de Meuron also celebrate the sensory qualities of stone in their Dominus Winery (Fig. 1.1) in Napa Valley, California, but with a quite different concept. These architects from Basle have explored the themes of material and surface to a

1.17

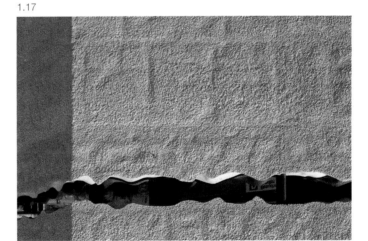

1.18

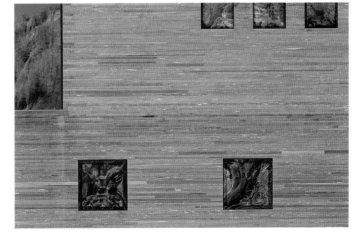

1.14 Church with Light in Ibaraki, Japan, 1989; Tadao Ando
1.15 Administration buildings of Südwestmetall in Reutlingen, 2002;
      Allmann Sattler Wappner Architekten
1.16 Administration buildings of Südwestmetall in Heilbronn, 2004;
      Dominik Dreiner
1.17 "Schaulager" in Münchenstein/Basle, 2003; Herzog & de Meuron
1.18 "Felsentherme" thermal baths in Vals, 1996; Peter Zumthor

degree matched by few others. Again and again they come up with surprising, new interpretations of different materials (some of which are presented in another context in this article). In the case of Dominus Winery they also use the natural stone found in the local environment as a way of integrating the building into its landscape. Yet the stone walls here do not have a solid, fixed appearance, but instead the air of a semi-transparent veil. Gabions, wire baskets filled with rubblestones, of the kind normally used to shore up slopes, are employed as the external skin, or are placed in front of facades; variously spaced – sometimes close, sometimes further apart – they enable the light to shine through. The stone, behind which there is sometimes a layer of glass (depending on room function), is used more like a skin than a traditional wall. In addition its storage mass is harnessed to even out temperature differences, important in a wine store located in a climate of hot days and cool nights. It is a stone facade construction that looks both modern and archaic.

Transparency, reflection, colour – different aspects of glass
The nature and contrast of two different materials – concrete and glass – becomes an impressive theme in Peter Zumthor's Kunsthaus in Bregenz (Fig. 1.21). The monolithic core, where poured concrete on walls and floors is polished, without coating and hence powerfully present in its materiality, is wrapped in a scaly cloak of etched glass. This "cloak" is structurally wholly independent of the building and assumes all essential functions of the external skin – from weather protection to daylight regulation. The structural separation of house and shell (visually, the components are linked by the etched glass ceilings) allows the concrete in the core – now freed from all functions of the external wall – to fully develop its sculptural character. At the same time, the architect succeeds in giving us a stunning visualization of the material qualities of the invisible material glass. Translucent but not transparent, the structurally uniform shell changes in appearance according to the position of the observer, daylight and light conditions. At times a mirror or gleaming, sun-reflecting surface, it appears dull and opaque on other days. Seen in a contre-jour lighting, the roof edge stands out from the volume like a glowing crown: contours merge, the transition between building and sky is blurred.

Glass, like few other materials, is the very symbol of the modern facade. Not only because we see it on just about every building, but because of the tremendous advances that have been made in glass technology over the last two decades. The previously unthinkable is now possible. For a long time absolute transparency was one of the biggest goals of modern architecture. Nowadays, however, with all the possibilities opened up by modern technology, the focus is less on dissolving the facade than on the material properties of a material that is invisible by nature: rendering its density and materiality visible. This also includes a thorough exploration of the varied range that lies between transparency and translucency – between being able to see through and shining through. This can be achieved by overlapping glass louvres or perforated metal sheet in front of glass, by printing, etching or coating the glass surfaces. All of these options and designs transform glass into a building material that seems more suited than any other to represent the complexity of modern society.

1.19

But what should architecture that reflects the Electronic Age look like? The Japanese architect Toyo Ito explores this topic in theory[4] and practice. Ito's key building is the media centre in Sendai, Japan (Fig. 1.20). Already the competition brief formulated the demand for a futuristic public building for the twenty-first century. In line with this requirement, in Toyo Ito's media centre, the internal floor plan functions are no longer clearly defined; instead, he has created areas geared almost entirely towards flexible uses. Hence, the building skin can hardly reflect the internal structure of the building. But it does represent its use as a site for electronic media and thus becomes by extension the symbol of the Computer Age, the virtual world. Toyo Ito experiments with varying degrees of transparency, which he achieves by printing different grids onto the glass surfaces, using figured glass and overlapping glazing panels in differing layers. The multi-layered spatial impressions that result, the mirroring effects and reflections, contribute towards translating virtual reality into real architecture.

A good decade or so beforehand, Jean Nouvel was one of the first architects to utilize the design potential of printed glass. His competition project for the Tour sans Fin in the La Défense arrondissement of Paris (1989) proposed a dematerialization of the structure by means of screen-printed glazing. The tower, which was never realized, was to be massive and rooted in the earth at the bottom and dissolve increasingly towards its crown by means of increasing density in the printed pattern, which would reflect more and more nuances of colour, an effect that the architect wanted to further enhance by using different types of glass. Herzog & de Meuron also use screen-printed glass to de-materialize the building volume of the new hospital pharmacy in Basle (Fig. 1.24). In this example, however, a uniform green dot pattern has been printed onto the glazed facade panels that envelop the entire structure all the way to the window reveals. The result is that the appearance changes according the distance of the observer from the building. From a distance the volume appears homogeneously green, up close one can discern the individual dots. The pattern is sufficiently coarse to reveal the insulating panels and fastening clips behind it: one has the feeling that the greenish veil reveals more than it obscures. The movement of the observer triggers a series of visual interference phenomena, which animate the volume and break up its hard-edged contours. The reflected images of the surrounding deciduous trees blend with the facades.

Matthias Sauerbruch and Louisa Hutton, too, did very careful calculations about the reflections on the glass. On the surface of the green-changing-to-red skin of the police and fire station in Berlin (see Fig. 2.4, p. 34, p. 67), they also reflect the neighbouring greenery. In other respects, of course, they pursue a quite different concept. They see colour as one of the key tools of expression in their architecture. In designing with glass, therefore, they are concerned less about transparency effects than about creating large colour patterns. And this hard see-through building material

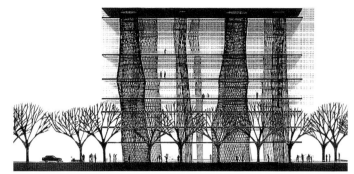

1.20

1.21

1.19 Art museum in Liechtenstein, 2000; Morger & Degelo, Kerez
1.20 Mediatheque in Sendai, 2001; Toyo Ito
1.21 Kunsthaus in Bregenz, 1997; Peter Zumthor

in particular has great potential for this, thanks to the recent advances in glass technology. By using coloured films in laminated glass, burning-in processes, and in particular the options opened up by screen-printing, all kinds of different effects can be obtained. The glass panels on the police and fire station are printed on the back with a grid of dots, a process in which almost any colour can be achieved through mixing, and a process which also gives a relatively neutral light in the interior.

David Adjaye uses the technique of laminating film into glass in his Idea Stores in London and so, too, does Rem Koolhaas in the Dutch Embassy in Berlin (Fig. 1.23). Both architects are relatively reserved in their use of colour – Adjaye in a repeating rhythm, Koolhaas in isolated areas, to add accent. But when the glass blocks of the embassy are backlit at night or when its conference room is bathed in deep blue light by day, the building exudes a sublime sensuality.

Plastic – an industrial material reinterpreted
In the Laban Centre of Modern Dance in London (Fig. 1.22) Herzog and de Meuron put on a spectacular display of the possibilities of industrial plastic. Here, too, subtle, understated use of colour plays a key role. On the outer skin of this dance institute these two material geniuses manage to turn simple webbed sheeting into a sophisticated, enigmatic creation whose contours blend into the sky. Only the backs of selected polycarbonate panels were coloured, which serves to further enhance the shimmering, pastel-like effect. Depending on the angle of the light and position of the observer, the material produces an ever-changing pattern of light moods, whereas in the interior the interplay with the second facade layer of translucent glass gives rise to a pleasant, delicate coloured light and a warm, positive atmosphere in the dance rooms.

Because of their product-immanent structure, i.e. as a filling between panes of glass, webbed inserts, corrugated sheet or fibre-reinforced, plastics are often well suited to transporting light moods or especially translucent effects. For decades, however, their use in building was restricted to purpose-built structures of lesser importance, to garages and canopies. Recently this has all changed. With improved ageing characteristics and a lower price, but also because of the material's aesthetic interest, plastic has earned itself a firm place on the facades of more prestigious buildings. Alongside the mostly panel-shaped semi-finished products, plastics in the form of membranes, as translucent textile or highly transparent, paper-thin sheeting are also enjoying what could be described as a boom. This is an area in which great technological advances have been made in recent years, and it has prompted a fundamental reappraisal of the building skin. This

1.22

1.23

1.22 Laban Centre of Modern Dance in London, 2003; Herzog & de Meuron
1.23 Dutch Embassy in Berlin, 2003; Rem Koolhaas, OMA
1.24 ISP - Institut für Spitalpharmazie in Basle, 1998; Herzog & de Meuron
1.25 Finnish pavilion at Expo in Hanover;
      detail of building skin, 2000; SARC Architects
1.26 Dutch pavilion at Expo in Hanover,
      detail of building skin, 2000; MVRDV
1.27 Icelandic pavilion at Expo in Hanover,
      detail of building skin, 2000; Ami Pall Johannsson
1.28 Dutch pavilion at Expo in Hanover,
      detail of building skin, 2000; MVRDV

is true in particular for the new Munich football stadium (see p. 114ff; p. 65) which looks like a giant abstract sculpture lying in the landscape, but not giving any hint of its real dimensions. Its outer skin made up of rhomboid-shaped air-filled cushions covered in a transparent membrane is wrapped evenly around the whole building volume. Light and colour are integral parts of the basic concept, above all their effects at night. For that is when this stadium, built as the home to two rival Munich-based football clubs, lights up like an enormous lantern in the colour of the team which happens to be playing. If it's red, you know Bayern München fans will be filling the stands; if it's blue, then the Munich Lions are having a home game. White remains the option for games not involving local teams. Cleverly the planners of this stadium have fully exploited the possibilities of modern technology to produce a contemporary building skin, creating an iconic landmark out of the essentially characterless material plastic sheeting.

1.24

Another exciting membrane structure, although one with a very different concept and appearance, was created a few years before by Tokyo architect Shigeru Ban – the Japanese pavilion at Expo 2000 in Hanover (see p. 120ff). Originally Shigeru Ban intended to use only paper for the skin of the pavilion, a plan that was not able to be carried out because of fire prevention regulations, so he turned instead to a solution which involved laminating the ultra thin membrane with plastic. Despite this change of course, Ban succeeded in creating a technically daring construction with a sensual aura and futuristic character. Where high-tech is the fascinating aspect about the football stadium, it is low tech that intrigues us in this Japanese pavilion.

A showcase of building skins
Shigeru Ban's Japanese pavilion was one of the most outstanding examples at Expo of innovative approaches to the building skin, at an exhibition that was in any case a veritable fireworks display of exciting new technology and aesthetics in this area. Experimentation is after all an integral component of any World Fair, and that particular one was filled with all kinds of examples of different sheetings, membranes, printed and etched glass, metal mesh and other skins. Some architects even took up the motif of flowing movement and the resulting image changes, and featured it in their design. MvRdV of Rotterdam, for example, had water flowing over textiles at various points on their Dutch Pavilion, the movement of the water creating a multitude of kaleidoscopic patterns, a constant shift between transparency and translucency. The liquid here lends the outer skin the appearance of a structured veil which becomes a carrier of meaning by seeming to enclose a secret (Fig. 1.28). Even Iceland's clear "ice cube" comes alive through the motion of water, which flows across its blue membranes on all sides (Fig. 1.27).
Yet another experiment in the skin, albeit completely different but no less sophisticated, can be seen in the Pavilion of Christ at Expo (von Gerkan, Marg und Partner, Fig 1.30), which has been reassembled as part of a monastery in Volkenroda in Thuringia since the fair closed. The walls on either side of the cloister are filled with all manner of everyday objects – selected according to the motto of the Expo – and displayed between two panes of glass. The result is an abstract cycle of images, reminiscent of the stained-glass windows in Gothic cathedrals. Different materials and objects,

1.25

1.26
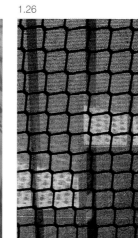

1.27

1.28

duck feathers and wood chippings, electric light bulbs and music tapes combine into a variety of patterns, casting a fascinating image of light and shadow onto the floor. The Hamburg-based architects thus bring out the essence of the objects, but also use the material and its structure as ornament.

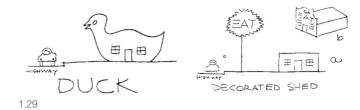

1.29

The decorated shell or the need for ornamentation
For nearly one hundred years, academic principles stated that architecture did not require ornamentation. Modernism had abolished it, or at least tried to abolish it. Nevertheless, even its leading proponents could not dispense entirely with decoration or at least tectonic ornament (see p. 14). Even Mies van Rohe's steel sections – superfluous from a structural perspective – are ultimately no more and no less than a kind of tectonic ornamentation. They have no other purpose than to provide structure (in the visual sense) to the building and to emphasize its verticality.
With its disdain for ornamentation, Modernism, which dedicated itself wholly to "the plastic effect of the building volume in light" instead of decoration, broke with a tradition that had endured for millennia. For people in all cultures around the world have decorated their homes since the beginning of time. This is true for monumental or public buildings and for residential buildings. And such ornamentation ranges from simple reliefs, to carvings, coloured tiles and elaborate frescoes, from the Greek or Chinese temple to the Arabic mosque, from the vernacular fresco painting in the European Alps to the azuelos, the coloured tiles used in Portugal.

In the 1960s, when urban buildings were increasingly covered in faceless, monotonous curtain walls, that is, when the skin had already been separated from the house and was moving towards degenerating into pure packaging, Robert Venturi substantiated this reality with his theory of the "decorated shed" (Fig. 1.29). Venturi divides the house into volume and facade, assigning the role of an autonomous meaning carrier to the facade. In contrast to the decorated shed he envisions a "duck", a building that derives its form from its function. The Post-Modernism of the 1970s is a first response to his challenge. Instead of addressing itself to the future, instead of taking the changed technological and societal conditions into account, however, this movement cast its eye backwards to the time before Modernism, when buildings still had a face (facade). This is probably also the reason why Post-Modernism didn't last. Like the trend that followed it, Constructivism, it shares the fate of all fashionable movements: it is transitory in nature.
Nowadays, however, the increasing fixation on the surface, together with innovative technology and the thirst for new fashions, is leading to an increase in the use of ornament and decoration to a level that has not been experienced for many years.
In an era of permanent sensory overload one has to create something new, something spectacular, to draw attention. As never before, the computer, the Internet and the new media have changed our aesthetic perception, our receptive capability and our options for designing. The colourful images, for example, are not only distributed globally in a matter of seconds, they are also copied and manipulated in countless variations. This cannot but influence architecture. In addition, there are new manufacturing processes and techniques,

1.30

especially in the context of glass coatings and the production of coloured glass and plastics, with colour gaining new significance. Colour is no longer used as monochrome accent, in the form of a wall painted in a strong colour, for example, but as decoration, to create colourful patterns.

This is evident, for example, in Francis Soler's apartment building in Paris (Fig. 1.31), directly across from the Bibliothèque Nationale. Soler decorates his rigorous, but carefully detailed box with colourful images superimposed onto the outermost of three glass layers: with details taken from a fresco by Giulio Romano in a Renaissance palazzo in Mantua! On each floor he adds another motif, stretched across two windows. Seen from the outside, the images create a light coloured pattern on the building (in daytime). From the inside, they appear like an oversized slide seen against the light – or like coloured glass windows in a Gothic cathedral (Fig. 1.32). But in contrast to the cathedrals they have no message to impart, no relation to the space. Meanwhile, the view of the outside is covered up, even distorted: occupants must live with the images, whether they want to or not. The building skin becomes fashionable packaging, clamouring for attention. Yet, unlike clothing, we can't just shed it whenever we feel the need to do so. Soler's uncompromising use of decoration thus also remains an extreme example, albeit one with great media impact.

The generally smaller buildings by Munich architects Hild and K. demonstrate a much more subtle treatment of ornamentation. They use ornamentation to explore boundaries, overthrow taboos and to provoke. In their small bus shelter in Landshut (Fig. 1.33) composed of sharp-edged Cor-Ten steel panels, which are self-supporting like a screen, ornamentation is a symbol for the randomness of cut-out patterns. For today's computer generated design and decoupage processes deliver any motif with equal ease regardless of whether it is a uniform grid or floral décor.

Jacques Herzog and Pierre de Meuron are true pioneers in using the building skin as an image carrier. With many of their buildings, even from a relatively early stage, these architects laid down a challenge to the theories of the modern movement, experimenting with the various possibilities of ornamentation (e.g. Ricola, Mulhouse), which for them "reflects the complexity of human understanding, including the dark, the criminal and the sexual moment"[5]. Herzog and de Meuron view architecture as an act of communication, not represented by fixed forms but by an oscillating field of perception[6], as a way of thinking that should offer many incentives for becoming aware of oneself and the world."[7] The exploration of material and surface is one of the principal themes in their architecture.

Their library of the Academy in Eberswalde (Fig. 1.35) is the most radical form of a decorated box. The severe, rectangular

1.31 1.32

1.33

1.29 Duck vs decorated shed, sketch; Robert Venturi
1.30 Pavilion of Christ at Expo in Hanover, now in Volkenroda, 2000;
      von Gerkan, Marg und Partner
1.31 House in Paris, 1997; Francis Soler
1.32 Chartres Cathedral, rose window in the facade of the north transept,
      c. 1240
1.33 Bus shelter in Landshut, 1997; Hild und Kaltwasser Architekten

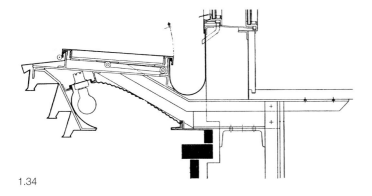

1.34

volume, clad in glass and prefabricated concrete panels, is covered on all sides with photographic reproductions. Each panel displays a photographic motif, each image is repeated 66 times in horizontal arrangement. From a distance, the two materials – glass and concrete – are difficult to tell apart. Up close, the glass is almost polished in appearance, while the concrete is restrainedly dull. In Eberswalde Herzog & de Meuron experiment with traditional perceptions and redefine the relationship of surface to volume by dissolving the facades into immaterial pictorial layers. They invited an artist, the photographer Thomas Ruff, to select the motifs of the photographs – perhaps, a questionable attempt at legitimization. The images are intended to tell a story and transform the facade into a projection screen. They are taken from history, science and art. Still: they communicate very little with regard to the use of the building.

No doubt, the architects achieved a provocative building with their library, which inspires comment and debate. At the same time, however, all this exuberant illustration does border on the realms of arbitrariness. What happens if the model designed by the leading figures of the architectural scene is duplicated hundred fold, if facades add to the flood of images that already exists?

A similar concept of decoration, although carried out on a somewhat more modest scale, is seen in Weil Arets' new university library in Utrecht (Fig. 1.36). He, too, joins the different materials of glass and concrete together, by covering them with the same pattern. Printed willow branches, which also have a role in screening the sun, lend the glass a delicate veil-like appearance; on the adjacent visual concrete surfaces they appear in the form of reliefs. In addition the architect uses the abstract plant motif to communicate a hidden message by referencing the green swathe that was originally planned for in front of the windows.

1.35

The facade in Utrecht, like the one in Eberswalde, wants to be more than a purely functional building envelope. When architects like Weil Arets, Jacques Herzog and Pierre de Meuron give back to the skins of their buildings a function as a carrier of images and meaning, they are drawing on an ancient tradition. In the past it was mainly the facades of grander buildings that had not only aesthetic function, but also communicated messages. In this sense they were a kind of early media facade, to use a modern term.

The facade as an information carrier
One very effective example of this is without doubt the Gothic cathedral and its rich sculptural programme on the portals and stained-glass windows (Fig. 1.32) which tells entire stories. Martin Pawley sees the windows of the churches as giant screens which with the help of natural light transmit visual information.[8] Similar functions, albeit without images, are ascribed to Islamic mosques, where artistic calligraphic inscriptions quote texts from the Koran. Today's architecture can hardly match such deep meaning, restricting itself instead to individual, sometimes superficial references which the uninitiated observer finds hard to interpret. Or it remains at the level of transmitting advertising messages, be they in the form of the client's logos, printed many times, or a flickering screen, for example.

Since the mid 1980s there have been a number of visionary attempts to realise electronic media facades with moving images, based on liquid-crystal technology or light diodes, such as the prize-winning competition entry (not built) by Rem Koolhaas for the Centre for Art and Media Technology in Karlsruhe (Fig. 1.41). Yet little has survived of most of these futuristic and much lauded designs, except for the purposes of advertising, as here the extra cost involved does seem to pay off. One such is the glass high-rise of Tokyo's Shibuya Station, whose entire main front was turned into a giant screen, using LCD membranes integrated into the glass. Round the clock this facade broadcasts marketing spots interspersed with news (Fig. 1.42). Such concepts, however, are an add-on, like the colourful advertisements of architecture, without an inner context, or even a relationship to the architecture. For this reason they are seen to best effect at night, when the building behind the illuminated advertising is hardly visible. Then, they and the bright shop windows and street lamps turn the often dismal daytime face of our cities into a sea of glittering lights, a truly fascinating display of colour and constantly changing images (Fig. 1.43). It is a phenomenon to which many inner cities owe their appeal, and which shows us that darkness is just as much part of the daily cycle as light.

Light and drama – architecture at night
Ever since it was discovered, electric light has been used to add drama to buildings, famous early examples being at the World Exhibitions of 1889 and 1900 in Paris. But architects of the classical modern – for example Erich Mendelsohn

(Fig. 1.34) and Bruno Taut – also used the night-time effect of light; Hitler's architect, too, Albert Speer used whole batteries of spotlights in the 1930s to create mystical-monumental cathedrals of light. In Europe special night-time facades are seen generally on specific types of building such as department stores, cinemas and also petrol stations. Apart from these examples, and the glass envelopes that light up to give impact to a city skyline at night, architecture has for a long time concentrated in its facade designs almost exclusively on daytime effect. This phenomenon is now gradually losing validity. More and more now we are seeing specialists such as light planners and artists being involved in projects to create a true architecture of the night. Sometimes the buildings take on an almost theatrical aspect. Kazuyo Sejima's Flagship Store for Christian Dior on Tokyo's fashionable Omotesando is an impressive demonstration of this trend (Fig. 1.40). By day a simple, almost reserved glass cube, the building at night turns into a beaming lantern, with colours changing subtly from floor to floor, an effect created by using different curtains and partition walls behind the glass facade.

Toyo Ito's Tower of Winds (Figs. 1.37, 1.38; now no longer in existence) is a prototype of pure light architecture. Here countless computer-controlled electric light bulbs, neon rings and spotlights, installed on a non-functional chimney, react to influences from the environment, to traffic noise and gusts of wind. Sometimes hectically flickering, at other times calm and with gentle transitions, a moving light show is displayed, a kind of visual environmental music.

Peter Cook and Colin Fournier, in cooperation with the Edler brothers of realities:united of Berlin, created a building skin enlivened with artificial light in their retro-futuristically designed Kunsthaus in Graz (Fig. 1.39). They used 925 ring-shaped fluorescent tubes, positioned behind the external skin of three-dimensionally shaped acrylic plastic, as pixels, each controlled from a central computer. In this way a kind of greyscale display is generated, which can also transport moving images. But these images can only be deciphered at a distance. In the project in Graz this is more of an artistic allegory of a media facade, an installation that deliberately looks archaic in comparison with what is today technically possible.

Light installations, even though it may simply be a matter of transmitting moving images, lend a new aesthetic dimension to a building skin, the potential of which is increasingly being discovered and explored. Often the designs are static displays, with colour being used more and more. Architects and light designers are decorating the facades of their building at night with sensual displays of light. A new kind of ornament is arising, an ornament that is switched on at night. This type of embellishment can also be switched off as required, and is thus less final than decoration printed onto a facade or set into it as a relief. As shown above, the applied ornament is

1.36

1.34 Herpich & Söhne furriers in Berlin,
     detail of facade lighting, 1929; Erich Mendelsohn
1.35 Library of Eberswalde Academy, 1999;
     Herzog & de Meuron
1.36 University Library in Utrecht, 2004; Wiel Arets

25

accepted much more today, a fact that points to a changing sociocultural environment and also to changing perceptions. Added to this is the waning validity of some of the rigid dogmas of the modern movement. Adolf Loos in his time pilloried ornament because he saw it as a waste of human endeavour, an argument that has little power in today's world of digitally reproduced images and industrialized printing methods. Yet no matter how electrifying some formal experiments with the building skin may be, as soon as facades are dramatised simply for the sake of it, key architectural qualities are lost. Architecture cannot be reduced to images and surfaces. This would rob it of its main raison d'être, that of creating space and providing answers to social questions. And architects run the risk of losing more ground in their influence on the building process. Sooner or later they are no more than packaging artists.

1.37

1.38

Notes:
1   Semper,Gottfried: Der Stil in den technischen und tektonischen Künsten, oder praktische Ästhetik. Ein Handbuch für Techniker, Künstler und Kunstfreunde. Frankfurt 1860
2   Ando, Tadao: Light, Shadow and Form. In: dal Co, Francesco: Tadao Ando – Complete Works. London 1995
3   Zumthor, Peter: Architektur denken. Basle/Boston/Berlin 1999
4   cf. Ito,Toyo: Blurring Architecture. Aachen/Milan 1999
5   cf. Dercon, Chris: Speech on the occasion of the opening of the exhibition "Herzog & de Meuron. No. 250. Eine Ausstellung" in Munich, 11.05.2006
6   cf. Mack, Gerhard: Building with Images, Herzog & de Meuron's library at Eberswalde. In: Architecture Landscape Urbanism 3: Eberswalde Library, Herzog & de Meuron. London 2000
7   cf. Interview with Jacques Herzog, "Architektur als Kunst ist unerträglich", Die Zeit no. 21, 13.05.2004
8   cf. Pawley, Martin: Theorie und Gestaltung im Zweiten Maschinenzeitalter. Braunschweig / Wiesbaden 1998

1.43

1.39   1.40   1.41   1.42

9   AIT documentation: Die Versachlichung des Materials. Vols. 1–3, Leinfelden–Echterdingen 1997
10   archithese 2/00: Textiles
11   Daidalos 56, June 1995: Magie der Werkstoffe
12   Detail 7/98: Facades, external wall
13   Hix, John: The Glasshouse. London 1996
14   l'architecture d'aujourd'hui 333, mars-avril 2001: ornement
15   Schittich, Ch.; Staib, G.; Balkow, D.; Schuler, M.; Sobek, W.: Glasbau Atlas. Munich/Basle 1998
16   Schulitz, Helmut C.: Die unvollendete Moderne. In: Schulitz + Partner: Bauten und Projekte. Berlin 1996
17   The Saint Louis Art Museum: Louis Sullivan: The function of ornament. New York 1986
18   Wigginton, Michael: Glass in architecture. London 1996
19   Schivelbusch, Wolfgang: Licht Schein und Wahn. Auftritte der elektrischen Beleuchtung im 20. Jahrhundert. Berlin 1992
20   Kunstmuseum Stuttgart: Leuchtende Bauten. Architektur der Nacht. Exhibition catalogue, Ostfildern 2006

1.37   Wind Tower in Yokohama, 1986; Toyo Ito
1.38   Wind Tower in Yokohama, 1986; Toyo Ito
1.39   Kunsthaus in Graz, 2003; Peter Cook, Colin Fournier with realities: united
1.40   Dior store, Omotesando in Tokyo, 2003; SANAA
1.41   Zentrum für Kunst und Medientechnologie (ZKM) in Karlsruhe, competition, first prize, not executed, 1989; Rem Koolhaas
1.42   High-rise at Shibuya Station in Tokyo
1.43   Times Square in New York

Is it all "just" a facade?
The functional, energetic and structural aspects of the building skin

Werner Lang

"Architecture is an art of pure invention. Unlike the other arts, [it] does not find its patterns in nature, they are unencumbered creations of the human imagination and reason. In consideration of this, architecture could be considered the freest of all arts were it not also dependent on the laws of nature in general, and the mechanical laws of material in particular. For, regardless of which artistic creation of architecture we look upon, it was primarily and originally always conceived to satisfy particular material need, primarily that of shelter and protection from the onslaught of climate and the elements or other hostile forces. And since we can gain such protection only through combining the materials nature offers us into solid structures, we are always forced to adhere closely to the structural and mechanical laws." [1]   Gottfried Semper, 1854

Despite changed cultural, economic, building technological and energetic parameters, the principal task of architecture is still to create a comfortable "shelter". In other words, the fundamental aim of building is to protect people from external climate conditions, such as intensive solar radiation, extreme temperatures, precipitation and wind. In construction, the building skin is the primary subsystem through which prevailing external conditions can be influenced and regulated to meet the comfort requirements of the user inside the building. Like the skin and clothing of humans, this raiment, too, fulfils the tasks demanded of it by performing a number of functions made possible by means of the appropriate design and construction. Any serious inquiry into this context must address the following questions, vitally important to the theory and analysis and to the planning and design:

1. Function: What is the practical purpose of the building/the building skin?
2. Construction: What are the elements/components of the building/the building skin and how are these elements assembled into a whole?
3. Form: What does the building/the building skin look like?

While these categories of observation and analysis have remained virtually unchanged for millennia, increased CO_2 emissions and the shortage of fossil fuels have precipitated a shift toward greater ecological awareness. As questions pertinent to sustainable building take centre stage in the planning process, this shift calls for a fundamental reconsideration of building concepts and the form and design of the building skin. Keeping this relationship in mind,

the following factor should be added to the above list:

4. Ecology: What is the energy consumption of the building/the building skin during construction, use and demolition?

In terms of comfort, functional properties take precedence over structural, aesthetic and ecological aspects. However, all four categories must be given equal weight in a "total building system," since they are interdependent and bear a direct influence on each other. Thus the physiological properties of an external wall are dependent on its structure, sequence of layers and material properties. The ecological characteristics in turn, are determined by functional i.e. physiological aspects such as insulating and shading properties. Questions of construction, too, such as the selection of materials determine the energy consumption in construction by virtue of their corresponding primary energy content. [2] All four aspects must be fully considered to create architecture that is – in the Semperian sense – guided by reason instead of being a "pure art of invention," which in adherence to the "universal laws of nature and mechanical laws of material [...] satisfies a material need," while asserting its membership in the liberal arts through quality in design. With all these aspects in mind, we shall begin by discussing the "material" aspects of the building skin. We begin by discussing the connection between the physical needs of the user and the resulting physical requirements of the building skin, followed by an overview of the functional properties and potentials of the building skin, and, finally, a detailed analysis of the structural and material implementation of these aspects.

The building skin as a separating and linking element between inside and outside: reflections on the function of the building skin

The building skin is the dominant system in all subsystems of a building – the load-bearing structure, mechanical services and spatial framework – not only in terms of design.

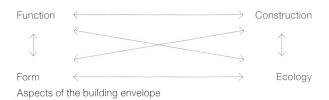

Function ⟷ Construction
Form ⟷ Ecology
Aspects of the building envelope

2.1   Teachers' seminar in Chur, 1999; Bearth + Deplazes (facing)

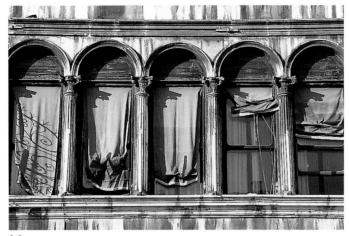

2.2

It must fulfil a multitude of vital functions and is a principal factor in the energy consumption of a building. Although facade and roof are subjected to climate stresses to different degrees, their functions are very similar, which is why they are sometimes difficult to distinguish. For the purpose of this discussion, these two areas are therefore combined under the overarching term building- i. e. external skin.

These functions are, among others:
· Lighting
· Ventilation
· Protection from humidity
· Insulation against heat / cold
· Wind protection
· Sun protection
· Glare protection
· Visual protection
· Visual contact / transparency
· Safety / security
· Prevention of mechanical damage
· Noise protection
· Fire protection
· Energy gain

The building skin has become increasingly important in recent years in the areas of research and development as a result of a growing awareness of environmentally sustainable forms of living. In the late 1960s and early 1970s, internal comfort was still largely a matter of high-performance air-conditioning systems. Since then, the external skin has become the key factor in efforts to conserve energy. The potential for decreasing energy consumption and above all, the debate surrounding the SBS syndrome [3] have changed our perspective. This is also reflected in the fact that, until recently, most building skins were conceived by architects, sometimes in collaboration with an engineer. Structural engineers were only consulted for elaborate construction projects. Today, several experts are involved in progressive projects aimed at optimizing the performance capacity of the building skin. New professions, e. g. daylight planner, facade engineer, energy planner and building aerodynamics engineer, have evolved as a result of the re-evaluation of the building skin and its importance for the energy household of buildings. We shall explore these issues with a focus on key functional demands such as lighting, heat- and sun-protection and their impact on comfort and energy consumption.

Comfort factors as parameters for building skin design

One of the primary tasks of the building skin is to regulate the prevailing conditions in the surrounding external atmosphere in order to ensure comfortable conditions in the interior. In view of the additional energy required for the operation of mechanical building systems, any such installation should be understood as a subsidiary system that acts to support the envelope in order to guarantee sufficient interior comfort. Hence, facade and roof must react to climate conditions in order to regulate how these might effect the internal building climate. The direct link between building skin and room climate calls for a precise definition of the term comfort, since this definition is the basis from which specifications for the conception of the external walls and roof are derived. The main factors are indoor air temperature

Building

Load-bearing structure

Technical services

Spatial sequence

Building skin

Facade

Roof

Ventilation systems

Sunscreen systems

Daylight systems

Insulation systems

Energy systems

Overall building system

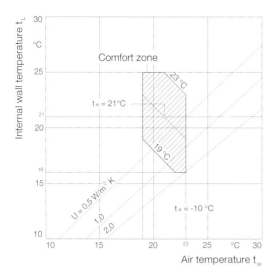

Comfort parameters[4]

User requirements	Energy Consumption in Administration Buildings	Climatic parameters
Indoor air temperature	Building skin	Outdoor air temperature
Surface temperatures	Heating energy	Air movement
Air change	Cooling energy	Relative outdoor air humidity
Relative indoor air humidity	Artificial lighting	Solar radiation
Luminance		
Lighting intensity		
	Building services	

Building skin parameters

and average surface temperatures, air change rates, relative indoor humidity, luminance and lighting intensity. These comfort factors, of which detailed definitions follow, should not be seen in isolation: they are closely related and interdependent. Indoor air temperature that is perceived as comfortable is very much dependent on relative indoor humidity, surface temperatures and on air movement in the room; it is also influenced by individual factors such as clothing and physical activity.

Indoor air temperature
The comfort zone for indoor air temperature ranges from 20–25 °C maximum. In summer, temperatures of up to 27 °C are still considered tolerable.[5] When internal wall surface temperatures and the relative indoor humidity are properly adjusted, indoor air temperatures as low as 18 °C are still perceived as comfortable.

Average surface temperatures
Whenever possible, these temperatures should differ by no more than 2–3 K from the indoor air temperature; the differential between various surface temperatures in surrounding areas should not exceed 3–4 K.[6]

Air change and air movement

While a minimal air change rate of 0.3/h is sufficient in unoccupied rooms, this value rises to 1.1/h during work hours. This corresponds to a fresh air intake of 40–60 m³/h per person.[7] Generally a value of 200 cm²/m² of floor area suffices for intake and ventilation openings for natural ventilation.[8] At the same time it is important to avoid draughts by ensuring that air velocity does not exceed 0.15 m/s.[9]

Relative indoor humidity
Depending on room temperature, the comfort zone for relative indoor humidity ranges between 30 and 70 %. Grandjean[10] establishes a more limited range of comfortable relative indoor humidity, between 40 and 60 %.

Luminance
The standard values for luminance at the work place are dependent on the activity, the room layout and the proximity of the workstation to windows. Typical values lie in the region of 300 lx for workstations near windows, 500 lx for standard cubicle offices and 700 lx for open-plan offices with a high degree of surface reflection or 1000 lx for open-plan offices with medium surface reflection.[11]

Lighting intensity
The quality of lighting in a room is not only influenced by luminance but also by glare. The lighting intensity should be approximately 2/3 to 1/10 of the interior field lighting intensity.[12] Hence, it is important to select and position glare protection elements in a manner that provides evenly distributed daylight without glare, while avoiding unnecessary cooling loads in the interior space.

All comfort-related parameters – with the exception of relative indoor humidity – can be directly controlled and regulated through the design of the facade and the roof and

2.2   Doge's Palace, Venice

	U-value	g-value	Diminution factor	Transmit-tance
Summer, clear skies	high	low	low	high
Summer, overcast	high	n/a	n/a	high
Summer, night	high	n/a	n/a	low
Winter, clear skies	low	high	high	high
Winter, overcast	low	n/a	n/a	high
Winter, night	low	n/a	n/a	low

Parameters and requirements for the building skin

2.3

this is the principal guiding factor in the conception of the building skin. Thus the indoor air and average surface temperatures are the product of the exchange between internal and external heat gains, on the one hand, and transmission- and ventilation heat losses through the building skin, on the other. Air change can be regulated through the number and dimension of ventilation openings. Luminance and lighting density are also influenced by the type, position and size of openings in the building skin. Close observation has demonstrated that a well-designed building skin is capable of producing a comfortable internal climate with the help of environmental energies even under less than favourable climate conditions.

Comfort and energy-related parameters of the building skin

U-value
The thermal transmittance (formerly U-value) indicates the amount of heat which passes through external wall structures in W/m^2K. For opaque wall and roof structures, typical values lie in the range of 0.3 W/m^2K, easily achieved with standard insulating materials of 12–16 cm thickness. Modern double glazing with insulating glass separated by an argon-filled cavity can easily achieve Ug-values of 1.2 W/m^2K. If using triple insulated glazing with argon filling, Ug-values of 0.7 W/m^2K can be reached; with krypton filling, 0.6 W/m^2K. For transparent and translucent external wall structures, one should take the potential of solar heat gain into consideration, as this can have a positive impact on the overall energy balance.

g-value
The total solar energy transmission (g-value) indicates the percentage of solar radiation (wavelength 320–2500 nm) transmitted through transparent or translucent external walls. This value is the product of the sum of transmitted radiation and heat emission from the internal pane into the room. The g-value of modern double glazing with insulating glass is around 60%, and roughly 50% for triple insulated glazing. If special coatings are used, as in the case of solar glazing; g-values of 40% or lower can be achieved for double glazing with insulating glass.

Diminution factor
The diminution factor indicates the proportion of incident radiation passing through a solar-shading system. It is given as a value between 0 and 1. The lower the value, the greater the diminution effect of the system. This value is dependent on the execution and installation angle of the shading system and provides information with regard to the heat gain in a room as a result of solar radiation.

Daylight transmission factor
The daylight transmission factor is a measure of the percentage of daylight present outside the building and perceivable by humans (wavelength 320–780 nm) that passes through the glazing. A typical daylight transmission factor for today's double glazing with insulating glass is around 80%, and for triple glazing with insulating glass it is around 70%. The constant changes in external conditions on a daily and yearly basis result in vastly different and in part conflicting requirements to which the external skin must respond in order to maintain comfortable conditions inside the building.

The performance of the building skin was a key concern even at a time when energy generation for internal comfort and conditioning was still linked to high levels of energy consumption. Historic architecture provides countless examples of impressive precursors to modern principles of sustainable building. Topics such as minimizing primary energy consumption and recycling building materials were basic considerations even in the past, because of limited availability. Recognizing its significance in relation to energy consumption and comfort, the building skin was designed primarily in response to regional climate conditions. In Central Europe, the thermal properties of structures and the thermal storage of the building skin were the functional focus of building in an effort to minimize energy consumption and optimize comfort. Daylight use was of secondary importance and the building technology of the time offered fewer options than are available today: hence, window openings were generally small in proportion to the opaque surface of the external wall. This particular aspect would only change with the advent of progressive glass manufacture in the 19th century. The increased use of glass in the second half of the 19th century went hand in hand with a greater focus on manipulators for sun and heat protection because of the radiation permeability of the material (Fig. 2.3). Many new principles were developed, especially for transparent wall construction, with the aim for adapting thermal properties to external conditions. Larger glass surfaces, high internal heating loads, changing user requirements, rising energy prices and the near-exhaustion of environmental resources, have made an investigation into the performance and function of the building skin more important today than ever before, if we wish to keep pace with changing demands and conditions. In addition to new developments in the area of insulated glazing and insulating materials, the implementation, research and development of manipulators in combination with a building skin design that meets the basic requirements are the focus of this investigation.

The impact of facade and roof design on energy consumption and comfort in the building interior

Heating energy consumption continues to be a key issue in housing construction, while cooling energy requirements are increasingly important in the context of office and administration buildings where internal cooling loads are rising. Components that protect against excessive heat gain in summer and unwanted transmission and ventilation heat losses in winter are therefore especially important. In conventional office buildings nearly 40% of total energy consumption is devoted to heating and a further 40% for the operation of air-conditioning systems for both ventilation and cooling. The remaining 20% is consumed for artificial lighting.[13] To increase comfort and reduce energy consumption, the cooling loads must be reduced by means of optimal sun protection, improved daylight use and daylight-dependent regulation of artificial lighting. Moreover, excess heat gains should be extracted via night cooling, a process that can be greatly facilitated with the corresponding building skin design and exposed thermal masses in the building interior, a combination that is equally effective for reducing transmission- and ventilation heat loss. Elements that are flexible, both in design and in use, are essential tools to meet the above-mentioned requirements. Depending on

the specific requirements, heat gains in a room or thermal transmittance losses in the facade can be minimized with shade-, glare-protection and insulating systems as well as by daylight-deflecting elements.

Today, basic demands for heat insulation as well as shade- and glare-protection systems that are both efficient and flexible in order to prevent overheating and glare in summer have already drastically reduced the energy consumption in buildings. Thus the average heating energy requirements in buildings constructed prior to 1968 lie near 260 kWh/m²a, while the corresponding value is approximately 60 kWh/m²a in new, low buildings.[15] Components for temporary sun and heat protection offer the greatest potential for a clear reduction in energy consumption, especially in the case of transparent or translucent facades. To translate this knowledge into minimal energy consumption and to utilize renewable resources, architects must carefully study the complex issues of material and energy exchange; moreover, they must know how to apply the information thus gained to planning and construction and consult specialized engineers.[16] The current energy savings potential can be realized through dense building, integrated power-heat systems and the correct placement and orientation of the building fabric. If the knowledge required to fully implement these solutions is either lacking or poorly executed, the building skin alone cannot compensate for the resulting deficits.

Sun protection systems

Independent of the heat insulation factor of a transparent facade, the placement of sun protection systems has a decisive influence on the energy consumption of buildings. Calculations on conventional facades with east and west orientation have shown that the energy consumed for cooling can be halved when external blinds are used, by comparison to a glass facade without sunscreen elements. Conversely, the use of internal blinds reduces the energy consumption by no more than 20%.[17] Sunscreen elements are required to prevent overheating in all building types, especially for buildings with high internal cooling loads and/or a high percentage of glazing, e.g. most administration or office buildings. Fixed, stationary systems do not allow for adjusting the shading element to the position of the sun, and this can result in functional disadvantages with regard to shading, transparency and daylight use. Moveable systems can be adjusted to respond to changing solar altitudes over the course of a day and in different seasons, allowing for individual control of the sunscreen elements, optimal shading and maximum use of daylight (Fig. 2.4).

It is important to point out the disadvantages of internal sunscreen elements, because the solar radiation absorbed by these elements is transmitted into the room. In summer, this results in unwanted additional cooling loads. In winter, the potential heat gain may be used to increase the room temperature. Systems mounted behind glass, and thus protected from the elements, are easier to build and to install. This is equally true for double-skin facades, where a great variety of manipulators can be installed behind a protective shield of single glazing. Since these systems are protected from dirt and pollution, they allow for the use

2.3   Multi-layered facade, Jaén, Andalusia

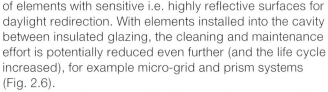

Solar radiation

Insulating glass

Incident
radiation 100%

Direct solar energy
reflection,
approx. 30%

Direct solar energy
transmission,
approx. 46%

Total energy
transmission,
approx. 58%

Secondary radiation
and convection to the
outside, approx. 12%

Secondary radiation
and convection to the
inside, approx. 12%

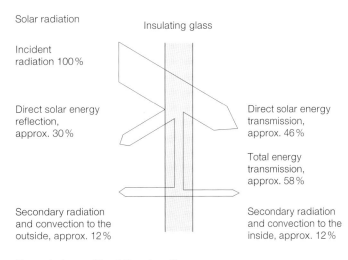

Energy balance of insulating glass [18]

2.4

of elements with sensitive i.e. highly reflective surfaces for daylight redirection. With elements installed into the cavity between insulated glazing, the cleaning and maintenance effort is potentially reduced even further (and the life cycle increased), for example micro-grid and prism systems (Fig. 2.6).
Despite the advantages offered by weather-protected shading systems, external sunscreen elements are still the most advantageous option due to the direct convection of heat gain to the outside. Nevertheless, it is important to consider climate conditions and wind resistance when selecting the relevant components, since high wind loads can lead to temporary system shutdown.

Anti-glare systems
The main task of anti-glare systems is to prevent extreme contrasts in lighting intensity, an issue that is especially important in office buildings with monitor workstations where visual comfort must be maintained. This is the principal difference between anti-glare and sun protection systems.
A variety of different systems can be used to mute and scatter intense light. These are:
• Curtains
• Horizontal blinds
• Vertical blinds
• Venetian blinds
• Screens
• Translucent glazing
• Electrochromic glazing
Whenever these systems are used it is important to avoid reducing daylight transmission to the point where artificial light has to be used or to impede visual contact between inside and outside. Textile anti-glare systems, screens and perforated aluminium louvres are practical options. The position of an anti-glare system in relation to the internal glazing layer determines the amount of heat gained in the interior as a result of radiation. By comparison to an office building with external sunscreen elements, sun protection glazing combined with an internal anti-glare system leads to an approximate increase in heating requirements of 20–30% as a result of the reduced radiation transmittance, and increased cooling energy requirements by 10–20% as a result of the heat gain in the anti-glare system.[19]

Daylight use
The use of natural daylight is increasingly important both in terms of the comfort and contentment of the users and with regard to reducing the requirements for artificial light. Daylight systems should be applied above all in areas where significant room depths preclude direct use of daylight (Fig. 2.7), and/or where the quality of lighting is a high priority, e.g. at computer workstations where optimal direction and distribution of light are essential. Daylight-dependent artificial lighting offers additional savings potentials. Measures to optimize the use of daylight should always be closely integrated with any sun protection systems to keep the daylight component of transmitted solar radiation as high as possible and the short- and long-wave spectrum of solar radiation as low as possible. The following systems are suited to meet these requirements:
• Glazing with selective coatings
• Reflectors that deflect daylight into the depth of a room
• Micro-grid systems with high reflective coatings

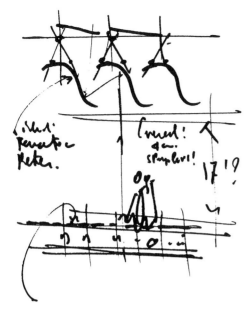

2.5

- Prism systems
- Light-diffusing glazing
- Glass louvre systems
- Holographic defractive system (HDS)

Thermal insulation systems
One option of regulating the resistance to thermal transmittance in a facade or roof structure in response to internal requirements and external weather conditions, is to employ materials and components capable of reducing heat loss through transmittance, convection or radiation. The common approach is to use materials with low thermal transmittance factors, low emission properties to decrease heat loss by radiation, and high-reflective foils or surface coatings to reflect heat radiation. Aside from reducing heat loss by transmittance, these measures can also help to increase the internal surface temperature of the exterior wall. While opaque skin structures with insulating materials of 12–16 cm in thickness display U-values below 0.3 W/m²K, similar values can only be achieved for transparent or translucent wall and roof structures through the use of temporary measures for thermal insulation. For a direct comparison, however, one should consider the option of using solar energy, since this factor is crucial in defining the energy balance of a facade. The radiation transmittance of an insulating material also influences the options for direct use of solar energy, e. g. for pre-heating fresh air or heating a massive external wall structure. Insulating systems are divided into functions according to their adaptability. Fixed systems, such as combined heat-insulating systems or rear-ventilated facade systems, do not allow the insulating properties of the building skin to adapt to seasonal and daily fluctuations in external temperatures and radiation conditions. This may become problematic when transparent or translucent insulating components are used and overheating in summer must be avoided. In moveable systems, such as sliding and folding shutters, the insulating material or component is installed either on the inside or on the outside of the existing skin structure. Transparent and translucent building components can be used to utilize heat gain in winter for preheating the air in the facade cavity, while evacuating the heated air via facade openings in summer. Opaque insulating systems do not offer this advantage of utilizing solar gains.

Natural ventilation
Aside from the above-mentioned parameters for regulating the energy balance, the building skin plays an important role in terms of the natural air exchange in buildings. Meeting requirements for air hygiene is the key factor in this context, with a special focus on the correct amount of ventilation to minimize heat loss by ventilation in times of cool outside temperatures. Free ventilation through existing openings in the building skin is generally sufficient for rooms whose depth does not exceed the height by more than 2.5. Dependent on the manner of opening, as well as the location and position of the operable element, this solution achieves air changes between 0.2 and 50 1/h.[21] Designing the building skin specifically with these natural principles in mind, e. g. the stack effect, can help to achieve natural ventilation even in the case of great room depths.[22]

2.6

2.4   Police and fire station in Berlin, 2004; Sauerbruch + Hutton
2.5   Menil Collection, sketch; Renzo Piano
2.6   Design Centre in Linz, 1993; Herzog + Partner

Other functional aspects

In terms of comfort and safety, sound insulation and fire protection are additional important properties of the building skin. With regard to sound insulation, the building skin should be designed to reduce external and internal noise to a comfortable level. This is achieved by using materials whose mass enables them to reflect existing sound. Another option is to generate sound insulation by absorbing sound energy and converting it into heat. The minimal values for acoustic insulation rates in external building components range from 50 to 75 dB.

As regards fire protection, the building skin must ensure the safety of the users, and prevent the outbreak of fire or explosions; it must also counteract the spread of flames, heat and smoke. Moreover, the structure must maintain its load-bearing capacity for a specified period of time and the layout must facilitate effective fire fighting measures. External skin construction can be classified above all with regard to the combustibility of its materials and the fire resistance period of building components and load-bearing components. The following aspects are covered by fire-resistance codes: walls, supports, floors, girders and stairs, which prevent the spread of fire and smoke as well as the penetration of radiating heat; transparent building components, i.e. glazing, which prevent the spread of fire and smoke but not the penetration of radiating heat; non load-bearing external walls; and doors and gates. For building skins it is therefore imperative to verify the building codes in each jurisdiction and to check specific guidelines for fire protection, which may limit the choice of building materials or construction type. For the purpose of fire protection, the focus is above all on load-bearing and room-enclosing walls, such as walls along emergency routes, in stairwells and on firewalls. These building components must deliver a fire resistance period of 30 to 120 minutes in the case of fire depending on building category and use. [23]

The building skin as power station

Before low-cost fossil fuels were widely available, the efficient use of heating energy and the principles of solar energy use were essential considerations in the design of buildings and building skins. Material selection, orientation of the building volume towards the sun, exposure, plans, and the design of facade- and roof surfaces were all harmonized with the conditions dictated by the site. These are, among others, the local climate, the topography, the availability of materials for construction and combustible material for building operation. Over many centuries, a culture of building evolved which demonstrates the direct link between functional requirements and external appearance, a link that is still visible today in traditional buildings (Fig. 2.8).

The drastic changes in the energy sector, in particular the ready availability of inexpensive fossil fuels and electricity, had a lasting impact on this traditional link. The relationship between local conditions and their impact on the built environment was more or less nullified (Fig. 2.9). Only the realization that fossil fuels are an exhaustible resource and that the burning of coal, oil and gas presents a grave danger for the environment and the population, prompted planners to change their attitudes. Throughout Europe, approximately half of the consumed primary energy is consumed for the

2.7

2.7   Reichstag in Berlin, 1999; Foster and Partners

Overview of possible insulating systems

Principle	Description	Position in rel. to external wall	
fixed systems		in	out
opaque systems	canopy, light shelf, louvres	o	x
	light grid systems	o	x
transparent/translucent systems	reflective glazing	o	x
	light-absorbing glazing	–	x
	light-defracting glazing	x	x
	prism systems	x	o
	holographic-optical elements	x	x
moveable systems		in	out
opaque systems	shutter	o	x
	hinged shutter	o	x
	sliding shutter	o	x
	folding shutter	o	x
	curtain	o	–
	louvres (wood, metal, plastic)	o	x
transparent/translucent systems	glass louvres	x	x
	prism systems	x	o
	holographic-optical elements	x	x

Improving the thermal properties of facades

Principle	Description	Position in rel. to external wall	
fixed systems		in	out
opaque heat insulation	integrated heat insulating system	x	x
	rear-ventilated facade, insulated	–	x
transparent/translucent insulation	solar wall heating	–	x
transparent/translucent face shell	winter window	x	x
	winter garden	–	x
	second-skin facade	–	x
	exhaust air facade	x	–
	solar air collector	–	x
moveable systems		in	out
opaque insulating elements	shutter	x	x
	hinged shutter	x	x
	sliding shutter	x	x
	folding shutter	x	x
	curtain	x	–
	louvres	x	x
transparent insulating elements	window leafs (e.g. coupled windows	x	x
	film element, foil	x	x

(in = inside; out = outside)

x component ideal for indicated function
o component marginally suited for indicated function
– component not suited for indicated function

Airborne sound insulation for different building components

Building component	Sound insulation factor R'$_W$ [dB]
plastic foam, porous, 5 cm	5
wood-chip board, 2 cm	22
insulating glass 2" 5 mm, compound glass 12 mm	33–35
single-layer brick wall, 15 cm, plastered on both sides	46–48
concrete wall 15 cm	53–55

Building material grades

Description for building supervision	Grade
fireproof materials	A
materials without combustible components, e.g. concrete, steel, natural stone	A1
materials with few combustible components, e.g. plaster, concrete blocks	A2
combustible materials	B
hardly inflammable materials such as preserved wood or textiles	B1
standard inflammable materials, such as wood planks	B2
easily inflammable materials, such as paper and films	B3

Description for building supervision

Grades	Abbreviation
fire-retardant	F30-B
fire-retardant and in the load-bearing components of non-combustible materials	F30-AB
fire-retardant and of non-combustible materials	F30-A
fireproof	F90-AB
fireproof and of non-combustible materials	F90-A

2.8

2.9

construction and operation of buildings. A radical reduction of energy consumption, coupled with the use of solar energies, is therefore the only logical and sensible solution to the problem of dwindling energy resources and environmental destruction.

Solar energy can be utilized twofold. Direct use is mainly concerned with orientation, plan and the design of the building and its components, especially the facade. Applied to the building skin, solar energy is used for natural ventilation (making use of thermal lift and the resulting pressure differences), for lighting interior spaces with daylight, and for heating interior spaces by harnessing the greenhouse effect (Fig. 2.10).

There is a wide range of systems from which to choose for collecting, distributing and storing the available energy. Buffer zones, transparent heat insulation, aerogel glazing and high-insulating glass with U-values below 1.0 W/m²K widen the field of options for direct solar use and reduce heat loss by comparison to conventional insulated glazing. Components and systems, such as massive wall components faced with translucent heat insulation, make it possible to use the solar energy stored during the daytime to provide heat in the evening and early night hours. As to daylight use, one should consider micro-grid systems, prism systems and HDS elements, which enable a more efficient use of daylight, especially for office and administration buildings where higher cooling loads and user comfort requirements come into play.

As its name indicates, indirect use refers to indirect application of solar energy through collectors, i.e. autonomous systems which can be integrated into the building skin. Indirect uses of solar energy include the heating of water and air for interior space heating or for domestic/industrial water consumption. The conversion of solar radiation into cooling energy is yet another application where solar collectors are used in combination with heat-absorption pumps or thermal/chemical storage systems. Photovoltaic elements have become increasingly popular in recent years for generating electrical power as a result of technological progress in this field, state subsidies and the development of panels that are easy to integrate. A wide range of applications has been developed for the building skin.

Unlike collectors that are mounted onto the building skin, these systems allow for full integration, both in terms of construction and design.[24] Aside from the functional advantages, this approach also results in cost savings, since no additional financing is required for the roof or facade surface covered in collectors.

Building materials, components and techniques must be carefully selected with the building concept in mind and harmonized with each other. Both in the area of the roof and the facade, the building skin offers a variety of options for applications capable of meeting nearly all energy requirements, provided the systems, combination and storage options are employed accordingly.

Structural aspects of the building skin

Aside from comfort and energetic requirements, the building skin must also fulfil a number of other functions as spatial component; these are primarily concerned with the structural design of the facade and roof construction. These functions are:

- Transfer of vertical loads, e. g. dead weight and superimposed loads
- Transfer of horizontal loads, such as the wind-induced pressure- and suction forces of impact loads
- Structural safety and prevention of mechanical damage
- Enabling the structural integration of components for direct and indirect use of solar energy or sun and heat protection of the interior space
- Enabling the structural integration of manipulators for the adaptation of the building skin to changing functional and user-dependent requirements

Beyond these aspects, questions related to design and visual appearance are in the foreground in the structural execution of the building skin. Construction and design are inseparably linked, because the structural design of the building skin determines the visual appearance of a building. Load-bearing components, such as beams, supports and walls, and the spacing between them define the rhythm, division and proportion of the building skin. The principal characteristics of an external wall construction, which define its design are the size, shape and arrangement of openings, the division, material selection and surface treatment of closed wall- and roof surfaces. With these parameters in mind, the following paragraphs address issues such as load transfer, structural arrangement, as well as options for constructional development with regard to their import for the visual appearance of the entire building.

2.10

Classifying the building skin with regard to constructional criteria

Based on an analysis of the constructional development and the properties of the building materials, the following criteria have been established to describe and classify envelope structures: [26]
- Load transfer (bearing/non-bearing)
- Structure of external wall in terms of shell arrangement (single-skin or multi-layered)
- Structure of external wall in terms of sequence of layers
- Radiation transmission (transparent, translucent, or opaque)

Other criteria, such as the placement and distance of the building skin in relation to load-bearing and bracing components such as girders, floors / ceilings and walls, are of secondary importance in terms of establishing typologies.

Load-bearing and non load-bearing skin structures
Perhaps one of the oldest principles of protecting oneself against the elements, wild animals or other risk factors is to create simple shell structures from stacked stones (Fig. 2.11) or stacked, hewn tree trunks, and to cover these structures with a roof of cantilevered stone slabs or wooden planks, or with wood- or stone shingles.
The load-bearing exterior skins are generally bend- and compression-resistant constructions, fashioned from clay, masonry or reinforced steel, but also from glass. Massive

2.8 Traditional buildings in Bavaria[25]
2.9 Situation today[25]
2.10 Museum für Hamburgische Geschichte, 1989; von Gerkan, Marg and Partner

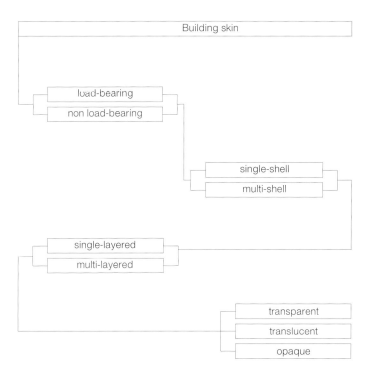

2.11

2.12

timber walls with logs or planks, typically found in traditional buildings in the alpine regions, should also be mentioned in this context. Half-timbered buildings are in a category of their own, since "load-bearing" and "space-enclosure" occur within the same layer, although the load transfer is effected by means of the wooden truss framework. Hence the nogging of the interstices is entirely flexible, notably with regard to the variability of modern skeleton structures. Modern external walls fashioned from solid wood are found, for example, in the so-called stacked-board structures, which have become more common in recent years in connection with resource-efficient building.

For roof constructions, the principal structures of interest in this context are domed-, shell- and vault constructions. In addition to these external i. e. roof structures, which are subject to compression, structures that are subject to tension also count among the "load-bearing" building skins. In the latter, load transfer is realized by means of synthetic sheeting or fabrics, i.e. via flexible and light tensile materials. The properties of these materials have been significantly improved in recent years owing to intensive efforts in research and development, and this has led to the increased use of tensile skin structures.

A second, equally ancient principle in the construction of building skins is the use of animal skins, leaves, blankets or woven elements, which – much like human clothing – are laid or stretched across simple load-bearing structures. To some degree, such structures are the precursors of contemporary curtain wall systems, in as much as they were the first instance of separating vertical load transfer from the other tasks of the building skin.

Today, most non load-bearing external wall structures are composed of wood, glass, metal, ceramic or natural stone shells, in which load transfer is realized via integrated support components. Modernism discovered glass as a building material for residential buildings at the beginning of the 20th century, developing fully transparent external wall structures by means of braced and skeleton constructions for load transfer. To render not only the building skin but the entire building transparent, the boundary between non load-bearing, transparent curtain facades and load-bearing, monolithic external walls has become less defined in recent years, since new construction methods enable glass to fulfil the tasks of load transfer and structural bracing (Fig. 2.12).

The separation of load transfer from the building skin's other tasks has broadened the field for employing a variety of materials and components in its construction. The possibilities for functional characteristics and visual forms of expression seem to be nearly unlimited.

The following facade types are predominantly used for modern office buildings:
• Post-and-beam facades
• Prefabricated (modular) facades (Fig. 2.13)

The two systems differ mainly in terms of manufacture and on-site installation. In both systems, panels and glazed sections are fastened in a linear fashion to a substructure. While the installation of the filling elements occurs only on the construction site in the case of a post-and-beam structure, larger elements of a component facade can be fully pre-assembled in a controlled workshop setting.

Single-skin and multi-layered skin structures
The second essential aspect to consider for a classification
is the structural development of the external skin. First and
foremost, it is important to differentiate between single-skin
and multi-layered structure. Essential functional properties, such as insulation or the adaptability of the building
skin to user requirements, are determined by this criterion.
Generally speaking, shells consist of pressure- and/or ten-
sion-resistant materials separated by an air buffer. While the
building's physical characteristics in monolithic constructions are determined by a single building material, the
performance profile of the building skin can be regulated
and optimized in multi-layered skins by means of employing different building materials. A multi-layered external
wall can, for example, be protected against sun, wind and
precipitation by a thin, light and weatherproof membrane,
with an insulating layer inserted beneath for good thermal
insulation. On the inside, a light structure with thin panels
provides the necessary, solid room enclosure. Condensation is easily eliminated by means of rear-ventilation – yet
another advantage in the building physics of such constructions. Typical examples are a single-skin external wall in
natural stone masonry in comparison to a multi-layered,
rear-ventilated external wall construction with external wood
facing. In this context, manipulators whose mechanical and
constructional properties make them into an additional layer
in front of or behind certain areas of the external wall, should
also be regarded as "shells." These are, for example, sliding and folding shutters, or rotating louvers for temporary
heat, sound, sun or visual protection. In the area of transparent shell constructions, multi-layered structures and the
integration of manipulators for flexibility in the control of the
functional facade characteristics have become more important. This applies especially to modern office buildings,
because rising demands on comfort, changed work habits,
rising internal cooling loads and changes in environmental
awareness combine to increase the demands made on the
execution of the building skin, which can no longer be met
by means of single-skin structures. The intensive and con-
troversial debate surrounding multi-layered glass facades
should be interpreted as proof that planners have indeed
recognized the importance of flexible external skin constructions and intend to make the most of the advantages they
offer with regard to minimizing energy consumption and optimizing comfort. [27]

2.13

Single-layer and multi-layer shell constructions
Another approach to classification is to analyse the layers
in a building skin, whereby single-layer and multi-layer
constructions are differentiated. In analogy to a structure
composed of different leafs or skins, the selection of different layers can contribute towards creating a structural
end product that is optimized in terms of function. The goal
is to provide comfort in the building's interior in the most
energy-efficient manner. A typical example of a single-
layer construction is an external wall executed in exposed
masonry, in which the functions of heat insulation, weather
protection and structural stability are performed by a single
material. Constructions of this type rarely correspond to

2.11 Stone houses in Gordes, Provence, 16th – 18th century
2.12 Covered courtyard in Munich, 2002; Architekten Betsch
2.13 Westhafen Tower in Frankfurt, 2003; Schneider + Schumacher

Criteria for building skin categories – examples

single-leaf • single-layer • transparent
1 Safety glass
2 Safety-glass fin

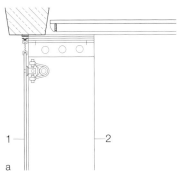

a

Railway station in London, Grimshaw + Partners

single-leaf • single-layer • translucent
Cast-glass block wall

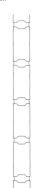

b

no title

single-leaf • single-layer • opaque
Reinforced-concrete wall

c

no title

single-layer • multi-layer • transparent
1 ETFE cushion, three layers with transparent
   internal layer
2 Air buffer, enclosed

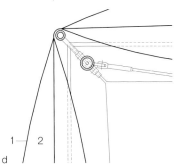

d

Pavilion in Doncaster, Alsop + Störmer

single-layer • multi-layer • translucent
1 Float glass, aerogel granulate, float glass

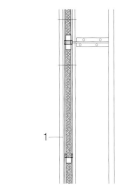

e

Studio in Munich, Herzog + Partner

single-layer • multi-layer • opaque
Wall construction: cement-fibre boards
                      Heat insulation
                      Concrete masonry

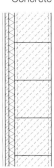

f

Film studios in Barcelona, Ferrater + Guibernau

multi-layer • single-leaf shells • transparent
1 Safety glass
2 Air buffer
3 Polycarbonate rib panel, transparent

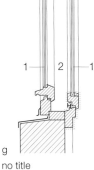

g

no title

multi-layer • single-leaf shells • translucent
1 "Cathedral glass", translucent
2 Air buffer

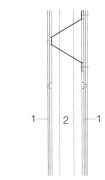

h

Steiff factory building in Giengen

multi-layer • single-leaf shells • opaque
Wall construction: Brick facing
                      Rear ventilation
                      Lightweight concrete wall

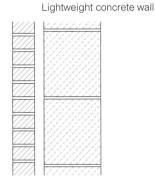

i

Office building in Lünen, Hillebrandt + Schulz

multi-layer • multi-layered shells • transparent
1 Safety glass, compound glass, float glass
2 Air buffer

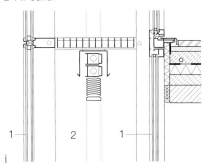

j

Administration building in Würzburg,
Webler + Geissler

multi-layer • multi-layered shells • translucent
1 Sun protection, safety glass, white enamelled
   underside
2 Safety glass, compound glass, laminated
   glass,
   ceramic printed

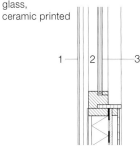

k

House in Almelo, Dirk Jan Postel,
Kraaijvanger • Urbis

multi-layer • multi-layered shells • opaque
Wall construction: Recycling brick
                      Rear ventilation
                      Wind screen
                      Insulation
                      Sand-lime brick
                      Interior plaster

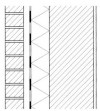

l

Foundation centre in Hamm,
Hegger Hegger Schleiff

current insulation requirements; when such buildings are renovated the practice is therefore to install additional, rear-ventilated shells or a heat-insulating layer. Common examples of multi-layer constructions are external wall systems in masonry, with interior and exterior layers of plaster, or non-ventilated flat-roof constructions in which various layers consisting of different building materials are linked into a solid composite layer.

Transparent, translucent, opaque
In addition to load transfer and structural development, light- or radiation transmittance is the third, most important criterion that defines the form and function of the building skin. In terms of the energy household and the possibilities for direct use of solar energy, this criterion is vitally important; but it has significant influence, too, in the area of daylight use and the greenhouse effect, as well as the risk of overheating in summer. Hence the potential for today's solar architecture should be studied specifically against this background. Both in the area of load-bearing and non load-bearing, as well as single- and multi-layered external wall constructions, there is a great variety of transparent and translucent facade systems. This abundance of different functional characteristics makes it possible to carefully adapt the heat and sun protection of the external skin to local conditions or individual requirements. Thus multi-layered glass facade systems combine good sound insulation and wind protection properties with a high degree of transparency, while the combination of translucent thermal insulation with massive thermal storage walls allows for a delayed use of the stored solar energy at night. Translucent facade components are increasingly popular for optimal daylight use; this function was provided even in the distant past by means of stretching animal skins and using thin alabaster and onyx slabs. By developing new applications for old principles, such as the tremendous variety of sliding elements in traditional Japanese architecture, the design and functional characteristics of the building skin can be optimized in the combination of transparent or translucent and opaque components.

The preceding paragraphs were devoted to creating an overview of the principal options for developing building skins that are highly different in terms of function by means of employing a wide range of constructions. When the options for combination are taken into consideration as well, we are presented with a tremendous variety of different skin systems, which can be conceived in correspondence to the desired functional requirements. At the same time, one has a clear sense of the enormous creative freedom that results from using vastly different materials, surface structures, colours, formats and proportions. Still, constructional solutions should never be based exclusively on the categories mentioned at the outset; the aim should be to develop a building skin that fully satisfies all the aspects relating to function, design and ecology. To this end, it is indispensable to establish a clear profile of the requirements, which the building skin must fulfil:
• What are the prevailing external climate conditions, how do they change over the course of a year and a day and which local conditions must be considered with regard to the surrounding built environment and the orientation of the facade or roof surface?

• What are the user requirements for the internal room climate? Are there any particular internal loads (cooling loads, contaminants or pollutants, etc.)?

To respond optimally to user needs and simultaneously minimize energy consumption during construction and operation, the building skin must therefore always be considered in terms of its reciprocal interaction with the construction and the building services. The following questions should be answered:
• Is the building skin adaptable to the changing needs of the user?
• What is the profile of the building's total energy concept? Can storage masses compensate for extreme temperature fluctuations?
• What are the options for utilizing environmental energies? Are there specific options for the direct and/or indirect use of solar energy? Is it possible to design the building skin to provide the required air change by means of natural ventilation? Is there an option of eliminating excessive heat gains in summer via the facade? Is there an option for integrated energy supply, e.g. by means of combined heat-power systems?
• Can materials with low primary energy contents be used? Do these materials require special protection, or do they have especially long life cycles?

In addition to these functional and ecological issues, the design of the building skin plays an important role in improving the quality of the site. Sustainable building skins are a matter of considering the conception of the building as a whole with a life cycle of many decades.

The building skin of the future

New forms of generating energy will influence the design of the building skin as much as future developments in how we work and in office technology. Research on new materials, manufacturing methods and facade components is vitally important. This may well revolutionize the performance and image profile of the building skin in a manner comparable to the invention of the float glass process in 1955. High-performance computers and new testing methods complement the options for glass applications in construction, advancing the production of transparent all-glass structures. The advanced development and optimization of synthetic materials exemplifies the potential changes, which the functional, structural and design characteristics of the building skin may undergo in the future. Thus the development of ETFE foils has made it possible to create multi-layered, wide-span membranes. The thermal properties of membrane structures were significantly improved, and transparent, extremely light and durable external wall and roof constructions became feasible (Fig. 2.14). Continued demand for high-performance and flexible facade systems will drive the development of the external skin from a static system to a multi-leaf and multi-layered building skin, equipped with manipulators. A variety of control functions, regulating thermal and visual comfort as well as the energy gain and consumption of buildings, will join and complement the traditional function of shelter. Hence, flexible skins are an increasingly important issue and the development of new, cost-efficient materials and components will play a significant role. Even today,

2.14

electrochromic glazing can alter the radiation transmission by applying integrated charges, while thermotropic glazing systems metamorphose from a fully transparent into a milky white skin as temperatures rise. The integration of the building skin and the building mechanics is of vital importance in the goal to successfully translate and realize innovative facade concepts. The *Mur neutralisant*, invented by Le Corbusier as far back as 1929, was eventually transformed into the modern ventilated facade as an example of linking building mechanics and external skin. This marked the beginning of a process in which the building mechanics were shifted to the external skin, thereby expanding its functional and visual scope. The self-regulating, polyvalent skin (Mike Davies), in which the many tasks of the building skin are carried out by a thin, multi-layered and multi-functional external skin structure, is one of the visions that points to a possible direction in future developments. However, individually controllable skins can only be understood by their users and adjusted to their satisfaction, if they recognize the link between their actions and the impact on the building climate. In other words, the regulation and adaptability of the skin must be achieved with control systems that are intelligently planned and easy to operate. Aside from the primary sheltering functions of the building skin, to which we have repeatedly referred, the facade will also gain importance as an information medium. New developments in the area of diode technology, the use of HDS elements and new methods for coating glass surfaces, will ensure that this function is also addressed with renewed interest (Fig. 2.15).

In view of the rapid development of new materials, planning instruments and production methods, as well as the countless options for combining existing materials and systems, the possibilities for the building skin seem limitless. Thus new procedures for determining material hardness have made the use of renewable raw materials in the area of innovative load-bearing concepts possible. To advance the issue of the building skin with a view to creating truly sustainable and enduring architecture, planning must be goal-oriented, responsible and sensible. A high degree of technical and creative ability is essential. The enormous potential of the building skin must be realized from a structural, functional, aesthetic and ecological perspective to promote advances in the development of architecture that is oriented towards the future.

Notes:
1   Müller, Werner; Vogel, Gunther. DTV Atlas zur Baukunst,
    Volume I. 4th edition. Munich: 1982, p. 15.
2   Published by the Swiss Association of Engineers and Architects (SIA):
    Hochbaukonstruktionen nach ökologischen Gesichtspunkten,
    SIA-Dokumentation D 0123, Zurich:1995.
3   Kröling, Peter: "Das Sick-Building-Syndrom in klimatisierten
    Gebäuden: Symptome, Ursachen und Prophylaxe".
    In: Innenraum Belastungen: erkennen, bewerten, sanieren.
    Wiesbaden / Berlin: 1993, p. 22–37.
4   Recknagel, Sprenger, Schramek: Taschenbuch für Heizung, Klima,
    Technik. Munich: 1999, p. 55.
5   While the lower boundary value of comfort is indicated as 22 °C in the
    DIN 1946, Part 2, VDI 2067 sets the standard internal temperature
    at 20°C.
6   Zürcher, Christoph, und Frank, Thomas. Bauphysik. Bau und Energie.
    Leitfaden für Planung und Praxis. Stuttgart: 1998, p. 15.
7   Daniels, Klaus. The Technology of Ecological Building. Basel [etc.]:
    1995, p. 39.

8   Arbeitsstättenverordnung § 5 – Lüftung sowie Arbeitsstättenrichtlinien
    § 5 Section 3, Freie Lüftung. Filderstadt: 1988.
9   RWE Energie AG, ed. RWE Energie Bau-Handbuch. 12th edition.
    Heidelberg: 1998, pp. 16/6.
10 Grandjean, Etienne. Wohnphysiologie. Zurich: 1974, p. 205.
11 For information on this topic refer to DIN 5035, Part 2, and to the ASR
    7/3 workplace guidelines on artificial lighting.
12 Bartenbach, Christian, und Witting, Walter. "Licht- und Raummilieu".
    Jahrbuch für Licht und Architektur. Berlin: 1995, pp. 13–23.
13 Tepasse, Heinrich. "Ganzglasgebäude im Simulator – Eine Kritik der
    neuen Energiekonzepte". Bauwelt 43/44 (1996): p. 2489.
14 Bundesarchitektenkammer (eds.). Energiegerechtes Bauen und
    Modernisieren. Basel / Berlin / Boston 1996, p. 19.
15 Johrendt, Reinhold; Küsgen, Horst: "Energiesparen bei Altbauten
    – vergessen?" In: Deutsches Architektenblatt (DAB),
    issue 9/2000, p. 1142.
16 For a discussion on practical application of environmental
    energies in architecture, see: Herzog, Thomas; Krippner, Roland;
    Lang, Werner: "Sol-Arch-Data". Deutsche Bauzeitschrift
    (DBZ), issue 4/98, pp. 97–102.
17 These values are based on the results of a calculation of energy
    requirements on a model. The model calculation was based on
    specific conditions. The values are not universally applicable for other
    buildings, since the energy requirements for cooling are dependent
    on room ventilation. See: Heusler, Winfried. "Energie- und
    komfortoptimierte Fassaden" Fassade 4 (1996), p 48.
18 The values given are typical values for insulating glass; they may vary
    according to thickness of glass, type of coatings and cavity fillings.
19 Gülec, T., Kolmetz, S., und Rouvel, L. "Energieeinsparungspotential
    im Gebäudebestand durch Maßnahmen an der Gebäudehülle".
    Bericht des Entwicklungsvorhabens IKARUS No 5–22.
    Forschungszentrum Jülich GmbH, ed. Jülich: 1994, p. 33.
20 Zürcher, Christoph; Frank, Thomas.
    Bau und Energie: Bauphysik. Stuttgart: 1998. pp. 140-145.
21 Daniels, Klaus. Gebäudetechnik. Ein Leitfaden für Architekten
    und Ingenieure. 2nd edition, Munich: 1996, p. 262.
22 "Das Dach als Klimamodulator – Zur Rolle des Daches als Bestandteil
    natürlicher Lüftungskonzepte". In: Detail, issue 5/1999,
    39th year, pp. 859–865.
23 Härig, Siegfried. Technologie der Baustoffe: Handbuch für
    Studium und Praxis. 12th fully revised edition, Heidelberg:
    1994, pp. 499–515.
24 Krippner, Roland; "Die Gebäudehülle als Wärmeerzeuger und
    Stromgenerator", in Building Skins, Munich: 2001. pp. 48–61.
25 Gebhard, Helmut. Besser Bauen im Alltag.
    Munich: Bayerischer Landesverein für Heimatpflege e.V., 1982.
26 For a discussion of the typological characteristics of external
    wall structures, see: Herzog, Thomas; Krippner, Roland.
    "Synoptical description of decisive subsystems of the building skin".
    Conference report of the "5th European Conference Solar Energy in
    Architecture and Urban Planning". Bonn: 1999. pp. 306–310.
27 Additional information on these themes is found in the following
    contributions: Lang, Werner: "Zur Typologie mehrschaliger
    Gebäudehüllen aus Glas". Detail, issue 7/1998, 38th year.,
    pp. 1225–1232. Lang, Werner; Herzog, Thomas: "Wärme- und
    Sonnenschutzsysteme aus Holz für Zweite-Haut-Fassaden". Detail,
    issue 3/2000, 40th year, pp. 428–433.

2.14 Apartment building in Tokyo, 1996; F.O.B.A.
2.15 Shop in Kobe, 2002; Barthélémy & Griño Architectes

2.15

The Building Skin as Heat and Power Generator

Roland Krippner

The use of solar energy has become increasingly important in the building trade in recent years. Different disciplines within the trade are researching this topic on various levels, in practice and experimentation as well as in theory and a variety of conceptual solutions. The urgent need to drastically reduce the consumption of energy and resources of built structures – and this applies to all buildings, from the single-family house to the exhibition hall – has given rise to new requirements and demands on utilization and construction. Naturally, the integration of solar energy with the building concept, be it for direct or indirect use, also has an impact on the building form, and the relationship between architecture and technology becomes even more significant. When technological solar energy systems are integrated into the building skin, it is vital to avoid looking at these technologies in isolation from the building. The information provided at numerous trade seminars and building fairs demonstrates that today's market already offers a broad range of proven, high-performance solutions. Where a gap still needs to be filled, however, is at the intersection of architecture and solar technology, to achieve what we might call "solar design".[1]

The link to solar energy technology
With regard to the (total) energy balance of buildings, the skin is the most important structural subsystem. For the integration of technological solar energy systems, the skin is the principal interface between architecture and solar technology, both structurally and visually. The principal characteristic of utilizing solar energy in buildings is that the relevant systems are visibly mounted on roofs and walls. Hence they are part of the skin and must also fulfil its traditional protective functions, while being adapted to constructional applications. Moreover, they have a major influence on the visual appearance. To create a technical and energy-efficient design that is also convincing on an aesthetic level, requires knowledge of fundamental technological and functional mechanisms, an understanding of building typologies and the ability to translate this information into an executable design.

Direct – Indirect use[2]
Solar energy occurs in various forms, of which radiation is an especially important energy source for buildings. One must differentiate between direct, i.e. passive use, and indirect, i.e. active use.
Direct use refers to the application of specific measures in the construction to collect, store and distribute incident solar energy, more or less without the implementation of technical devices. Building specific parameters for regulating the interior climate and the energy household include the basic principles of solar heating and cooling and of daylight use. Indirect use refers to additional technical measures for absorbing, distributing and, if necessary, storing solar energy; i.e. collector technology and heat pumps employed to complement heating and cooling measures, as well as photovoltaics and wind energy as power generators. These applications can be allocated to a multitude of technical systems, which represent a broad spectrum of building-specific use of solar energy. The study of technological solar systems presented on the following pages focuses first and foremost on (flat) collectors and pholtovoltaic modules.

Natural supply of solar radiation
Solar radiation varies widely over the course of a day and a year, and is also strongly influenced by prevailing weather conditions. Radiated energy can differ up to a factor of 10 on two consecutive days, reaching at times up to 50× higher values on a clear summer day than on an overcast winter day.
Furthermore, in Central Europe the daily and seasonal supply of solar radiation does not coincide with the peak times for heating or energy requirements. Thermal storage can compensate for short-term shifts. Seasonal changes, on the other hand, pose a major problem: In Germany nearly three quarters of annual radiation occurs in summer, and storing the energy thus gained is only possible by means of elaborate, subterranean storage installations. These restrictions in availability impose technical and economic limitations on the use of solar energy.
Practical applications in buildings are determined by two principal parameters: surface exposure, i.e. the cardinal orientation and angle of the surface, and the absence of shade. Solar radiation (global radiation) is composed of the direct radiation of the sun and of diffuse, indirect radiation resulting from radiation reflected from the sky and surrounding surfaces (sky radiation). In Central Europe, over fifty per cent of the total annual radiation is in the form of diffuse radiation. This percentage is even higher in urban and industrial regions due to smog. Within Germany, there are slight differences in incident energy according to geographic location: generally speaking, conditions are more favourable south of the Main River.[3]

3.1   Office building at Freiburg central station, 2001; Harter+Kanzler

Solar thermics[4]
Types of collectors
A solar collector is the generic term for technical systems that absorb radiation, transform it into heat and distribute it to a fluid carrier medium (water, air). The component where the energy transformation and heat transmittance occurs is called a (solar) absorber. Collectors are most commonly used for water heating and space heating. In addition there are a number of specialized building applications for the generation of process heat (e. g. commercial applications such as in a car wash or commercial laundry) and for cooling. The collector is the central component of a solar-thermal installation. In combination with classic building installations (pipes, heat exchangers, pumps, storage), collectors create a total energy system. Depending upon the type of use, different system configurations are available for selection. Among conventional collectors for domestic use, we differentiate between solar absorbers, flat-plate collectors and evacuated tube collectors (ETCs).

Solar absorbers
The simplest form of a collector is the surface-mounted absorber, predominantly made of black rubber or synthetic mats. They are usually installed on flat roofs or roofs with a shallow slope. While solar absorbers are very cost-efficient, they also yield a relatively low degree of energy.
They are most frequently used to heat water in open-air public pools, where the radiation supplies and heat requirements tend to overlap. Solar roofs with an open absorber made of high-grade stainless steel are also availa-

ble as complete systems; here the solar collector is partially or fully integrated into the roof surface. These selectively coated metal surfaces can also be used for curved roof shapes.

Flat-plate collectors
Flat-plate collectors are the most common type of collectors. In contrast to conventional solar absorbers, flat collectors have a metal absorber, usually in copper, covered with transparent and hail-proof safety glass. For the absorption layer, so-called selective coatings are used today, instead of matte black lacquers (Fig. 3.4). These coatings absorb nearly all the available solar radiation (up to 95%) and transform it into heat while keeping heat radiation loss to a minimum (emission grade $\leq 12\%$). Air collectors are special types of collectors. As a carrier medium, air has the advantage of being usable for space heating or drying directly, that is, without a heat exchanger. Moreover, there is no risk of frost formation, and hence, corrosion, and the requirements for sealing the building component against leakage are less stringent. By comparison to water, air has a lower specific heat capacity, diminished by a factor of 4. This means that such installations must operate with large air volumes coupled with correspondingly large channel diameters and high-performance fans.

Evacuated tube collectors
In the evacuated tube collector, the vacuum created between absorber and casing noticeably reduces both convection and heat-conduction losses. The vacuum must be renewed

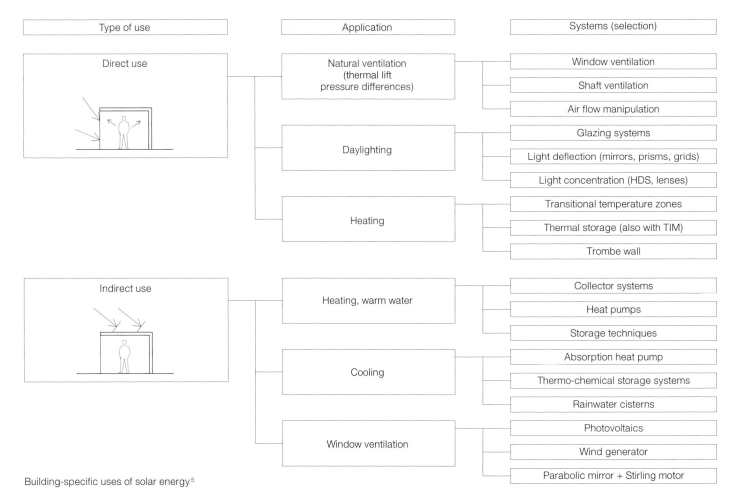

Building-specific uses of solar energy[5]

3.2

at specific maintenance intervals and demands a high degree of leakage protection in the construction.

In the case of the evacuated tube collector, the absorber is integrated into an evacuated glass tube. The vacuum tubes are arranged in parallel rows inside a collector module. Each module holds up to 30 glass tubes, combined inside an insulated connector box and linked to the solar cycle. We differentiate between two principle techniques: the direct link with a co-axial twin tube located inside the absorber for separate routing of the in- and outtake of the thermal carrier as well as the indirect, "dry" link with a heat pipe, in which carrier medium and solar cycle are uncoupled. The modular design offers the advantage, among others, of exchanging individual tubes without disrupting the operation of the entire system. Evacuated tube collectors have demonstrably low heat losses, especially advantageous for high operating temperatures (process heat).

Climatic parameters and applications
Collector orientation and angle
The orientation and angle of a collector surface are essential parameters for achieving good heat yield. Since optimal exposure is difficult to realize in every instance, some degree of reduction must be taken into account whenever the surface deviates from a straightforward southern exposure, although these reductions are much less drastic than is generally assumed. There are a number of useful options with which good coverage can be achieved during the prime usage period. We should point out that collectors are not equipped to utilize radiation levels that fall below 200 W/m^2. Aside from the installation size, the type of use also determines how the collectors must be installed. Thus, systems targeted at heating water should be oriented for maximum exposure to solar radiation in summer, while installations aimed at complementing space heating should be oriented toward the low azimuth angle of the winter sun. Accordingly, angles should be steeper (60°) for favourable amounts of radiation for south-facing surfaces in winter and shallow (20°) in summer. Angles of less than 20° should be avoided, because this would interfere with the self-cleaning ability of the glass surfaces.

Despite the impact of orientation and collector angle, studies have shown that in summer an angle of approx. 40° results in only slight radiation losses in a comparison of south-east to south-west exposure. In the case of full east i.e. west orientation, a shallow angle of approx 20° has been shown to be more favourable since this position ensures longer exposure to heat radiation. In winter, any deviation from full southern exposure leads to more significant losses in radiation yields. While solar radiation of up to 85% of the optimal value is sensible in summer, the limit in winter lies closer to 90%.

Angle and orientation of the collector surface can easily be adjusted in the case of flat roof installations, although it is important to avoid reciprocal shading of the collector elements. In summer, the distance between components should be at least 1.5-times their height and in winter 5-times their height.

Radiation strength is noticeably reduced on vertical facade surfaces. While southern exposure and unshaded conditions can yield up to 90% in winter, only half of the optimal value is available to such installations in summer.

Angle	0°	20°	40°	60°	90°
Orientation					
East	> 95%	93%	86%	72%	46%
South-east	> 95%	> 95%	93%	81%	50%
South	> 95%	**100%**	95%	82%	49%
South-west	> 95%	> 95%	93%	81%	50%
West	> 95%	93%	86%	72%	46%

Energy gain according to different angle and orientation of collector in summer (April to Sept.) [6]

Angle	0°	20°	40°	60°	90°
Orientation					
East	58%	57%	53%	45%	32%
South-east	58%	75%	83%	83%	69%
South	58%	82%	96%	100%	88%
South-west	58%	75%	83%	83%	69%
West	58%	57%	53%	45%	32%

Energy gain according to angle and orientation of collector in winter (Oct. to March) [7]

3.2   Arco, Trentino

3.3

3.4

Applications

In Germany, solar collectors are ideal solutions for heating pool water or water for other uses in consideration of the given geographic and climatic conditions. Simple solar absorbers for heating pool water are efficient already at temperatures of up to 25 °K above ambient temperature, since reflection losses are relatively small in this area.

Warm water preparation

The working temperature for warm water preparation lies approximately between 30 and 60 K. Standard flat-plate collectors with single glass covers and selective absorber coatings will yield good results in these applications. Since the energy requirement tends to diminish nearly constantly over the course of a year, the high radiation values in summer are especially efficient. When calculating the dimensions of a collector installation, it is important to harmonize the system to the actual energy requirements (number of users, consumption, and equipment) and to consider the specific target for heating. The warm water requirements of a 4-person household with optimal southern exposure can be supplied by a roof collector surface of no more than 5–6 m² and a 300-l water tank. Due to the reduced radiation yield, comparable collectors on a facade would have to cover a 20 to 25 % greater area. This would cover normal use of warm water in summer. With a good cost-use-ratio, between 50 to 60 % can be thus covered on an annual average. Properly sized and designed flat-plate collector installations, used at 30 % of their full capacity, can be expected to yield energy gains ranging between 250 and 350 kWh/m²a; evacuated tube collectors achieve up to 450 kWh/m²a.

Space heating

In Germany, there is a pronounced discrepancy between radiation supply and space heating requirements over the course of a year due to the seasonal changes we have already discussed. While nearly 60 % of the space heating demand falls into the peak heating period, from November to February, the incident radiation supply during that same period on a surface with a southern exposure represents only about 12 to 15 % of the annual radiation supply. This means that – in comparison to warm water preparation – the applications for space heating have higher requirements per se.
To transmit useable heat into the heating cycle, the operating temperature for space heating must lie between 40 and 90 K. This application is best served by flat-plate collectors with selective coating and by evacuated tube collectors. To cover up to 35 % of the annual heating requirements of a well-insulated single-family house, an absorber surface of approximately 0.5 to 0.8 m² (evacuated tube collector) is needed per 10 m² of heated space; in the case of flat-plate collectors the average is 0.8 to 1.1 m². Solar space heating systems with combined warm-water preparation can be expected to yield a total energy gain of approximately 200 kWh/m²a.

Photovoltaics [8]

Photo-solar cells

Photovoltaic (PV) installations are technical systems that transform solar radiation directly into electricity. At the core of such an installation are the solar cells that are combined into modules. These systems produce DC voltage that needs to be transformed into 230-AC voltage with a 50 Hz frequency for standard household appliances with the help of a DC-AC

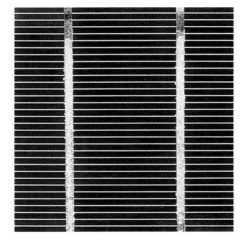

3.5

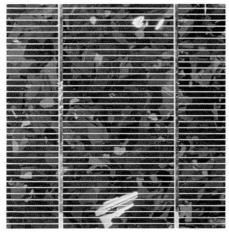

3.6

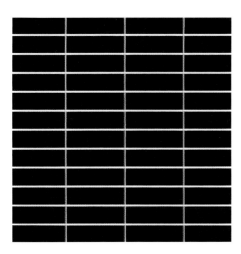

3.7

3.8

converter. Solar systems that produce electricity are usually operated as networked (network-coupled) systems connected to a supply network that serves as storage; so-called off-grid systems are rare; in these systems excess electricity is stored in accumulators (e. g. rechargeable batteries).

Material and composition
The basic material of standard solar cells is the semi-conductor silicon. Cells composed of mono- and polycrystal-line silicon are produced in coating thicknesses of 200–300 μm (0.3 mm), while so-called thin-film cells and amorphous silicon cells have a thickness of only 1–6 μm. Solar cells have a relatively low efficiency factor, which depending on cell material can vary by up to a factor of 3. For standard (silicon-) cells the maximum theoretical efficiency factor is roughly 28%. Performance is affected primarily by radiation intensity, surface area and cell temperature. The following figures provide a simplified overview of available solar cells.

- Monocrystalline silicon cells, with an extremely pure and completely even crystalline grid structure: expensive and elaborate to manufacture, these cells reach efficiency ratios of between 15 and 18% (Fig. 3.5)
- Polycrystalline silicon cells, characterized by a lack in purity of material and partially even crystalline grid structure: easier to manufacture and thus less expensive, these cells reach efficiency ratios of 13 to 15% (Fig. 3.6)
- Amorphous silicon cells, thin-film cells, in which the crystals are mostly random: cost- and material-efficient manufacture, these cells achieve efficiency ratios of 5 to 8%; this cell type is ideal for large surfaces (Fig. 3.7)
- Thin-film cells, new cell technology, copper-indium-diselenid (CIS) and cadmium-telluride (CdTe) cells: low material requirements, also suitable for steam-application on large areas of nearly any type of surface and in any shape; achieve efficiency ratios of up to 9.5% (CIS) (Fig. 3.8)

The development of hybrid cells, a combination of monocrystalline and amorphous silicon cells, and stacking cells, in which two are three layers are stacked on top of each other (tandem or triple cells), is leading to an improvement in efficiency. To improve the performance of such stacked cells still further, one solution is to design each of the layers in a triple cell, for example, for a different spectral zone (short, medium and long-wave radiation).
Approximately 30 to 50 crystalline cells are usually combined into larger, prefabricated units. These photovoltaic modules are multi-layered, that is, the cells are either embedded in synthetic resin between glass panes or between glass and a synthetic laminate, whose backing can be opaque, translucent (obscured glass/light-deflecting film) or transparent (clear glass, transparent film) depending upon requirements. Amorphous silicon cells can also be mounted on pliable carriers such as plastic sheets or foils. In addition, milled, semi-transparent cells are also available, and printing processes with CIS cells are equally possible.

3.3 »TU Arena«, Tübingen, 2004; Allmann Sattler Wappner
3.4 Technical college, Bitterfeld, 2000; scholl architekten
3.5 Monocrystalline silicon cells
3.6 Polycristalline silicon cells
3.7 Amorphous silicon cells, semitransparent
3.8 CIS cells

3.9

The performance of a photovoltaic installation is indicated with values in Wp or kWp, with p as the "peak" factor or maximum performance, which can be transferred to the circuit to which the installation is connected; however, this is a relative value. This value is generally calculated on the basis of an incident radiation of 1000 W/m² at cell temperatures of 25 °C. In practice, the true performance tends to be at approximately 90 % of this rated performance.

Structure and colour
The structural characteristics of photovoltaic modules are the form and arrangement of cells as well as the fine tracks that connect them. Most crystalline cells are designed in square formats (holohedral or bevelled) with a length ranging from 100 to 130 mm; in the meantime, PV-cells are available in nearly all primary shapes and their variants. Light transmittance can be varied by adjusting the space between the cells (usually between 3 and 15 mm). While amorphous and monocrystalline cells present a homogeneous image, polycrystalline cells are characterized by a multi-fractured, structured surface with differing light reflections. In addition to the standard colours blue and anthracite, monocrystalline cells especially offer many different variations with regard to the appearance of colour. The colour of a solar cell is changed by means of applying thin interference layers onto its surface in a steam process, which results in a (minor) deterioration in the efficiency ratio.

Climatic parameters and installation principles
The annual performance of a photovoltaic installation is also determined by the orientation and angle of the module surface. In contrast to thermal collectors, radiation of less than 200 W/m² can still be harnessed for solar power. In Germany, the highest annual radiation volume is available to south-facing fixed systems installed on an angle of 30° or less. While minor deviations of up to 5 % are achieved in south-east and south-west oriented roof installations at angles of up to 45°, performance diminishes drastically in vertical facade surfaces. For network-coupled installation (1 to 5 kWp), one can expect average power generation of 700 kWh/a per installed kWp/a, depending upon geographical and climatic conditions. For average household power requirements of approximately 3500 kWh/a, nearly half of the annual requirements, or more, can be covered with an average installation size (2 to 3 kWp). It is important to note, however, that the percentage of power for direct use amounts only to 20 to 25 % as a result of the time lapse in the power generation. The rule of thumb for a rough estimate of a PV installation is that 1 kWp requires a generator surface of approximately 10 m². Depending upon the cell type, the required surface fluctuates between 7 and 9 m² (monocrystalline), 8 and 11 m² (polycrystalline) or 16 and 20 m² (amorphous). The required surface for CIS cells is 11 to 13 m², for CdTe cells, 14 to 18 m². It must also be taken into account that the space requirements have an influence on the accumulated energy consumption of the PV system, as in the case of modules with low efficiency ratios in particular more attention has to be paid to the frame or support.[10] It is important to avoid any shading of photovoltaic surfaces, since even small shadows (cast for example by an antenna) result in noticeable reductions in performance. Since all units of a system connected in series are reduced to the smallest performance in the entire system, partial sections in shade

Angle	0°	30°	60°	90°
Orientation				
East	93%	90%	78%	< 60%
South-east	93%	96%	88%	66%
South	93%	**100%**	91%	68%
South-west	93%	96%	88%	66%
West	93%	90%	78%	< 60%

Energy gain according to different angle and orientation of photovoltaics installation (100% = 1055 kWh/m²a) [9]

can demobilize larger module surfaces. Parallel connections can limit such losses in performance. In principle, fixed and moveable elements are distinguished in the integration of photovoltaic modules into the building skin. As an alternative to fixed mounted units, one can also use moveable, uniaxial (Fig. 3.9) and biaxial tracking systems. The rotational axis can be vertical or horizontal, depending upon the orientation and the specific installation conditions. In theory, biaxial tracking PV modules are capable of utilizing twice as much solar radiation per year as optimally orientated fixed systems. However, since the performance of uniaxial tracking systems is only slightly less than that of biaxial systems, one must consider not only the more elaborate (and expensive) mechanics but also the additional requirements for integrating such systems into the building structure. It is important to evaluate and test the overall cost-benefit-ratio for tracking systems, as nearly 50% of average annual radiation is present in diffuse radiation. In the case of semitransparent modules, the performance can be increased by using holograms to focus the radiation on the photovoltaic cells.

On integrating solar systems into the building skin
Total surface potential
Estimates on potential surfaces in Germany show that out of a total gross roof surface of 4345 mill. m^2, approximately 30% are suited for the integration of solar systems in or on the roof, depending on orientation and shading. At a rough calculation in terms of facades, without differentiating according to usage types, a total surface of 6660 mill. m^2 would present approximately 6%, that is 400 Mio. m^2 of facade surfaces with south-east to south-west orientation suitable for integration measures. In terms of the entire building skin, these figures result in a theoretically usable surface of more than 1700 mill m^2 for the integration of thermal solar and photovoltaic systems.[11] Conversely, up until the end of 2004 the total surface covered by collectors was 5.8 mill. m^2. While sales of collectors rose each year by 25–30% up to 2001, the increase has fallen back to 15% in recent years. By contrast trends in sales of photovoltaics have increased almost tenfold.[12] This has been greatly assisted by the "100,000 roofs-solar-power-program" and the "Renewable Energies Law". Despite this positive development, the total percentage of solar thermal power and photovoltaics is approximately 0.35% of available roof and facade surface. In other words, we are not taking full advantage of a potential that represents not only a major technical challenge but could also lead towards true solar architecture.

The task of integration
Integrating solar technical systems into the building skin means that a component has to become an integral part of the roof and the building skin, whereby the component must fulfil functional and structural tasks as a part of both. Hence the visual and constructional integration of solar components must guarantee that the installation on or in the external skin does not conflict with the requirements and characteristics of the building skin, but complements and supports the latter in an optimal manner. Design is not an over-arching principle in this instance. An important factor for the integration task is the targeted thermal i.e. photovoltaic solar energy use and the resulting scale of the systems. The dimensions of the system have considerable impact on the external image of the buildings and must there-

fore be harmonized with the visual principles at work on the roof and facade surfaces.
Many buildings display a lack in sensitivity and/or an absence of understanding of the "building's character" when it comes to the task of integration, which tends to manifest itself in a poor adaptation of the "interventions" into the overall structure. This illustrates all too clearly the necessity to consider aspects of design in addition to the requirements that arise from the system technology and practical concerns for construction. For this reason, the following paragraph focuses on design principles and options for integrating solar systems into roofs and facades. To begin with, we shall explore the complex topic of design independently of technical and constructional aspects.[13]

Visual integration
Whenever we speak of design in architecture, the term is often limited to (formal) aesthetic criteria.[14] But form and colour alone do not determine how appropriate an "integration" might be. Material and the construction of the building skin, as well as the size and proportions of its individual elements are additional relevant parameters. To visually integrate solar systems into the building skin, one must first analyze the principal and typological characteristics of roof and wall. This is far more challenging in terms of facades than roofs. While one phase of investigation is generally sufficient for a roof (excluding roof extensions and conversions), at least three steps seem to be required for facades. Roofs offer a tremendous potential for utilizing solar energy. Roof design – shape, angle and covering – is strongly influenced by regional factors, i.e. climate and local materials, and has a lasting impact on the image of cities and villages. With regard to the visual integration of collectors and photovoltaic modules, architects are not alone in commenting on random component placement on the roof, the destruction of homogeneous surfaces, discrepancies in style, and the lack of proportion between the component dimensions and the smaller roof covering units, as reasons for poor quality in design.
A study of basic design options based on roof forms reveals that orthogonal forms, such as shed roofs and gable roofs, offer a range of options, which, although not necessarily greater, is frequently more harmonious than in the case in hipped and mansard roofs, where installations across the entire surface are less practical because of the ridges and the resulting sections.
Clearly, the design (of a solar system) has considerable impact on the visual appearance of the building skins, and in this context facades are notable for presenting a multitude of additional aspects by comparison to roof surfaces. In their role as the "face" of the building, they reveal design principles, structural parameters and layout principles of the surfaces to a much greater degree. These attributes are expressed by proportion and articulation, by architectonic decoration and are reflected in the differentiation, exaggeration and modulation of the facade and its components. The result is a broad spectrum of designs, which are moreover defined by building materials and the era in which they were realized.
As visual messengers (image carriers), facades play a special role and collectors and PV modules installed on facades

3.9   Paul Löbe Building, Berlin, 2001; Stefan Braunfels

3.10

are very much design elements, in contrast to those mounted on roofs. Moreover, when such elements are integrated into partial components of the facade, e.g. balcony balustrades, operable elements, etc., their visual prominence creates higher demands on the design. Hence the integration of technological solar systems calls for a close study of the typological facade characteristics to achieve a gradual understanding of potential options for mounting.

A satisfying design solution is largely determined by the necessary harmonization of the overall concept with each detail; this includes issues such as the surface material and colouring. Thus the surfaces of solar installations, smooth and reflecting surfaces in metal and glass, are generally faced with roof-covering and facade materials with rough surfaces and "warm" tones.
In terms of formal and aesthetic criteria, the products now available on the market offer a broad spectrum of design options with a wealth of alternatives (polygonal and polychrome), as manufacturers strive to respond to the wishes of architects and clients. Thus the wide range of colours is often emphasized as a special advantage in the case of photovoltaics. Still, the use of additional colours and shapes in building skins is not without risk and should be carefully considered. However, with regard to the visual integration of PV modules, colour choice (in addition to colours such as blue, gold, magenta and black, intense research is being conducted to expand the palette) does not play such a dominant role. Especially blue and anthracite are perfectly "convincing" as architectural solutions since they harmonize very well with most technical, that is synthetic and natural building materials such as concrete, steel, glass as well as wood and clay brick.[17]
It is important to note that not every potential surface – i.e. an optimally or sub-optimally oriented surface – is suited for the visual integration of solar energy systems. Clearly, the options are much greater when planning a new building than for installations on existing structures.[18] In terms of consistent and convincing integration, this means that one must consider the typological and structural characteristics of the building skin and identify continuous, self-contained surfaces. Additional building sections on top of, in front of and inside the building must also be considered as these often present yet another challenge to achieving a good integration.

Structural integration
With regard to the structural integration, the optimal adaptability of the systems to different skin structures is another important aspect. It is important to differentiate between principal installation options of technical solar systems on wall and roof. In addition to location (external and internal), the position with regard to the water-conducting layer is an essential criterion. These basic principles result in a variety of requirements that must be analyzed for each specific installation situation. Issues relating to construction and the physics of the structure, such as the interaction between component depth, roof- and wall installation as well as the location of the system in relation to the respective functional layers (load transfer, insulation, moisture protection, etc.) have to be clarified. Decisions with regard to detail measurements, building component dimensions, the design of connecting geometries

3.10 Single-family house in Hegenlohe, 2004; Tina Volz, Michael Resch

Position	Full coverage	Ridge	Verge	Eaves	Area
Single piece					
Continuous					
Symmetrical					
Asymmetrical					
Mulitple					
Symmetrical					

Positioning of technical solar systems on roofs. Shed roof model.[15]

Position	Parapet	Skylight	Parapet + Skylight	Soffit area	Floor height
(Partially) symmetrical					
Continuous					
Grouped					
Regular					
Asymmetrical					
Irregular					
Combined					

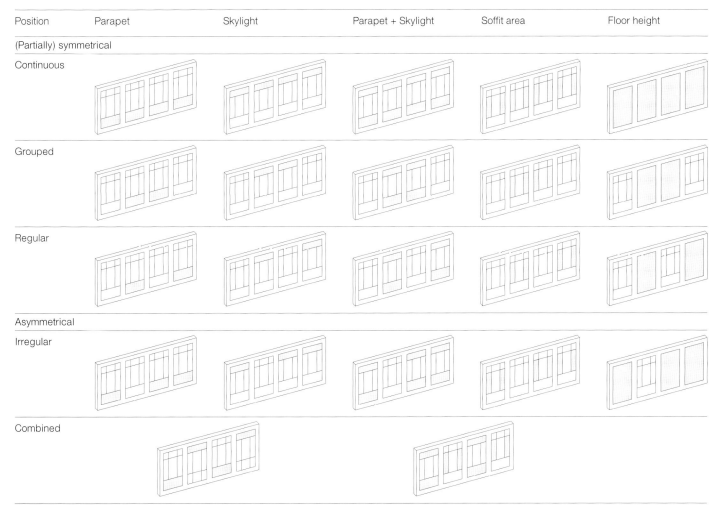

Positioning of technical solar systems on facade. Placement in openings.[16]

3.11

and profile sections all influence the visual appearance of the building skin and must be evaluated as to their impact on the structural layout and overall integration.

Roof[19]

For the roof area, the basic principles of integration can be applied simultaneously to solar thermal and photovoltaic systems.

For steep-pitched roofs, one must differentiate between additive solutions mounted on top of the roof covering and integrated solutions (Fig. 3.10) mounted at the level of the water-conducting layer. For flat roofs there are a number of options for free-standing installations.

In rooftop installations, the systems are usually mounted with a metal substructure parallel to the existing roof covering, whose insulating function is thus maintained. Any pipes and cables are laid above the roof skin. This additive solution tends to present few problems in terms of adaptation. However, this solution does not permit the utilization of substitution effects. In addition to its own weight, the substructure must absorb wind pressure and suction forces and transfer them into the roof truss. Depending upon load, roof fastening can be realized by means of roof hooks attached to the rafters or roof hooks independent of rafters. Since the collectors represent a very real additional load, the load-bearing capacity of the structure must be tested and, if necessary, reinforced.

By contrast, integrated collectors and PV modules replace the conventional roof covering and must therefore take on the protective function of the roof skin. In this solution the mounting system must guarantee sufficient weather protection. Especially the junctions to the roof covering between components must be both rain- and snow proof, and must be able to absorb any heat expansion. The market offers a broad palette of roof solutions ranging from the total-energy-roof to conventional brick-connection-method and customized covering frames, which are attached to the existing substructure; the transitions to roof covering, verge, ridge and eaves are realized with metal sheets and sealing gaskets. The connecting and linking cables are installed in the cavities between the rafters in integrated roof installations.

When the roof slope falls below a minimal range, a waterproof sub-roof is required to guard against rain seepage; for PV modules especially, it is important to provide sufficient rear-ventilation for the underside of the installed components to prevent condensation. Systems that combine solar thermals and photovoltaics are now available. These systems offer the advantage of simple options for combinations without having to change the frame, fastening and insulation system. Photovoltaic systems are now also available in modules with considerably reduced dimensions, e. g. solar roofing tiles. Conventional connection techniques simplify the task of mounting and adaptation and create a direct relation to the existing modular principle. Above transitional temperature areas such as atria, corridors, etc., photovoltaic elements can be installed as semitransparent sunshades on (sloping) glass roof constructions under consideration of safety regulations for overhead glazing.

For installations on flat roofs, a special substructure is required which serves to determine the mounting angle and, above all, to absorb the own weight and onslaught of wind forces. Since the weight of the supporting or substructure may result in considerable additional loads, the load-bearing capacity of the roof must be tested prior to installation. The choice of anchorage depends on the static test result: in the case of heavy load anchorage, the system is mounted with concrete plinths onto the flat roof to avoid an expensive and potentially damaging penetration of the roof skin. In the case of insufficient load-bearing capacity, the loads must be distributed to structural components capable of bearing the loads via a special substructure. Photovoltaic installations are also available as integrated systems for flat roofs, for example as a usable protective layer over the roof skin. Surface-laminated cells on conventional roof- and insulation strips can be used as a roof skin. The extremely low self-weight of these systems makes it possible to install them on roofs with low load-bearing capacities.

Facade
Since the early 1990s, the term solar facade has become more frequent in research and practice. It is frequently used to denote solar thermal installations in which the function of the wall as climate protection and buffer is complemented by the additional function of acting as an active heat source. Yet these are not the complete (or integrated) solutions offered for roofs, because the facade must meet additional requirements such as daylight use or visual contact to the outside. Despite its reduced performance and higher demand on design, facade integration opens the door to additional options, for example, in cases where poor exposure and the shape of a steep-pitched roof or insufficient load-bearing capacity of a flat roof, do not allow for roof installations. Generally speaking, one differentiates between additive and integrated solutions for facades, which can be installed vertically or on an angle. Due to different system

weights, deviations in building height and component size as well as the various integration options that result from these parameters, collectors and PV modules are treated separately in terms of facade integration.
Solar collectors can be integrated into warm- and cold facades as additive components arranged in small units and as large-format collector surfaces (Fig. 3.3). The great variety of external wall solutions available on the market means that fewer standardized installation systems are available for facade integration than for roof integration. In massive wall constructions, the building height of the collector generally dictates an additive installation on top of or in front of the water-bearing layer. Depending on the insulation thickness, the component may also be attached directly on the load-bearing layer or between wood studs, which means that the entire system can be integrated into insulating layers with external skin that are standard today.
Many manufacturers now offer fully integrated systems – especially for post-and-beam facades – in which flat-bed collectors and PV modules are simply a further building component in addition to windows, fixed glazing and opaque balustrade components. This component is easily adapted to different modular integration systems. Collectors especially require greater effort and cost for installation on standard dimensions and shapes in comparison to roof installation.

Low building height and relatively great adaptability as well as a number of design options (different formats, colouring

3.11 Office and factory building in Kassel, 2002; Hegger Hegger Schleiff

Installation of technical solar systems – Facade

	Vertical installation with distance to water-bearing layer
	Vertical installation directly on top of water-bearing layer
	Vertical installation integrated into water-bearing layers
	Vertical installation between water-bearing layer and internal surround
	Vertical installation – Internal with distance behind water-bearing layer
	Vertical installation – Angled with distance in front of water-bearing layer
	Horizontal installation with distance in front of water-bearing layer

Installation of technical solar systems – Roof

	High pitched roof with distance in front of water-bearing layer
	High pitched roof directly on top of water-bearing layer
	High pitched roof integrated into water-bearing layers
	High pitched roof between water-bearing layer and internal surround
	High pitched roof – Internal with distance behind water-bearing layer
	Flat roof, elevated on top of water-bearing layer
	Technical solar system
	Water-bearing layer
	Internal surround

Installation of technical solar systems in relation to water-bearing layer[20]

and structure) make photovoltaics particularly well suited to facade integration. The dual function of wall surround and sun protection can be coupled with protective and regulative functions to benefit from building technological and economic synergy effects. Photovoltaics in the facade can offer an economical and aesthetic alternative to materials such as natural stone or stainless steel despite diminished yield potentials. In principal, a differentiation is made between the installation in front of opaque and transparent/translucent surfaces. Photovoltaic modules can be integrated into opaque, non-ventilated facades and in ventilated facades; in both cases it is important to ensure a low operating temperature. Since the efficiency ratio diminishes with increasing temperatures, at least 5 cm should be allowed for constructions with rear ventilation. In addition to framed standard components, frameless PV modules are integrated into post-and-beam and component facade structures. As the modules match the optical and functional properties of glass, they are easily installed with standard glass fastening techniques; single or multiple linear bearings, point fastenings and integration into structural-glazing systems are all possible. In front of transparent/translucent facade surfaces the photo(voltaic) cells can be integrated into the composite window structure as space enclosure. Depending upon the layer density, however, diminished light transmittance and reduced total energy transmission coefficient must be considered in addition to the temperature rise in the cells (Fig. 3.11). The second layer, i.e. the external layer in double-skin facades or – with an interstitial space – as sunshade, offers another option for installation. In this case, sufficient rear-ventilation is guaranteed; and in the case of double-skin facades the resultant heat can be put to additional use. The combination of photovoltaic power generation and sun shading opens the door to a rich variety of uses for fixed (canopy roofs, cantilevered roofs; Fig. 3.12) or moveable systems (awnings, louvres). In shading applications, especially, daylight incidence and heat transmission, sun- and glare protection as well as visual contact to the outside can be controlled by varying the joint dimension between the individual cells.

Perspectives for the future
Much has happened in the area of using solar energy for buildings, both in terms of (energy)technology and in the construction field. There is a building boom, but the results are rarely what could be called "solar design", that is, the aesthetic qualities of the buildings continue to be a largely unsolved problem. And yet the enormous potential of materials, semi-finished products and systems as well as the corresponding integration- and combination options, provide architects and engineers with a variety of opportunities for designing and implementing innovative solar technologies. As far as the task of integration is concerned, there is still a lack of typological studies of the building skin, which would be an important basis and evaluation tool for the visual integration of solar technical systems. Even though such studies seem primarily necessary for existing buildings, they provide helpful guidelines in the planning of new buildings as well. Buildings are complex structures for which there are no universal answers to the question of selecting the appropriate means. Individual solutions must always be viewed in the context of the whole. To achieve a positive result, it is essential to analyze the totality of all relevant information in the search for an optimal solution.

Like all technical innovations, solar technology changes the look of buildings, and this applies to new buildings and to conversions of existing structures. One essential task is to focus not only on the functionally efficient and structurally correct integration of solar-technological components in the building skin, but also to ensure that they have a positive aesthetic effect, that is, to ensure that they are visually integrated into the overall architectural concept. The challenge is to find adequate design solutions for these technical innovations – new forms of expression for modified performance parameters.

Many promising ideas and examples have already been created along the "solar" path towards a new, building culture that is equally sustainable on an ecological, technical and aesthetic level; still, much remains to be done, both in terms of quantitative application and in terms of qualitative translation.

Notes:
1   Herzog, Thomas: "Solar Design". In: Detail. Zeitschrift für Architektur + Baudetail, 39th year, issue 3/1999, pp. 359–362.
2   RWE Energie Bau-Handbuch.12th edition. Essen: RWE Energie AG, Bereich Anwendungstechnik,1998, chapter 17, pp. 3ff.
3   Annual global radiation (2002, on a horizontal surface), e.g. in Flensburg 983 kWh/m²a, Frankfurt/Main 1053 kWh/m²a, Munich 1183 kWh/m²a. Deviation from the long-term mean between 1981 and 2000 was max. 5 %. Sonnenenergie, , May 2003, p.64.
4   Active solar energy use. In: Marko, Armin; Braun, Peter O. (eds.): Thermische Solarenergienutzung an Gebäuden.
     Für Ingenieure und Architekten. Part II. Berlin: 1997, pp. 195–393 and RWE Energie: Bau-Handbuch, 2004, chapter 17, pp. 7–44.
5   Source: Prof. Thomas Herzog, TU Munich
6   RWE Energie Bau-Handbuch, 12th edition, Essen 1998, chapter 17, p. 22.
7   ibid., p. 23
8   ibid., pp. 39–52 and Müller, Helmut F.O.; Nolte, Christoph; Pasquay, Till: "Die Mittel aktiv zu sein.Von der Aufgabenstellung zur Lösung". In: Danner, Dietmar; Dassler, Friedrich H.;

Krause, Jan R. (eds): Die klima-aktive Fassade. Leinfelden-Echterdingen: 1999, pp. 105–113
9   RWE Energie Bau-Handbuch, 1998, chapter 17, p. 42 and product documentation SGG Prosol, Solar-Module für Gebäude, Saint-Gobin Glass Solar, Aachen
10   cf. Corradini, Roger; Wagner, Ulrich: Ganzheitliche Analyse von zukünftigen Photovoltaik-Systemen, part 1. In: Technik in Bayern, vol. 10, 2/2006, p. 32–33.
11   Quaschning, Volker: Systemtechnik einer klimaverträglichen Elektrizitätsversorgung in Deutschland für das 21. Jahrhundert. Düsseldorf: VDI-Verlag, 2000, pp. 44–50
12   Stryi-Hipp, Gerhard: Photovoltaik-Produktion in Deutschland. Kapazitäten, Lieferfähigkeit, Engpässe und Wettbewerbsfähigkeit für PV 'Made in Germany'. In: 20. Symposium Photovoltaische Solarenergie, Kloster Banz, Staffelstein. Conference volume, Regensburg: 2005, no page.
13   Krippner, Roland: Architektonische Aspekte solarer Energietechnik. In: SOLEG – Abschlussbericht, ed.: Schölkopf, Wolfgang, Munich: 2001, p. 3.12-1–3.12-29. Project coordination ZAE Bayern and Herzog, Thomas; Krippner, Roland.
14   Krippner, Roland: "Ökologie vs. Ästhetik?" In: DBZ – Deutsche Bauzeitschrift, 48th year, issue 9/2000, pp.114–118.
15   cf. Note 13, p. 3.12–16.
16   cf. Note 13, p. 3.12–20.
17   Busse, Hans-Busso v.; Müller, Helmut F.O.; Runkel, Susanne: Photovoltaik. Integration einer neuen Technologie in die Architektur. Forschungsbericht. Dortmund: Universität Dortmund, 1996, pp. 10ff.
18   Krippner, Roland: "Zwischen Gebäudetypologie und Denkmalschutz". In: Bauhandwerk/Bausanierung, 21st year, issue 3/1999, pp. 43–46 and Schittich, Christian (ed.). In: DETAIL Solares Bauen, Munich: 2003, p. 37, Note 15.
19   For a description of assembly systems for roof and facade integration, see also: Solarthermische Anlagen. Leitfaden für Heizungsbauer, Dachdecker, Gas-Wasserinstallateure, Elektriker, Fachplaner, Architekten und Bauherren. Published by the DGS, Deutsche Gesellschaft für Sonnenenergie, Berlin 6/2001 and Photovoltaische Anlagen. Leitfaden für Elektriker, Dachdecker, Fachplaner, Architekten und Bauherren. Published by the DGS, Deutsche Gesellschaft für Sonnenenergie, Berlin 2/2002.
20   cf. Note 13, p. 3.12–24

3.12 Lehrter Station, Berlin, 2006; von Gerkan, Marg und Partner

3.12

Materials in the building skin – from material to construction

Modern architecture is using building materials in new and innovative ways. Not only industrially produced materials such as glass, plastics, metals and concrete, but also traditional building materials like wood and stone. In the building skin this is leading to interesting examples where the fascination derives from both the nature of the materials themselves and the way in which they are processed and utilized. The emphasis is not so much on building to suit the material used, but on the impact a particular building material creates, its material and visual qualities. Today conventional solutions are giving way to individual concepts, often demanding processing techniques and designs that challenge architects, planners and construction firms alike.

Building processes are shifting from the building site back to the factory. An example of this is the prefabricated ventilated aluminium skin, covered in plastic sheeting, used for the Micro-Compact Home in Munich (see p. 102ff). Technology from the aerospace and automotive industries was employed in its manufacture. To produce the stainless steel mesh used on the Administration Building in Heilbronn (see p. 80ff), a special mesh-weaving machine was developed, which meant integrating an entire production process into the planning of the building. Other projects involve producing special profiles and frames, entire assemblies or individual components, or using standard products in new and imaginative ways. Projects like the Cycling Stadium in Berlin (see p. 86ff) demonstrate how standard series products for industrial use can be successfully transferred to architectural applications. And polyurethane foam, more familiar in roof renovations, has also made the transition to the building skin in the house in Zurndorf (see p. 132ff). By contrast, in the case of the Music Academy in Santiago de Compostela, the holes created when the blocks were drilled out of the quarry have been left in the surface of the finished stone slabs (see p. 190ff). No further surface finishing was carried out, and it is this unique structure that gives the facade its distinctive, individual look.

These examples show only a selection of the options available in designing the building skin. Set out on the following pages is how this was achieved in the individual projects, i.e. that part of the process which is seldom covered in architectural publications. Once again we see how important careful workmanship is, if the final result is to match the original idea of how the material should be used.

Metal

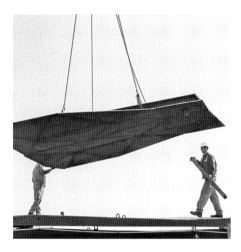

Corten steel plate
After welding the steel plate was sandblasted and evenly oxidized. Subsequent treatment of the surface with hot paraffin gives additional depth.
Fixing method: The different angles give the individual steel plates sufficient static height to form a rigid folded structure.
Point spacing to the system surface: +10 cm, 0 cm, -10 cm; total: 20 cm

Quantity: 1160 triangles, fitted together in groups of twelve and then welded on site.
Size of triangles: edge length between 1.10 and 2.80 m
Plate thickness: 14 mm

Documentation Centre in Hinzert
Architects: Wandel Hoefer Lorch + Hirsch, Saarbrücken (see p. 70)

Stainless steel rod mesh
Fixing method: The stainless steel mats are attached to prefabricated, height-adjustable metal frames of galvanized steel and connected to each other with steel springs.
Thickness of overall mesh: 10 mm
Weight: 9.4 kg/m^2
Aperture: 61.5%

Cycling Stadium in Berlin
Architect: Dominique Perrault, Paris (see p. 86)

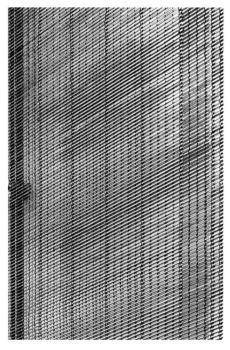

Stainless steel strip mesh
Fixing method: A GRP grid and a load-bearing frame of galvanized wide-flange T-sections support the mesh. The grid is fixed to locking plates located at the junctions and which rest on the reinforced concrete floor. On site metal strips were interwoven by hand on long and cross joints in the panel elements to form a seamless surface.

Rainwater is carried away between the support grid and the steel frame via a double layer of bitumen.

Width of strips: 50 mm
Thickness of strips: 0.4 mm
Size of individual woven lengths:
1.0 × 6.0 m

Administration Building in Heilbronn
Architect: Dominik Dreiner, Gaggenau
(see p. 80)

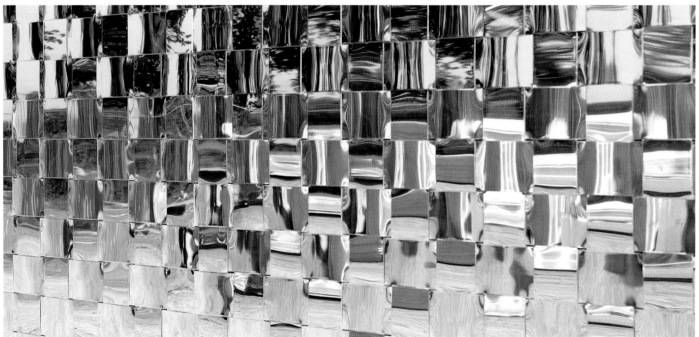

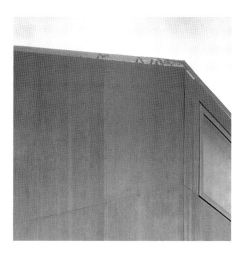

Perforated stainless steel sheet
Fixing method: The panels are bolted to steel tubes. Coated polyester fleece behind carries away rainwater.
Size: up to 1.2 × 4.13 m
Weight: 10.1 kg/m²
Aperture: 35.43 %

House in Dornbirn
Architects: Oskar Leo Kaufmann + Albert Rüf, Dornbirn (see p. 76)

Copper sheet
Rolled copper sheet was used as well as perforated sheet and expanded copper sheet. As the copper cladding oxidises, its colour changes to dark brown or black; parts of the facade directly exposed to the weather gradually develop a green patina over time.
Fixing method: On the roof the sheets are affixed to stainless-steel frames and mounted onto a support of height-

adjustable pegs. On the facades the panels are fitted as a curtain wall.
Size: max. 3.60 × 1.18 m
Thickness: between 1.5 and 3.0 mm
Weight: copper sheet, 13.5 kg/m²,
expanded copper 12 kg/m²
Aperture: 15 %

Service Centre in Munich
Architects: Staab Architekten, Berlin (see p. 94)

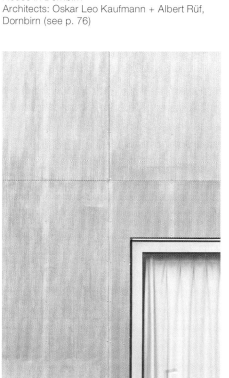

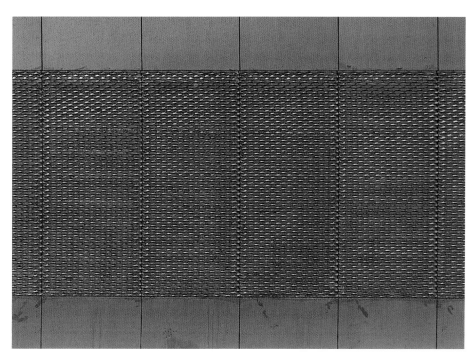

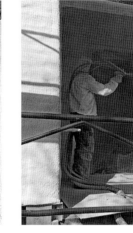

*Domed aluminium discs
polished and naturally anodized*
Fixing method: First the mounting plates were fixed to the outer layer (which was strengthened in the area in which the discs are attached). Then the discs centred on these plates and fixed. The lower plate is additionally sealed to protect against penetrating moisture. Slightly different spacings between the discs even out the varia-

tions in the building volume.
Base: Sprayed concrete facade with sealing layer, externally insulated, rendered and finished with a coloured plastic sealant.
Diameter: 660 mm
No. of discs: approx. 17000
Rise: 90 mm

Selfridges in Birmingham
Architects: Future Systems, London (see p. 104)

Polyurethane foam
The walls have a moisture-diffusing UV-protecting layer.
Fixing method: The foam was sprayed onto the load-bearing frame of OSB.
Thickness: between 920 and 1470 mm
Insulation properties: 0.34 W/m^{2}K
Price per m^2: €900 material/assembly

House in Zurndorf
Architects: PPAG Architekten, Vienna (see p.132)

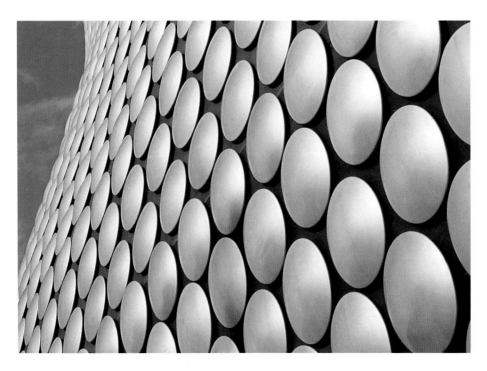

EFTE sheeting
(Ethylene/tetrafluoroethylene copolymer)
Fixing method: The cushions, each made up of at least two layers, were pretensioned and stabilized by means of excess pressure in the enclosed air volume. Twelve air-pumping stations keep the operational pressure of the cushions constant at around 300 Pa (roof) to 400 Pa (facade). The cushions are affixed with aluminium profiles which clamp the weatherstrip edge in an EPDM rubber profile to the steel frame.
Size of rhomboids: between 2.0×7.0 m to 4.6×17.0 m
No. of rhomboids: 2874
Thickness of sheeting: 0.2 mm
Weight: With a density of 1.75 kN/m³, the resulting weight per unit area is under 1.0 kg/m² for two sheeting layers of one cushion.
Fire rating: Fire-resistant building material B1, melting point at 275 °C

Allianz Arena in Munich
Architects: Herzog & de Meuron, Basel
(see p. 114)

Glass

*Rhomboid glass elements
flat, convex and concave*
Increased strength as a result of the curvature.
Fixing method: Each pane is fixed by means of two clamps on opposite sides. The panes stay in position even under conditions of severe earth tremors, the frame itself slides at the edge connection with the panes. For added safety stainless-steel sheet is inserted in the groove in the edge of the outer pane.
Frame: diagonal post-and-beam facade; the inner faces were sealed with silicone to ensure a proper seal despite the raking angle of the posts.
Size of rhomboids: 3200 × 2000 mm
Thickness: 2 × 6 mm laminated safety glass; panes of float glass, partially pretensioned by warming to produce deformation
Rise: 150 mm
U-value: 2.6 W/m^{2}K
Solar screening: UV-filter foil between laminations in the glass
Fire rating: Fire-resistant glass was used in the area where there is a risk of fire spreading from adjacent buildings.

Prada Flagship Store in Tokyo
Architects: Herzog & de Meuron, Basel
(see p. 138)

Glass louvres
Coloured screen printing, applied to the back.
Fixing method: The fixed glass panes are suspended in aluminium-coated fixings which are attached to the anchor rail by means of a bracket (aluminium-coated). The opening louvres which are positioned in front of the windows are seated in a moveable fixing with drive mechanism.

Base: Mineral-fibre thermal insulation, 120 mm black lining, 250 mm reinforced concrete
Height/width: 65 mm/1.0–2.5 m
Thickness: movable louvres, 2×6 mm laminated safety glass, fixed louvres, 6 mm toughened safety glass
Weight: 15 kg/m^2

Fire Station and Police Station in Berlin
Architects: sauerbruch hutton, Berlin

Translucent glass blocks
Fixing method: The glass blocks are fixed to the steel frame. Also the glass blocks on the joints are connected via a steel profile which rests on an EPDM profile.
Quantity: approx. 13000 blocks
Size: $430 \times 430 \times 120$ mm
Weight: 16 kg per glass block

Department Store in Tokyo
Architects: Renzo Piano Building Workshop

Wood

Wooden shingles
Shingles made from untreated Western Red Cedar. Quality class 1, sawn.
Fixing method: The wooden shingles are fitted onto counterbattens. Plastic sheeting provides the seal, behind this are ribs of glued laminated plywood which are fitted together to form a curved space frame.
Between the ribs is the thermal insulation of mineral wool.

Length: 450 mm
Width: between 100 and 250 mm
Row spacing: 14 cm, triple-layer

Board of Ipé hardwood
Fixing method: The boards rest on squared timber bolted to a raised, height-adjustable steel frame.
Width / thickness: 105 mm / inside 20 mm, outside 30 mm
Dry weight of Ipé: 1 150 kg/m³

Holiday House on Øvre Gla
Architects: 24h architects, Rotterdam

Ferry Terminal in Yokohama
Architects: Foreign Office Architects, London
(see p. 178)

Natural stone

Mondariz granite, untreated
The coarse structure of the blocks
comes from the marks left after the
stone was drilled out of the quarry. No
further surface treatment was applied.
Fixing method: Granite blocks
anchored to the steel frame
Size: 1750 mm high bands of different
widths
Thickness: 300 mm

Music Academy in Santiago de Compostela
Architect: Antón García-Abril, Madrid (see p. 190)

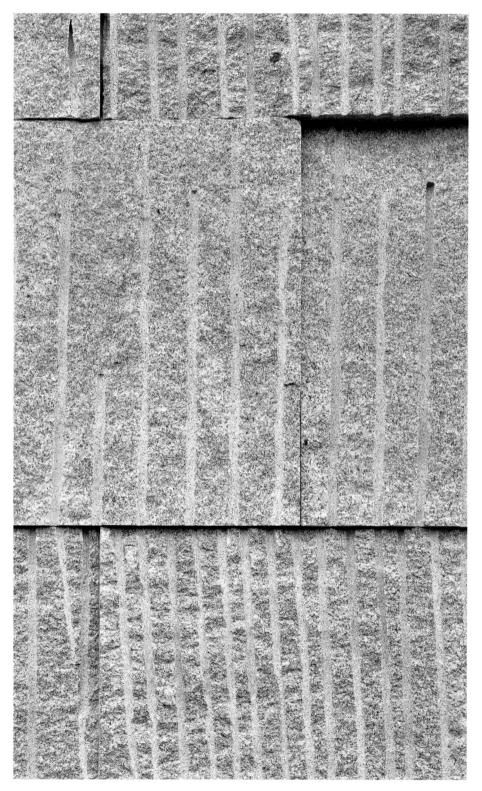

Documentation Centre in Hinzert

Architects: Wandel Hoefer Lorch + Hirsch, Saarbrücken

Floor plan · Sections
scale 1:500
Wire model

1 Exhibition space
2 Seminar space
3 Office
4 Reading recess
5 WC for disabled
6 WCs
7 Services
8 Library
9 Kitchenette
10 Store
11 Hats and coats

In the idyllic landscape around Hinzert in the Hunsrück, south-west of Trier, few traces remain to remind one of the terrors that took place there in the years 1939–45, when more than 13,000 people underwent the torments of a concentration camp. After the war, the camp was cleared away, and the fields were restored to the local farmers. All that remained was a small memorial cemetery, recalling the political prisoners who had been subject to torture and who had done forced labour there. In order not to forget the camp and its prisoners, an architectural competition was held to create a documentation centre. The architects' winning concept proposed the design of a building and exhibition that form a single whole. The expressive outer skin in oxidized steel is both load-bearing structure and facade. At the end facing the former camp, it opens on to the landscape with a large glazing, on which a historical photo of the prisoners' barracks is printed. The skin consists of 1,160 triangular steel plates cut by means of computer numerical control (CNC) to different sizes. From these, 12 large elements were prefabricated in the workshop to be subsequently welded together on site. The angles between the individual plates were calculated in such a way that the elements provide the necessary structural height, and the folded structure has adequate stiffness. After welding, the steel surfaces were sandblasted and evenly oxidized. Subsequent treatment with hot paraffin lends a sense of additional depth and a certain lustre. The internal finishings are also distinguished by timber cladding with a triangular articulation. The supporting construction is thermally separated from the steel structure. Along most of the length of the walls, the inner and outer skins are discrete elements, creating a space that is used to accommodate ancillary functions, an archive and reading recesses.

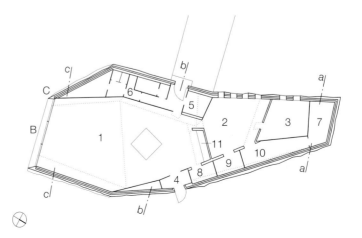

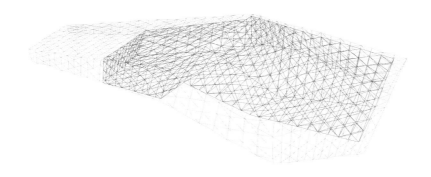

aa

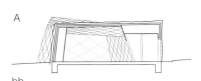

A

bb

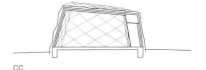

cc

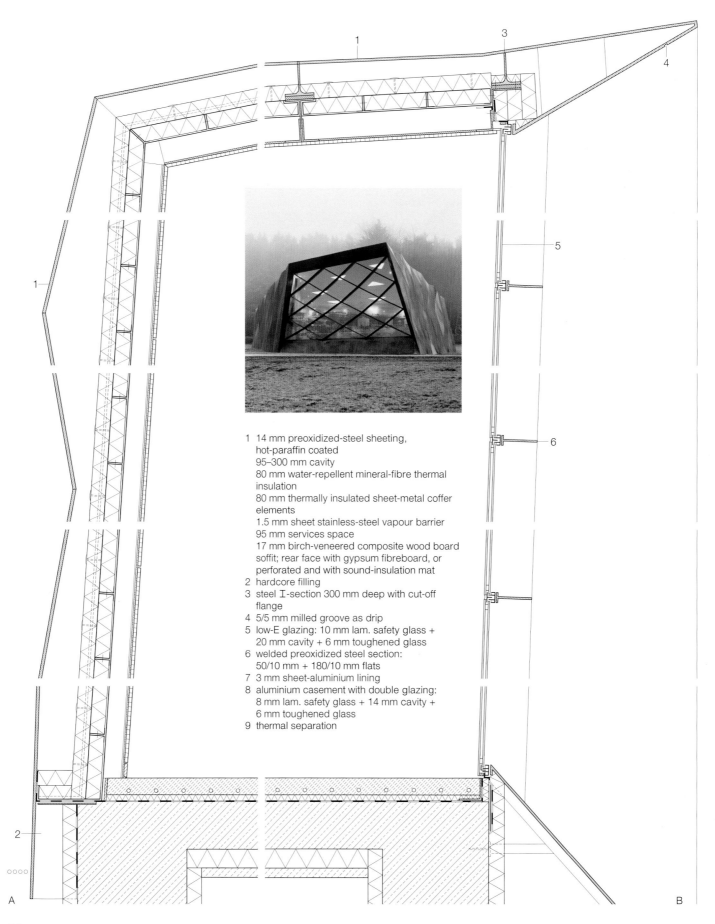

1 14 mm preoxidized-steel sheeting,
   hot-paraffin coated
   95–300 mm cavity
   80 mm water-repellent mineral-fibre thermal
   insulation
   80 mm thermally insulated sheet-metal coffer
   elements
   1.5 mm sheet stainless-steel vapour barrier
   95 mm services space
   17 mm birch-veneered composite wood board
   soffit; rear face with gypsum fibreboard, or
   perforated and with sound-insulation mat
2 hardcore filling
3 steel I-section 300 mm deep with cut-off
   flange
4 5/5 mm milled groove as drip
5 low-E glazing: 10 mm lam. safety glass +
   20 mm cavity + 6 mm toughened glass
6 welded preoxidized steel section:
   50/10 mm + 180/10 mm flats
7 3 mm sheet-aluminium lining
8 aluminium casement with double glazing:
   8 mm lam. safety glass + 14 mm cavity +
   6 mm toughened glass
9 thermal separation

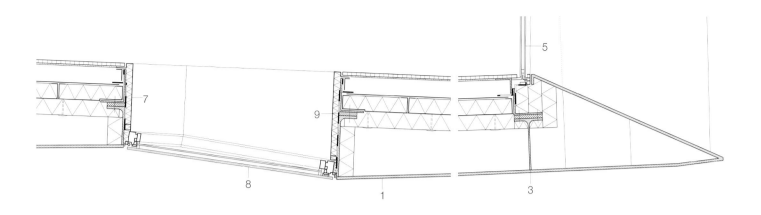

C

Museum Liner in Appenzell

Architects: Gigon/Guyer, Zurich

The zigzag form of a gleaming roofscape rises above the peaceful saddle roofs in the community of Appenzell. The long, monolithic volume with shed roofs set at right angles to its longitudinal axis houses an art museum. A winding circulation path guides the visitor through ten exhibition rooms that are arranged in pairs and grow progressively smaller towards the northern end. This internal rhythm is transferred to the external form: as room depths change, the height and width of the shed roofs also change, as each pair of rooms is lit entirely from a north-facing band of windows. Two large openings in the exhibition area allow for visual contact to the outside and facilitate orientation on the inside. The narrow faces of the building, where the foyer and the reading room are located, offer views of the surrounding landscape through large-format glazing. The monolithic exterior of the museum is underscored by the facade cladding in glass-bead-blasted stainless steel panels, which span across the entire volume. The museum entrance is the only feature to project out from the scaly carapace of the skin; its exposed concrete facade indicates the massive solidity of the volume. The structure of the rectangular steel panels, mounted to overlap one another, echoes the shingle motif on traditional houses in the region. Like the shed roofs, the matte grey steel shingles on the longitudinal facades adapt to the changing scale of the interior spaces. To the north, the longish panels become increasingly shorter, until they are nearly square in shape. Depending on the viewpoint of the observer, these shifts in proportion manipulate the visual effect of the length of the building, whose face seems to change with the seasons. From precious, gleaming metal to dull, monolithic rock – the appearance of the skin is in flux and yet these changes define its character.

Site plan   scale 1:2000
Detail section of shed roof
scale 1:20

74

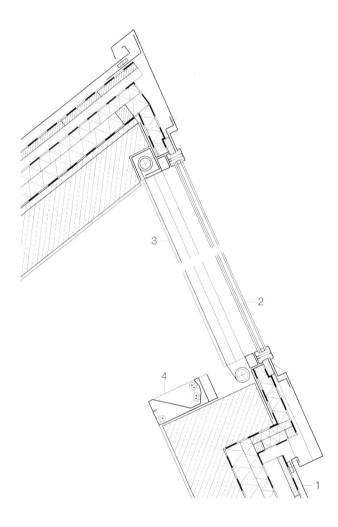

1 roof construction:
   covering:
   3 mm stainless-steel
   sheet
   glass-bead-blasted finish
   bitumen sealant
   27 mm planed
   timber formwork
   50 mm roof battening
   waterproof foil
   mineral fibre layer
   60 mm compression-
   resistant layer

80 mm mineral-wool layer
vapour barrier
cement leveling course
250 mm reinforced
concrete
15 mm plaster
2 double glazing:
   8 mm safety glass +
   cavity + 2× 12 mm
   lamenated safety glass
3 guide rail for solar shading
4 ventilation/
   strip lighting

House in Dornbirn

Architects: Oskar Leo Kaufmann + Albert Rüf, Dornbirn

This house in Dornbirn, Austria, presents itself at first sight as a closed shell – not unlike an oyster – concealing its interior life from prying eyes. What is more, it speaks a quite different language from that of the traditional surroundings. The double-pitched roof seems to be the sole link with the style of the neighbouring developments. Drawn over the street face and the roof are seamless, perforated and riveted sheet stainless-steel panels. Rainwater flows through the perforations and runs off over a coated polyester mat. Beneath the matting is an additional layer that reduces the noise caused by precipitation. Access to the house is directly from the street. A staircase leads down from the entrance to the kitchen-cum-living room at a lower level. Here, the impression of a building closed to the outside world is reversed. A nine-metre-long glazed facade opens on to the garden. The two levels of the dwelling are dominated by exposed concrete walls and ceilings. The wooden window frames form a contrast to these cool, sobre surfaces. In the attic, on the other hand, warm tones prevail. The walls and ceilings are in a timber form of construction clad with poplar-veneered plywood. Via a linear landing space with cupboards, there is access to the bedrooms, where an area of glazing set flush with the roof plane affords a view of the sky.

Sections
Floor plans
scale 1:400

1 Carport
2 Kitchen-cum-dining room
3 Living room
4 Floor opening with metal-mesh safety screen
5 Study
6 Landing with cupboards
7 Bedroom with bathroom
8 Void

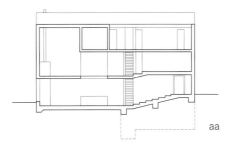

aa

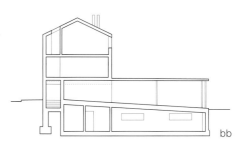

bb

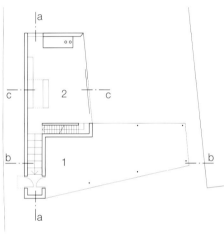

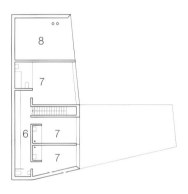

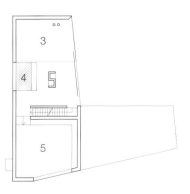

1 roof construction:
  2 mm perforated stainless-steel sheeting
  50/25/3 mm steel RHSs in ventilated cavity
  sealing layer: polyester matting
  90/25 mm wood open boarding on battens
  windproof paper; 15 mm oriented-strand
  board
  2× 120 mm mineral-wool insulation between
  100/240 mm glued lam. timber beams
  15 mm oriented-strand board; vapour barrier
  50/20 mm battens
  10 mm poplar-veneered plywood
2 double glazing: 10 + 8 mm float glass +
  16 mm cavity
3 glued lam. softwood lined with oak boarding
  on both faces
4 120–250 mm reinforced concrete floor slab,
  sealed
5 oiled oak sliding door with double glazing:
  10 + 8 mm float glass + 16 mm cavity
  2 mm sheet-aluminium external lining to frame

6 toothed strip for electric operation
7 electric motor for sliding door
8 250 mm waterproof concrete floor slab,
  sealed
9 double glazing in aluminium frame:
  6 mm toughened glass + 16 mm cavity +
  lam. safety glass (2× 6 mm toughened glass)
10 electric lifting gear for roof light
11 wall construction:
  2 mm perforated stainless-steel sheeting
  waterproof layer: polyester matting
  50/25/3 mm steel RHSs in ventilated cavity
  windproof paper
  15 mm oriented-strand board
  2× 120 mm thermal insulation
  20 mm oriented-strand board
  vapour barrier
  50 mm services cavity
  10 mm plywood
12 wire mesh safety layer in stainless-steel frame
13 200 mm exposed concrete wall

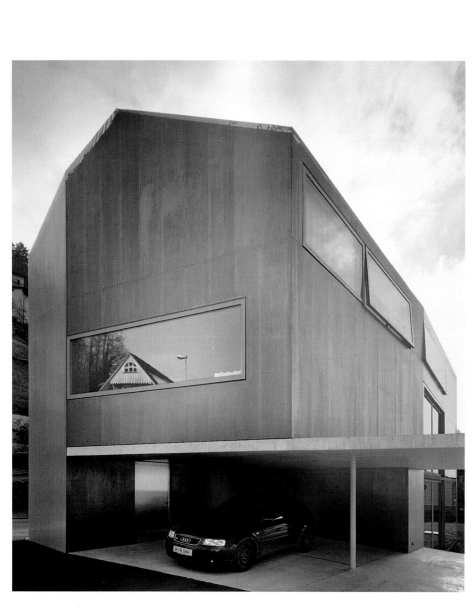

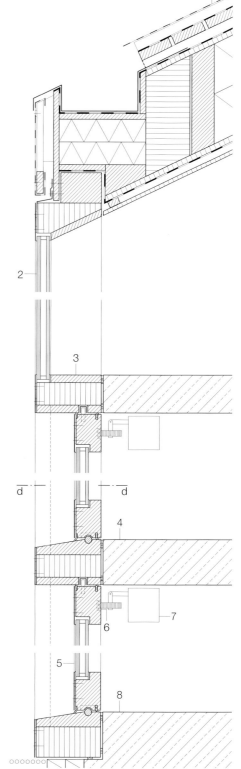

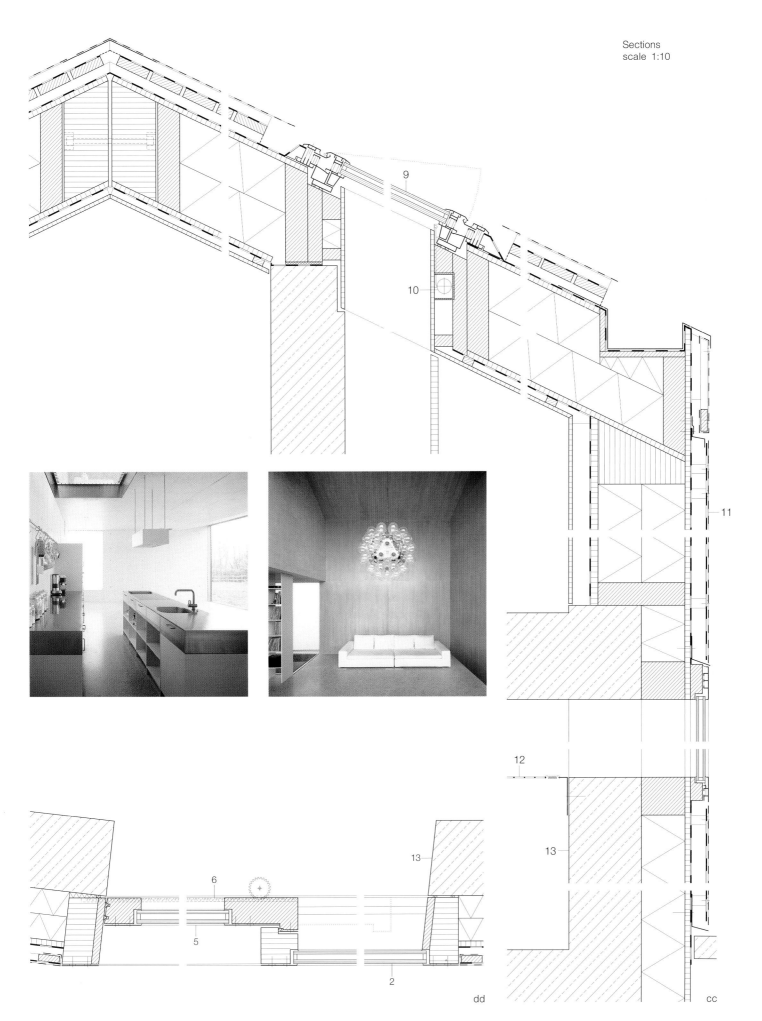

9

10

11

12

13

6

5

2

13

dd

cc

Administration Building in Heilbronn

Architect: Dominik Dreiner, Gaggenau

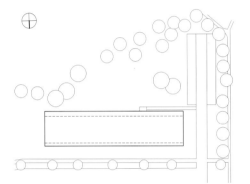

The park-like surroundings to the headquarters of the German Südwestmetall organization are reflected in the stainless-steel lattice mesh drawn over the end faces and the roof. Depending on the lighting mood, therefore, the contours of this 76-metre-long and 18.5-metre-wide development may appear dematerialized or clearly articulated. The two long faces of the building are fully glazed and set back to different extents, creating continuous veranda-like spaces.

The unusual metal skin consists of 0.4 mm stainless-steel flat strips 50 mm wide tightly woven into linear bands on a specially developed machine like a weaver's loom. The lattice mesh is supported on a GRP grating. The roughly 1 × 4 metre elements are fixed to the galvanized steel supporting structure via disc anchor pieces at the abutments. Along the longitudinal and lateral joints between the mesh sheets, the metal strips were woven by hand, so that one has the impression of a seamless cladding layer. The long glazed faces of the cube, set between the raised ground floor and the roof, reveal the same sense of clarity. The flush casement sections between the panes of glass are barely evident, and the sliding doors open behind the glazed front. The internal space is articulated by four light-coloured cubic elements, which house the kitchens, sanitary facilities and ancillary spaces. Grey and white tones, in combination with exposed concrete, glass, stainless steel and sisal, lend the space a restrained elegance.

Thermal activation of the structure is the central feature of the indoor-climate control. The roof slab is used in winter for heating and in summer for cooling. A system of bore holes in the earth, with heat-exchange units and an electrical heat pump, helps to minimize energy needs. It was possible to obviate all structures on the roof.

Site plan
scale 1:2000
Sections
Floor plan
scale 1:500

1 Entrance
2 Seminar space
3 Kitchen
4 Chair store
5 Foyer

6 Restroom
7 Kitchenette
8 Printing / Binding
9 Library
10 Conference space

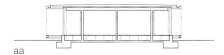

aa

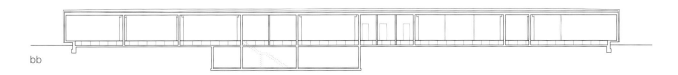

bb

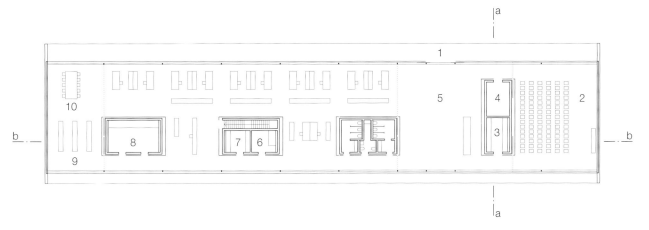

Section   scale 1:20

1 stainless-steel perforated sheeting
2 stainless-steel mesh (50/0.4 mm flat strips) on
   28 mm GRP grating (40/40 mm mesh)
   two-layer bituminous roof seal
   100–200 mm polyurethane thermal insulation
   to falls on vapour barrier
   350 mm reinforced concrete roof slab
3 supporting structure for GRP grating:
   80/80/9 mm steel T-sections and
   2× 30/30/3 mm steel angles

4 Ø 82.5/5 mm and Ø 51/5 mm tubular
   steel bearers with
   60/6 mm lugs welded on for 3
5 stainless-steel mesh on GRP grating
   two-layer bituminous seal
   100 mm polyurethane thermal insulation
   vapour barrier
   200 mm reinforced concrete wall
6 50/6 mm and 110/6 mm galvanized steel flat
   fixing lugs

7 30 mm galvanized steel T-section
8 19 mm medium-density fibreboard,
   epoxy-resin coated
   100/60 mm wood bearers
9 sisal carpet
   35 mm screed on bearing board
   raising pieces in hollow floor
10 5/44 mm stainless-steel skirting
11 subfloor operating motor for
   sliding glass door

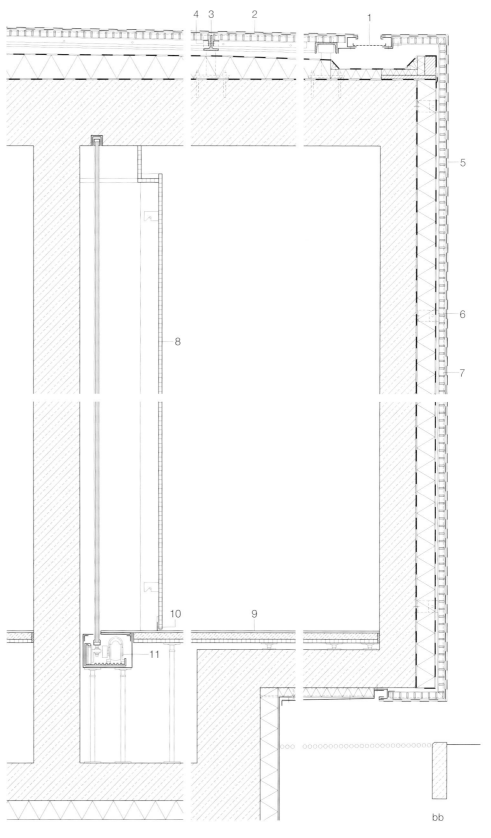

bb

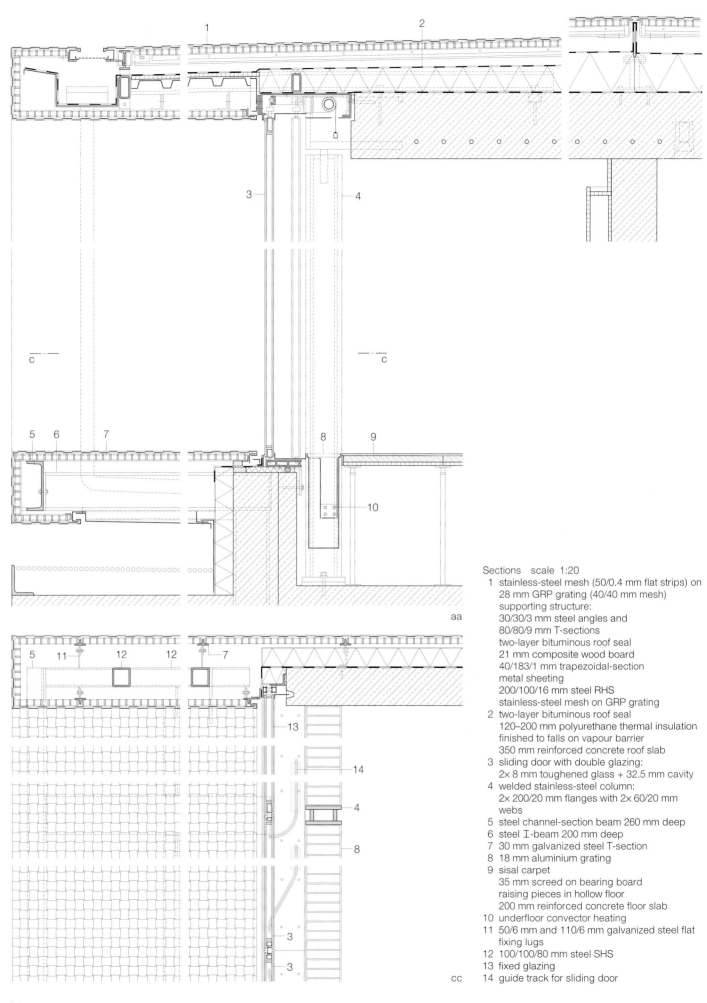

1 2

c —— —— c

aa

3
4

5 6 7 8 9

10

5 11 12 12 7

13

14

4

8

3

3

cc

Sections   scale 1:20

1 stainless-steel mesh (50/0.4 mm flat strips) on
   28 mm GRP grating (40/40 mm mesh)
   supporting structure:
   30/30/3 mm steel angles and
   80/80/9 mm T-sections
   two-layer bituminous roof seal
   21 mm composite wood board
   40/183/1 mm trapezoidal-section
   metal sheeting
   200/100/16 mm steel RHS
   stainless-steel mesh on GRP grating
2 two-layer bituminous roof seal
   120–200 mm polyurethane thermal insulation
   finished to falls on vapour barrier
   350 mm reinforced concrete roof slab
3 sliding door with double glazing:
   2× 8 mm toughened glass + 32.5 mm cavity
4 welded stainless-steel column:
   2× 200/20 mm flanges with 2× 60/20 mm
   webs
5 steel channel-section beam 260 mm deep
6 steel I-beam 200 mm deep
7 30 mm galvanized steel T-section
8 18 mm aluminium grating
9 sisal carpet
   35 mm screed on bearing board
   raising pieces in hollow floor
   200 mm reinforced concrete floor slab
10 underfloor convector heating
11 50/6 mm and 110/6 mm galvanized steel flat
   fixing lugs
12 100/100/80 mm steel SHS
13 fixed glazing
14 guide track for sliding door

Cycling Stadium in Berlin

Architects: Dominique Perrault, Paris
Reichert, Pranschke, Maluche, Munich
Schmidt-Schicketanz und Partner, Munich

The cycling and swimming complex is located between the Friedrichshain and Prenzlauer Berg districts in Berlin. It was so designed that the free-spanning steel roofs would resemble lakes amidst a newly planted orchard of 450 apple trees. The three-storey halls, sunk 17 metres deep in the ground, project barely a metre above ground level. They are part of an extensive underground sports complex, which includes another indoor pool, a gym and multipurpose hall, as well as the necessary auxiliary rooms.

The building skin of the cycling stadium is composed of a circular steel roof 142 metres in diameter and 48 trussed girders in a radial arrangement. In combination with the bracing ring girders, the steel construction forms a massive wheel that is supported on 16 concrete columns at its main ring girder. The entire roof surface and the facade area over the depth of the roof structure are uniformly clad with a metal mesh. The wire mesh elements are bolted to a prefabricated substructure composed of steel angles and flat steel; the horizontal elements are connected via steel springs, which can be opened for maintenance work.

On clear, sunny days the stainless steel mesh creates extraordinary effects through the reflection of light. Depending upon the angle of vision, the moisture-proof roofing sheets in the horizontal and the facade panels in the vertical shimmer like a dark, barely perceptible backdrop through the steel mesh.

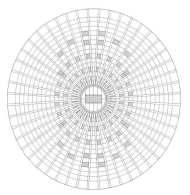

Plan of roof
Longitudinal section
through cycling stadium
and swimming hall
Plan of garden level
scale 1:3000

1 Cycling stadium
2 Swimming hall
3 Foyer
4 Office tract
5 Triple-use sports hall
6 Multipurpose hall
7 Athletes' area
8 Swimming pool
9 Parking

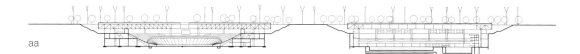

aa

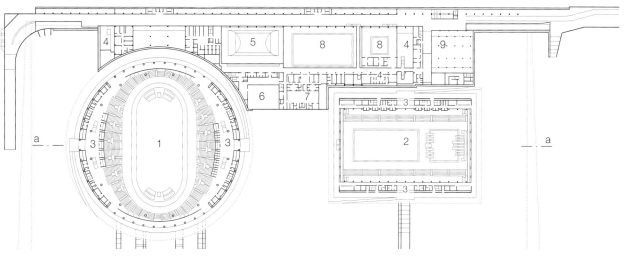

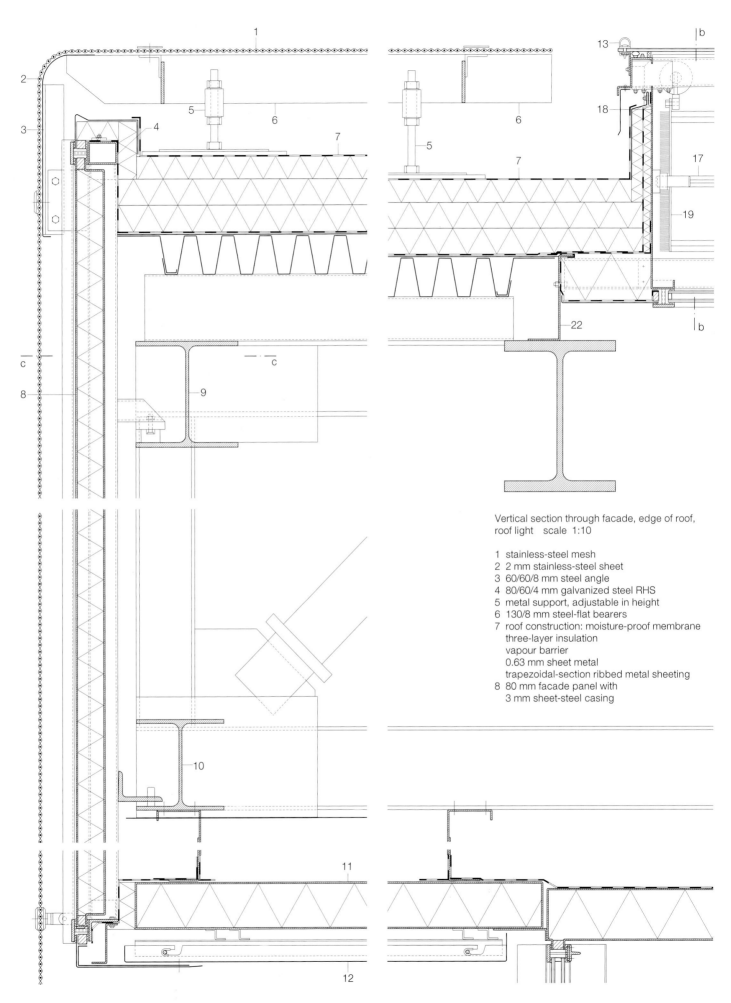

Vertical section through facade, edge of roof,
roof light   scale 1:10

1 stainless-steel mesh
2 2 mm stainless-steel sheet
3 60/60/8 mm steel angle
4 80/60/4 mm galvanized steel RHS
5 metal support, adjustable in height
6 130/8 mm steel-flat bearers
7 roof construction: moisture-proof membrane
   three-layer insulation
   vapour barrier
   0.63 mm sheet metal
   trapezoidal-section ribbed metal sheeting
8 80 mm facade panel with
   3 mm sheet-steel casing

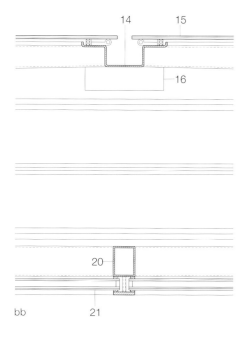

9 upper chord, I-beam 280 mm deep
10 lower chord, I-beam 240 mm deep
11 120 mm panel, galvanized and plastic coated
12 soffit panel
13 quarter-turn
14 gutter, 3 mm sheet steel with 2% falls
15 lam. safety glass of 8 mm partially tensioned
   glass
16 2 steel flats 60/10 mm
17 sunscreen louvre
18 3 mm steel-sheet casing
19 brush seal
20 80/60/3 mm steel RHS
21 double glazing with
   8 mm laminated safety glass lower pane
22 4 mm steel-sheet case

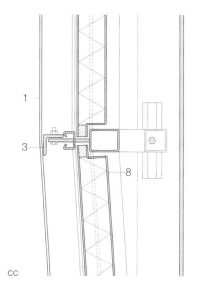

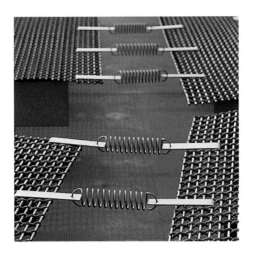

Support for metal mesh
Top view · Cross-section
scale 1:5

1 stainless-steel mesh
2 110/30/2 mm steel flat
  with 2.8 mm dia. tension spring
3 38 mm dia./7.1 mm steel tube

4 threaded rod
5 600/300/5 mm steel base plate
6 400/700/10 mm protective mat
7 110/8 mm steel plate
8 130/8 mm steel plate
9 60/60/6 mm steel angle
10 84.3 mm dia. stainless-steel disc
   screwed to 9

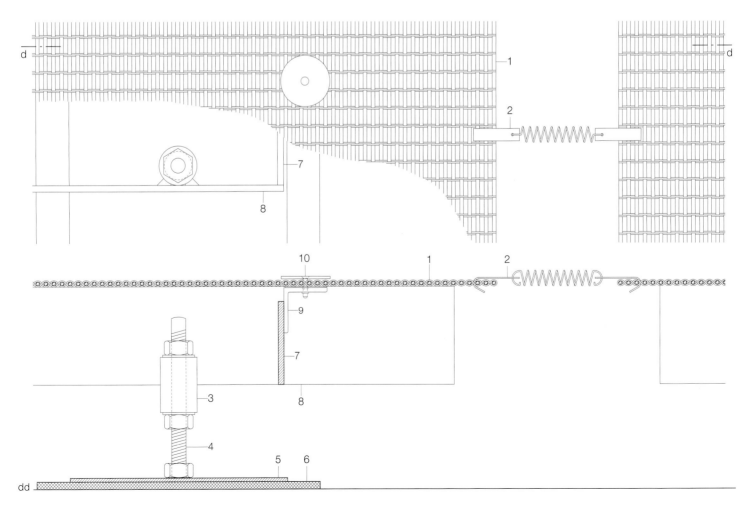

Glasgow Science Centre

Architects: Building Design Partnership, Glasgow

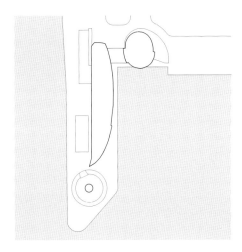

Site plan
scale 1:5000

The Science Centre in Glasgow is the most elaborate and largest Millennium project in Scotland. Situated on a strip of land between the river Clyde and a harbour basin, the complex is surrounded by water on three sides. The core of the complex consists of a spectacular rotating tower and two elliptical volumes that house an IMAX theatre and the so-called Science Mall with over 5000 m² of exhibition area. The facades of the exhibition buildings draw the eye with their matte, shimmering surfaces in titanium, which envelop the sculptural forms. The meticulously finished, smooth panels surround the volume like a second skin, their regular structure supports the even reflection of the surfaces.

The long exhibition building, whose form consists of a segment wrapped around an axis, faces the river with a glass facade cut into the building skin, while the face on the harbour side is fully clad. The shape of the titanium panels follows the course of the load-bearing structure, whose main girders cross on the diagonal. To achieve a uniform surface, the panels were fitted together into larger, diamond-shaped pre-formed elements before mounting. By contrast, the skin of the IMAX building is adapted on-site to the curvature of the volume and mounted in individual rows. Here, too, the shape of the titanium skin results from the load-bearing structure. The setting and the futuristic effect of the volumes is enhanced even further by the reflections on the surrounding water surfaces. As a material, titanium creates associations with utopian architectures and Space Age aesthetics in the visitors' minds.

Facade panel of exhibition building
Isometric projection

Sectional detail of panel joint
scale 1:10

1 500/500/0.4 mm sheet titanium-zinc panels
2 1 mm stainless-steel sheet
3 vapour barrier
4 63/45/1.5 mm steel angle
5 110 mm thermal insulation
6 vapour barrier
7 105/250/1.25 mm trapezoidal-section ribbed steel sheeting
8 composite wood board
9 35 mm thermal insulation
10 8 mm perforated plywood
11 323.9 mm dia./12 mm steel tube
12 adaptor

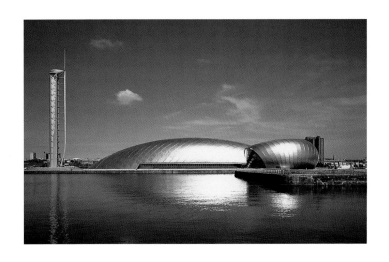

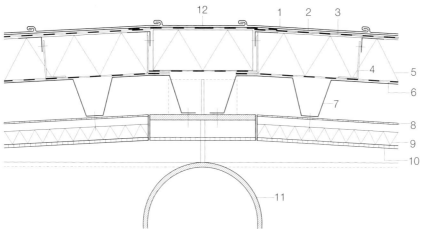

Service Centre in Munich

Architects: Staab Architekten, Berlin

Like a bar of copper, this 84-metre-long "infrastructure unit" lies at the feet of the statue of Bavaria in Munich. The unpretentious building replaces a provisional structure that had existed for many years on the Theresienwiese, a large, oval city-centre site that has remained otherwise undeveloped and which is used for fairs, including the Oktoberfest. Thanks to the untreated copper skin and the low height of this building at the edge of the open area, the development is hardly conspicuous. The distinct material quality and coloration of the skin serve to integrate the structure into the surroundings. Over the years, the oxidation of the smooth-rolled surface will help the centre to blend with the colours of the green slope to the rear. The copper panels, up to 3.75 × 1.00 m in size, are laid flat on the aluminium supporting structure. On the roof, they are fixed to stainless-steel frames. The hermetically sealed outer skin is the outcome of strict safety requirements, designed to protect the building against vandalism not only during the Oktoberfest, but in the long months in which it stands mostly empty. Appearances are deceptive, however. Behind the folding shutters are window strips and concealed doors integrated almost invisibly in the outer skin. Vertically sliding gates in the south facade open to reveal generously glazed access areas for the police, first-aid services and the Oktoberfest organization. The internal space is surprisingly well lit, since the broad-mesh expanded-metal screen that shields the interior from prying eyes allows daylight to penetrate to the rooms beyond. In addition, there are skylights in the flat roof over the corridors. On the western side, four courtyards are cut into the building, which is fully glazed around these areas. In this way, daylight is brought to the lower floor level, which accounts for more than half the volume of the building.

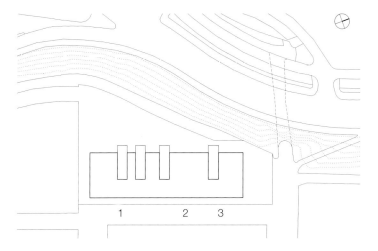

Site plan
scale 1:2000
Sections · Floor plans
scale 1:750

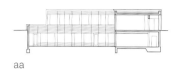

bb

aa

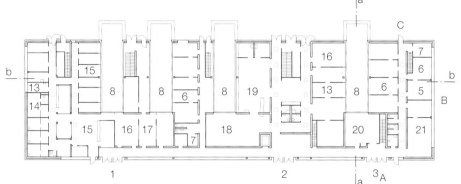

1 Police
2 Red Cross
3 Festival organization
4 Changing room
5 Press centre
6 Office
7 Kitchenette
8 Courtyard
9 Services
10 Store
11 Staff room
12 Lost-property office
13 Doctor
14 Police cell
15 Interrogation
16 Operations centre
17 Emergency calls
18 Surveillance/Video
19 Treatment room
20 Media centre
21 Youth office

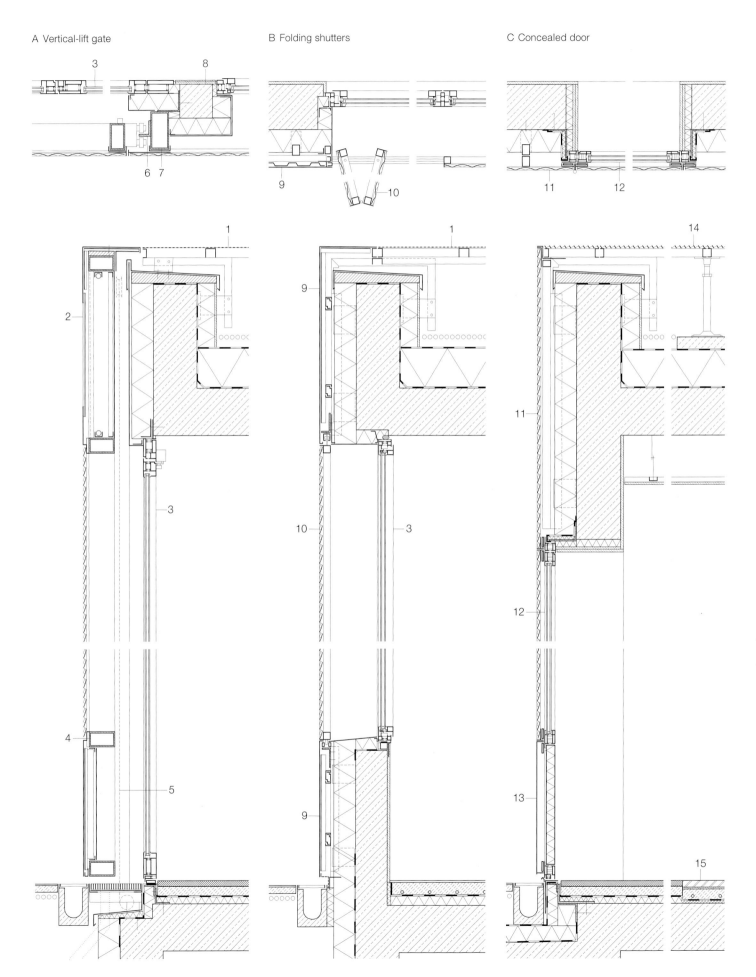

A Vertical-lift gate

3
8

6 7

B Folding shutters

9

10

C Concealed door

11 12

1

2

3

4

5

1

9

10 3

9

14

11

12

13

15

Horizontal sections · Vertical sections
scale 1:20

1 1.5 mm perforated copper sheeting
   50/40 mm stainless-steel channel frame
   60 mm bed of gravel; separating layer
   200 mm thermal insulation
   two-layer bituminous seal
   250 mm reinforced concrete roof slab
2 4 mm perspex lettering
3 aluminium casement/door with double glazing:
   2× 4 mm lam. safety glass + 18 mm cavity +
   2× 4 mm lam. safety glass
4 140/80/6 mm steel RHS frame
5 cable drive
6 70/80 mm steel angle guide track

7 200/100/8 mm steel RHS
8 180/180 mm reinforced concrete column
9 1.5 mm copper sheeting
   25 mm trapezoidal-section sheet aluminium,
   adhesive fixed
   30 mm aluminium fixing rail
   45/55 mm aluminium RHSs
   56/120 mm aluminium channel shoes
   120 mm rock-wool insulation
10 1.5 mm expanded copper mesh
   40/40/2 mm aluminium SHSs
11 1.5 mm expanded copper mesh
   45/50 mm aluminium RHSs
   45/55 mm aluminium RHSs
   56/120 mm aluminium channel shoes
   120 mm rock-wool insulation

12 steel door with extended hinge flaps and
   double glazing:
   4 mm float glass + 18 mm cavity + 2× 4 mm
   lam. safety glass
13 1.5 mm copper sheeting
   50/15/5 mm aluminium RHSs
   47 mm thermal insulation with 2 mm
   aluminium sheeting on both faces
14 3 mm expanded copper mesh
   50/40 mm stainless-steel channel frame
   raising pieces, adjustable in height
15 35 mm cast-stone pavings
   10 mm bed of mortar; 55 mm screed
   separating layer;
   20 mm insulation
   250 mm reinforced concrete floor slab

Pavilion in Amsterdam

Architects: Steven Holl Architects, New York
Rappange & Partners, Amsterdam

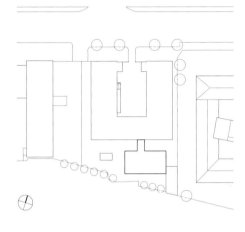

Site plan
scale 1:2000
Plan of the Pavilion
scale 1:500

The conversion of an historic warehouse into an administration building required an expansion of the existing structure to accommodate an underground car park, a cafeteria and an auditorium. An extension, unique in form and colour, was added for this purpose to the rear of the original building, which lies directly on one of the canals that are a typical feature of Amsterdam. The pavilion has the appearance of an artistic composition, deliberately geared towards experiencing architecture with the senses. The theme of the design is one of layering. The building skin is a three-dimensional, geometric collage of materials, shapes and colours, visually linked across staggered openings and transparent layers. The dramatic staging of open versus closed, visible versus hidden, is transformed into a play of perception through the movement and changing viewpoints of the observer. In contrast to the red brick of the historic structure, the new addition is clad in green copper sheeting, whose nuanced colouring is the result of varying oxidation processes. The patinated, perforated sheeting forms the outer layer of the multi-layered facade construction. It is suspended some 30 cm in front of the actual solid external wall and fixed to a steel structure. Depending upon viewpoint, the observer can glimpse the veiled building volume through the small perforations. Openings of different sizes in the semi-transparent metal skin allow a view of the outer wall of the building, partially faced with coloured MDF panels and window openings. The red and green panels shine through the green perforated sheet, emphasizing the multiple layers of the skin. On the inside, the facade is enclosed with perforated, beech veneer MDF panels and aluminium sheeting, also perforated. As a result of the layering, the openings in the individual layers overlap in some areas, so that some windows lie behind the semi-transparent internal cladding. The rear face of the panels is coated with fluorescent paint in these areas, which creates a diffused glow of colour in certain light conditions. The effect of light and colour of this facade extends into the surroundings: the shimmering colour reflections are mirrored in the greenish water of the canal. The play of light and colour of the translucent facade is particularly dramatic at night.

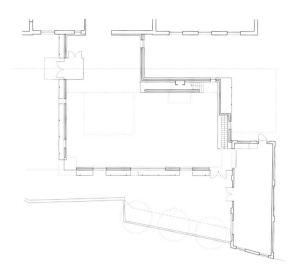

Vertical section
scale 1:50
Horizontal section
scale 1:20

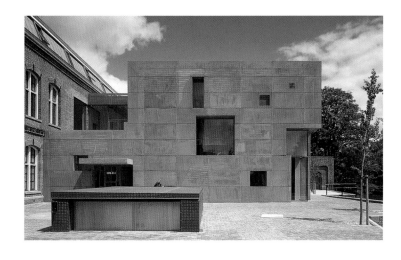

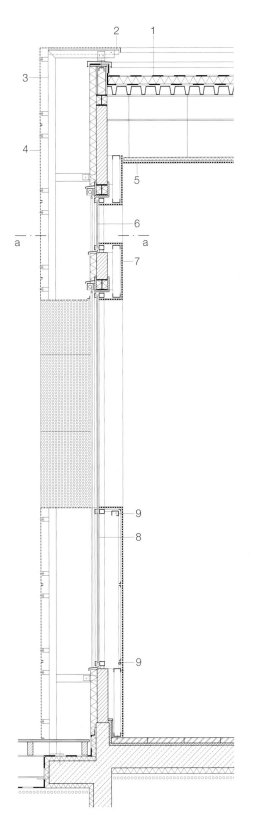

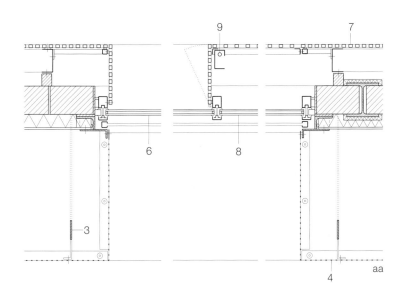

1 roof construction:
  waterproof roof sheeting
  100 mm thermal insulation
  vapour barrier
  trapezoidal steel sheet
  I-section
2 60/60/5 mm steel T-section
3 100/6 steel flat
4 4 mm patinated copper sheeting,
  perforated
5 suspended ceiling:
  16 mm perforated MDF
  with birch veneer
  30 mm insulation
  T-section

6 double glazing,
  transparent
7 wall construction:
  16 mm perforated MDF
  with birch veneer
  steel channel
  timber profile
  150 mm sand-lime brick
  thermal insulation
  80 mm rigid foam panel
  glass fibre panel with artificial
  resin coating
8 double glazing,
  translucent
9 lighting

Micro-Compact Home in Munich

Architects: Horden, Cherry, Lee Architects, London
Haack + Höpfner Architekten, Munich

The Micro-Compact Home is a lightweight, transportable dwelling that can be adapted to different locations. In a short space of time, new living space can thus be created, either temporary or permanent. The idea for this home was developed as part of a seminar at the Technical University of Munich, involving cooperation with the Tokyo Institute of Technology. The spatial arrangement is influenced by traditional Japanese tea-house architecture, while current technology from the aerospace and automotive industries was used in its realisation.

An important component in this prefabricated cube is its ventilated, aluminium skin, covered in plastic sheeting. This envelope can even be customised by printing different designs on the UV-resistant sheeting, before sticking it onto the anodised metal surface. The Micro-Compavt Home has a solid wood frame, infilled with OSB panels with rigid polyurethane insulation between the panels. Additional high-grade vacuum insulation panels are built into the roof. In the interior the sandwich frame is coated with PVC. From the outside, the joints on the facades reflect the spatial arrangement of this tiny cube (sides 2.65 m long). All the functions of a normal home are accommodated within. The wet areas (sanitary and kitchen installations) are aligned along a single axis, while the entrance area and floor space for the kitchen (also serving as seating for the sunken dining area) are located in the centre. The sleeping deck above the table can be folded upwards when not in use. All available cavities were used for drawers and pull-out shelving, to maximise space utilisation.

A small privately financed group of seven such residential cubes has been on test in the north of Munich since the end of 2005. The sponsor's logo is prominent on the outside of each home.

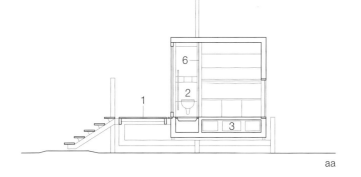

aa

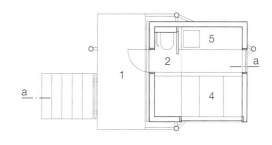

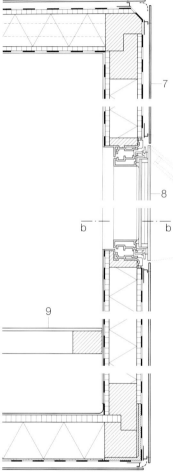

Section · Floor plan
scale 1:100

1 Terrace
2 Entrance / shower
3 Storage space
4 Dining area
5 Kitchen
6 Sliding door

Sectional details
scale 1:10

7 3 mm aluminium covered with
UV-resistant plastic sheeting
10 mm ventilation space
4 mm bitumen seal, 12 mm OSB
rigid foam insulation between
100/60 mm and 100/120 mm
wooden uprights
12 mm OSB, 3 mm PVC

8 top-hung aluminium window
($U = 0.6$ W/m^{2}K) with double
glazing: 11 mm cavity between
2× 4 mm toughened glass
9 raised floor construction:
5 mm injection-moulded polyurethane surface, 2 mm GRP on
60 mm timber frame

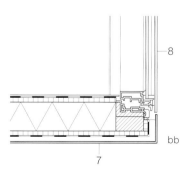

Selfridges Department Store in Birmingham

Architects: Future Systems, London

Selfridges' new department store is a striking landmark in Birmingham's city centre: a bright blue facade covered with polished aluminium discs which seem to float on its surface. Like sequins on a dress, these discs change their appearance according to time of day and weather conditions, while also lending the building a distinctive granular texture and air of lightness. In order to maximise sales space in the store and have better control over lighting of the products, windows were kept to a minimum.

The organic volume of the building entirely fills the plot it stands on; it provides more retail space than originally specified in the master plan, and also bridges a significant rise in floor height from one end of the site to the other. All of this was achieved at no more expense than for a conventional department store, such as the one next door. In these terms, the giant blue "blob" has both functional and commercial logic.

The three-dimensionally curved skin of the building covers the entire volume, also enclosing the technical services on the roof. The walls are a cost-effective solution of sprayed-concrete facade, insulated on the outside and then finished with a coat of coloured synthetic sealant. Fixed on top of this, via an adjustable connection, are the aluminium discs. This connection detail consists of a holding plate, affixed centrally, and a domed cover plate. First every tenth disc was fixed in horizontal bands, and then the remainder positioned accordingly in between. The slightly different spacings between the discs even out the variations in the curvature of the shell. All 660 mm in diameter, the 15,000 identical discs were produced in series – pressed, spun, and finally polished to a mirror finish and naturally anodized.

Section · Floor plan   scale 1:1000

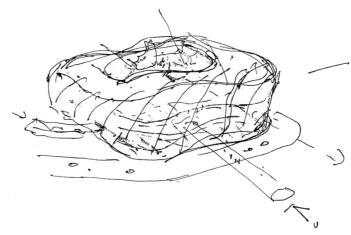

104

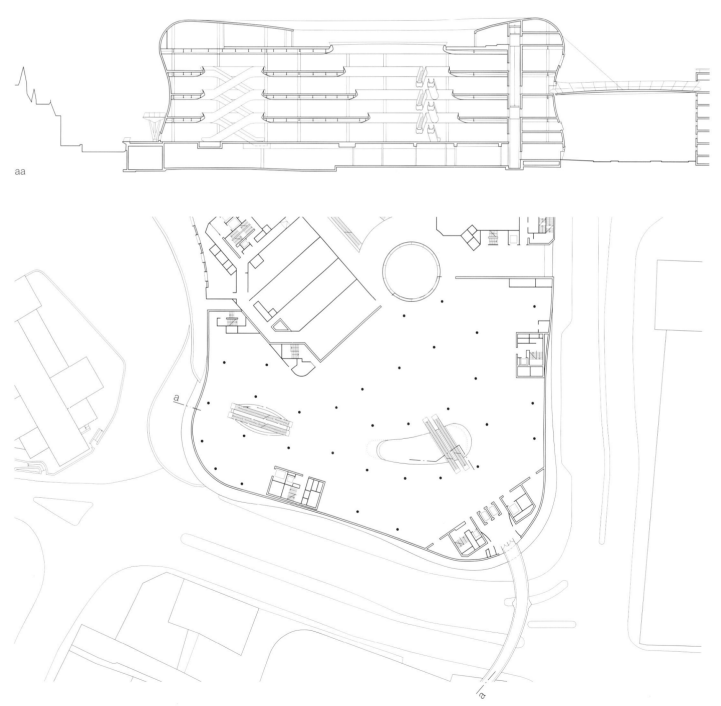

aa

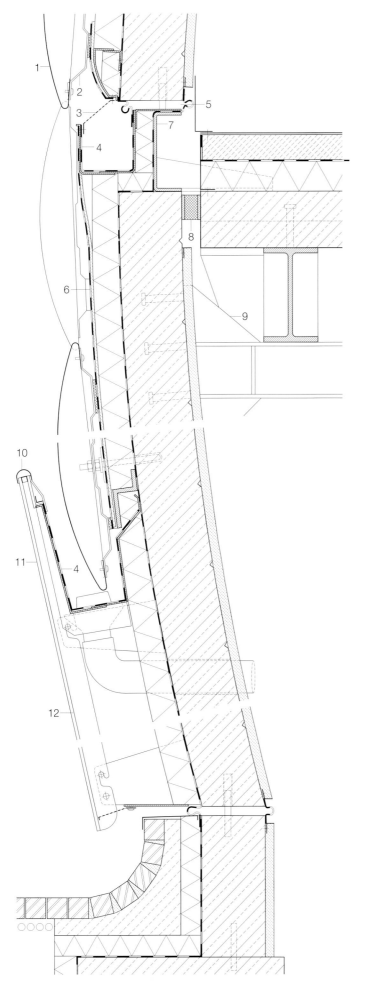

Facade section
Abutment of floor slab to
base of facade
Sectional details through
entrance
scale 1:10

1 660 mm dia.
  aluminium disc
  polished and
  naturally anodized
2 anodised aluminium
  plate
3 insect screen
  aluminium mesh
4 aluminium gutter
  with welded-on
  membrane
5 expansion joint
6 plastic sealant
  10 mm render
  75 mm insulating
  mat
  plastic sealant
  175 mm sprayed
  concrete
  20–30 mm plaster
7 channel-section steel
  with anchor pin for
  concrete element
  above
8 fireproof cover
9 bracket for suspend-
  ing the sprayed-
  concrete elements
10 stainless-steel profile
11 3 mm polished stain-
   less-steel panel
12 bracing, aluminium
   sheet
13 stainless-steel profile
14 150/250 mm steel
   RHS
15 medium-density
   fibreboard lining
16 glass fin
   16 mm toughened
   glass
17 9 + 15 mm laminated
   safety glass
18 entrance door
   19 mm toughened glass
19 aluminium ramp
20 in-situ concrete on
   ribbed metal sheet-
   ing, with pale-blue
   pigmented top layer

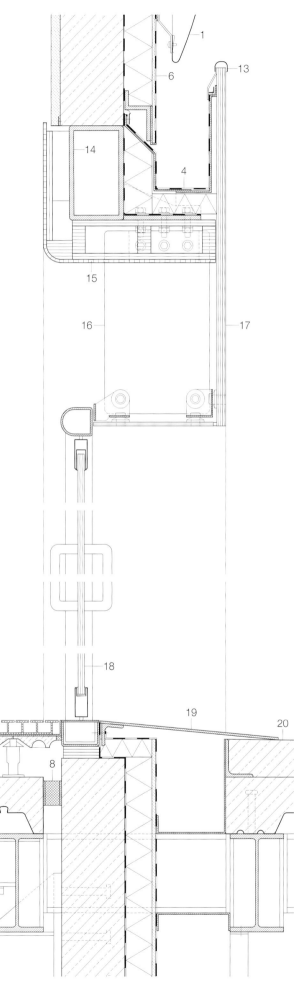

Sectional detail through window
scale 1:10
1 660 mm dia. polished aluminium disc
   naturally anodized
2 wall construction:
   plastic sealant
   10 mm render
   75 mm insulating mat
   sealant
   175 mm sprayed-concrete element
   20–30 mm plaster
3 stainless-steel section
4 aluminium gutter
   with welded-on membrane
5 150/250 mm steel RHS
6 9 + 15 mm laminated safety glass
7 glass fin, 16 mm toughened glass
8 medium-density fibreboard window lining
9 sheet aluminium with
   welded-on membrane

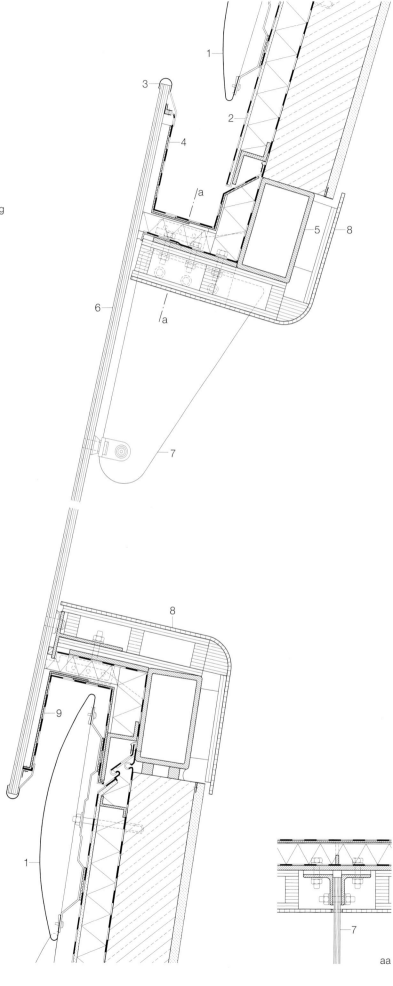

A Summer Space

Architects: Johl, Jozwiak, Ruppel, Berlin

Light reflections dance across the surface reminiscent of a mosaic of round glass blocks, on whose cylindrical surfaces the rays of the sun are refracted a hundredfold. Depending on the viewpoint, the spherical skin reflects the green of the surrounding trees or the shifting colours of the sky, and it takes a second look to discover the basic module of the construction: a PET bottle. In the interior of the "plastic igloo" the relief of multi-coloured screwtops lends a subtle colour to the light penetrating through the translucent plastic skin, lending a unique ambience to the space. PET bottles are no longer sold primarily as the product they were intended for, but for their function as containers for a variety of beverages, after which they usually make their way to the recycling depot. Their potential as a quality object for practical use has been demonstrated by students at the Technical University in Berlin with this design. The goal of the term project was to utilize not only the specific potential of the chosen material, but to draw out its aesthetic qualities as well. On a circular plan, the bottles are stacked into a cone. To protect the interior from wind and rain and to ensure structural stability, a transparent scaffolding film was integrated and attached between bottle head and screwtop. The shape of the skin was almost predetermined by the arrangement of the bottles. The result is a spherical vault, an archetypal form of building skin. Three thousand bottles were linked via the transparent film; the entrance opening is stablized with moulded fibre board.

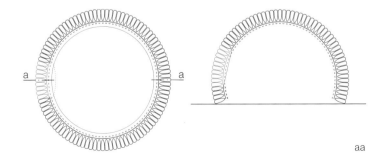

Plan
Section
scale 1:100
Sectional details
scale 1:10, 1:5

aa

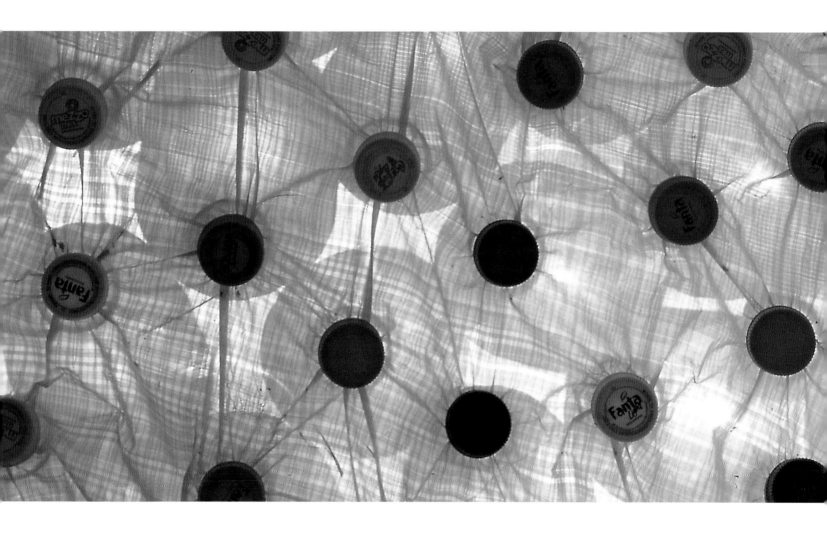

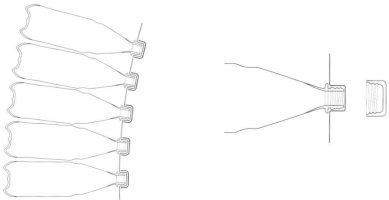

Eden Project near St Austell

Architects: Nicholas Grimshaw & Partners, London

Cornwall, in the south-west of England, is one of the most temperate regions in the British Isles. With palm trees and flowering rhododendron, it is the ideal location for a botanical garden. The Eden Project, the largest of its kind in the world, features international species – trees, bushes and flowers from three different climatic zones – and attracts thousands of visitors each day. During the construction period alone, the site drew some 500,000 visitors, and in the first two months after the gardens were opened, 400,000 people came to see the botanical and architectural attractions.

The archetypal building skin stretches across the staged microcosm like a second sky. The lightness of the material makes one forget the huge dimensions of the domes, which nestle in the hollow of a disused loam pit. With structural spans of up to 124 metres, the basic form of the construction is a series of intersecting geodesic domes. This geometry offers a number of advantages: it facilitates a lightweight yet rigid structure; and it is easily prefabricated with a plug-in jointing system that offers a high degree of precision and can be delivered to the construction site as a series of small components. A lightweight structure was essential in view of the poor load-bearing capacity of the soil. The dome construction is divided into two layers. The outer skin is based on a hexagonal framework, the inner layer on a triangular and hexagonal grid. At the lines of intersection between the domes are complex, three-chord, triangular steel trusses. The covering consists of light ETFE cushions, which are inflated by compressors. The overall weight of the construction is less than that of the air it encloses.

The scheme was designed as part of an ecological system and to sharpen the awareness of visitors to the importance of plants. For that reason, the display focuses not only on exotic species; it also features the fruits of familiar plants: paprika, tobacco, cotton, coffee, tea, etc. – without the plants themselves. This selection is particularly interesting to young visitors, for whom special guided tours are available. Adult visitors can participate in a number of seminars and workshops.

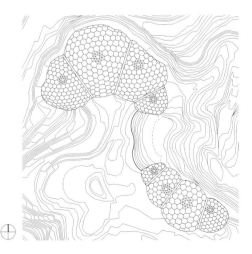

Site plan
scale 1:5000

Sectional details
Standard node
scale 1:20

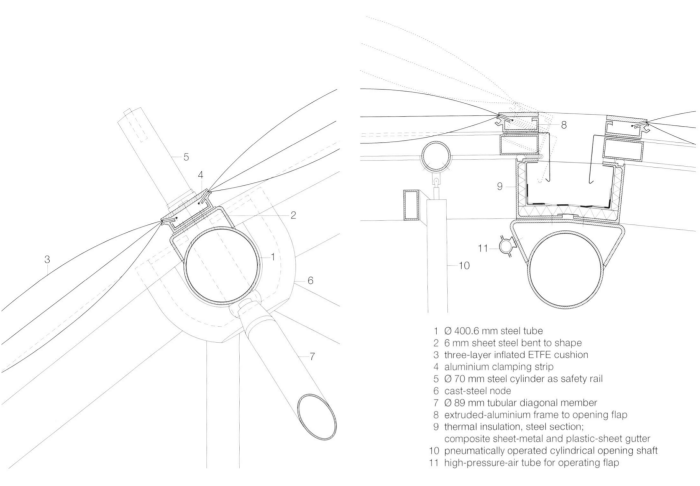

1 Ø 400.6 mm steel tube
2 6 mm sheet steel bent to shape
3 three-layer inflated ETFE cushion
4 aluminium clamping strip
5 Ø 70 mm steel cylinder as safety rail
6 cast-steel node
7 Ø 89 mm tubular diagonal member
8 extruded-aluminium frame to opening flap
9 thermal insulation, steel section;
   composite sheet-metal and plastic-sheet gutter
10 pneumatically operated cylindrical opening shaft
11 high-pressure-air tube for operating flap

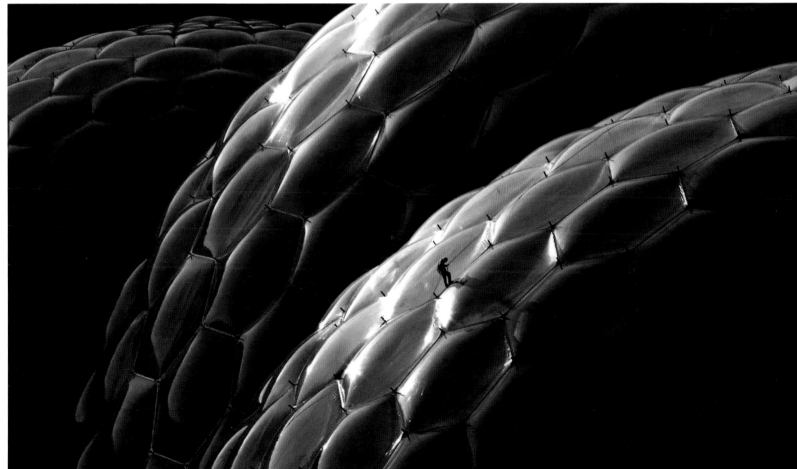

Allianz Arena in Munich

Architects: Herzog & de Meuron, Basel

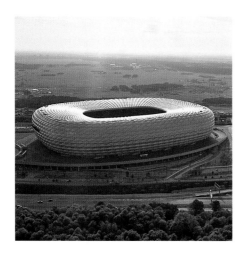

What immediately stands out about Munich's new football stadium is its unusual envelope. This rounded form looks like a piece of abstract sculpture lying in the landscape near the motorway junction on the north side of the city. When a match is on, the entire synthetic skin of the stadium lights up in red or blue, depending on which of the two home teams is playing (Bayern München or TSV 1860). This device helps the rival clubs, both co-sponsors of the stadium, identify with their new grounds. White light remains the option for games where no local teams are involved. Inside the stadium, colour is restricted to a neutral grey: the fans themselves turn the seating bowl into a bright spectacle when the steeply banked tiers of seats are full.

By day the skin, which is divided up into diamond-shaped cushions, appears shiny, transparent and homogeneous. Yet behind there are different load-bearing systems: Cantilevered steel lattice girders form the primary structure of the roof, while the secondary support structure for the roof and vertical facades, structurally separate from the primary frame, is a rhomboid grid of steel girders, with field diagonals varying from 2×7 metres to 5×17 metres. The 65,000 m² skin is made up of 2,874 individual ETFE cushions, each one matched by only one other of identical geometry. The cushions are fixed in aluminium profiles that clamp the weatherstrip edge to the secondary construction. The gutters between the cushions are sealed with flexible plastic profiles and welded at the junctions. Twelve air-pumping stations keep a constant internal pressure in the cushions, raising it as required depending on wind and snow loads. The lower part of the facade is printed with a pattern of dots that intensifies towards the bottom to gives a semi-transparent look. On the upper part, by contrast, the cushion "covers" are made of white ETFE.

As the lower edge of the cushion facade starts a good four metres above the ground, the risk of damage through vandalism to the delicate 0.2 mm thin foil is minimised. High above the outer edges of the pitch the inner perimeter of the roof sheeting is finished with a continuous 370-metre long cushion. To avoid too much shading of the turf, the cushions on the southern part are fitted with transparent ETFE sheeting, which allows virtually all the UV portion of sunlight to permeate, thus giving good growing conditions for the grass. At night 1,058 facade cushions are lit up by fluorescent lights inside. Specially developed cover plates of acrylic glass act as a colour filter to create monochrome lighting or bi-colour stripes and diamond patterns.

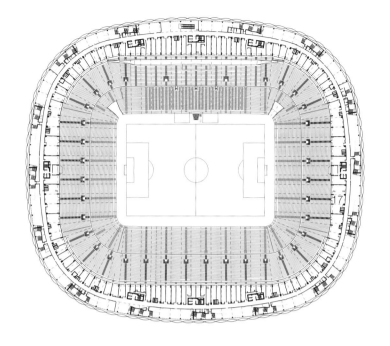

Plan of Level 5
Section
scale 1:2500

Section through roof over west stand
scale 1:50

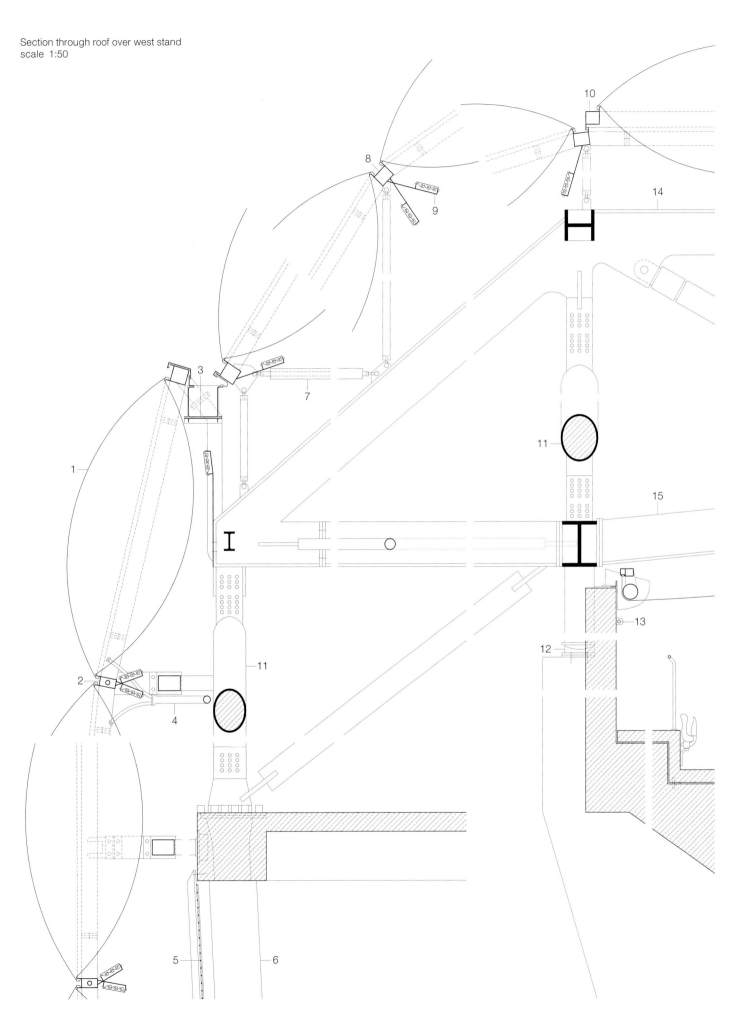

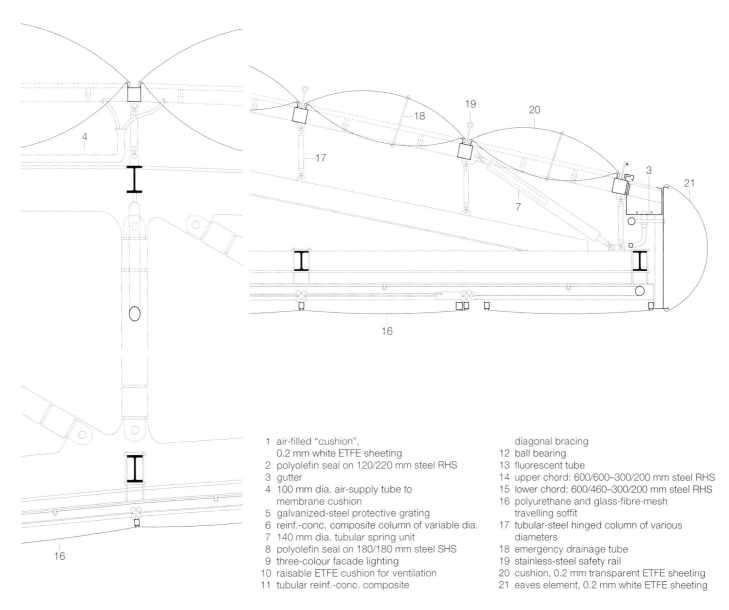

1 air-filled "cushion",
  0.2 mm white ETFE sheeting
2 polyolefin seal on 120/220 mm steel RHS
3 gutter
4 100 mm dia. air-supply tube to
  membrane cushion
5 galvanized-steel protective grating
6 reinf.-conc. composite column of variable dia.
7 140 mm dia. tubular spring unit
8 polyolefin seal on 180/180 mm steel SHS
9 three-colour facade lighting
10 raisable ETFE cushion for ventilation
11 tubular reinf.-conc. composite

diagonal bracing
12 ball bearing
13 fluorescent tube
14 upper chord: 600/600–300/200 mm steel RHS
15 lower chord: 600/460–300/200 mm steel RHS
16 polyurethane and glass-fibre-mesh
  travelling soffit
17 tubular-steel hinged column of various
  diameters
18 emergency drainage tube
19 stainless-steel safety rail
20 cushion, 0.2 mm transparent ETFE sheeting
21 eaves element, 0.2 mm white ETFE sheeting

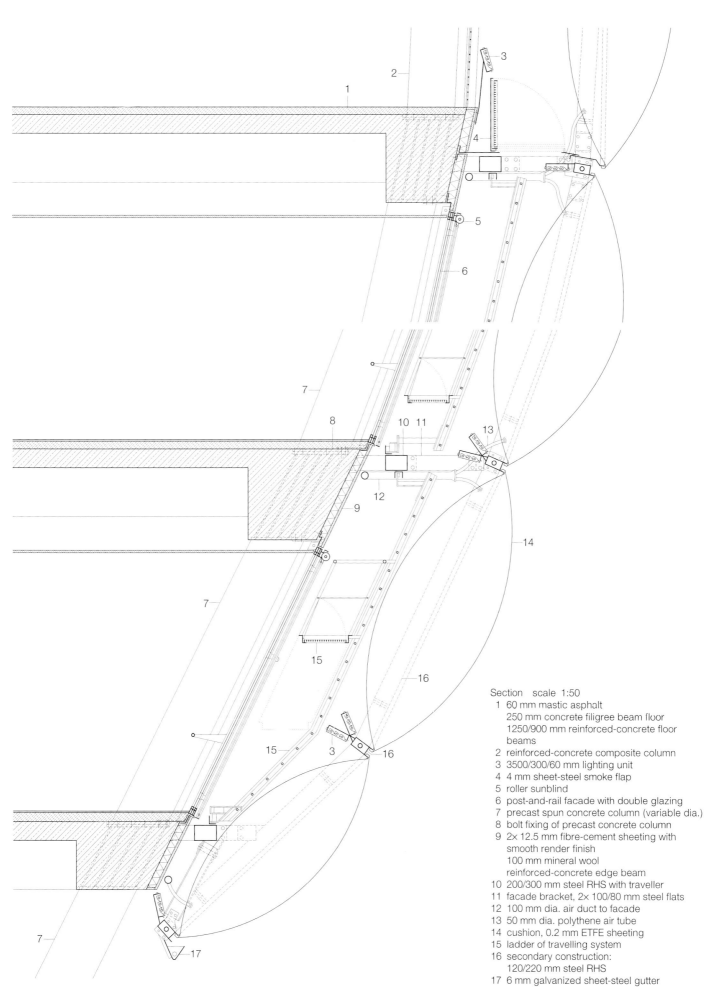

Section   scale 1:50

1 60 mm mastic asphalt
   250 mm concrete filigree beam floor
   1250/900 mm reinforced-concrete floor
   beams
2 reinforced-concrete composite column
3 3500/300/60 mm lighting unit
4 4 mm sheet-steel smoke flap
5 roller sunblind
6 post-and-rail facade with double glazing
7 precast spun concrete column (variable dia.)
8 bolt fixing of precast concrete column
9 2× 12.5 mm fibre-cement sheeting with
   smooth render finish
   100 mm mineral wool
   reinforced-concrete edge beam
10 200/300 mm steel RHS with traveller
11 facade bracket, 2× 100/80 mm steel flats
12 100 mm dia. air duct to facade
13 50 mm dia. polythene air tube
14 cushion, 0.2 mm ETFE sheeting
15 ladder of travelling system
16 secondary construction:
   120/220 mm steel RHS
17 6 mm galvanized sheet-steel gutter

Japanese Pavilion in Hanover

Architects: Shigeru Ban Architects, Tokyo

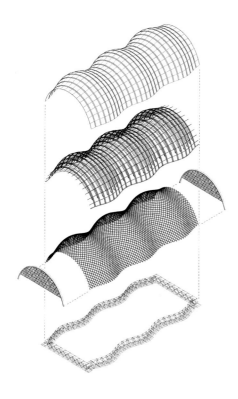

Axonometric:
membrane
curved timber ladder-girders, cable stayed
cardboard-tube lattice-grid shell with
cardboard-honeycomb end walls
ground-level foundations in:
sand-filled steel construction

Plan · Sections
scale 1:1000

1 Entrance
2 Covered waiting area
3 Administration
4 Ramp
5 Green dome
6 Exhibition islands

Shigeru Ban is known for his use of unusual materials, which he has strikingly incorporated in his architecture on many occasions. This is certainly true of the Japanese Pavilion he designed for EXPO 2000 in Hanover. Since the structure was largely constructed of paper, it was possible to dismantle it at the end of the exhibition and recycle it completely.
The lattice shell of the main hall consisted of a grid of cardboard tubes made from recycled paper. The end walls were in a cable-tensioned cardboard honeycomb construction, while the roof skin consisted of a five-layer fireproof and waterproof paper membrane, specially developed for this project. The ground-level foundations were in the form of a steel and scaffold-board construction filled with sand. Since building permission is not foreseen for paper or cardboard structures in Germany, extensive trials were necessary before work could begin. In view of the pronounced creep behaviour of paper, the structure had to be reinforced with curved timber ladder-girders, which, together with the steel stays, performed the main load-bearing function. To provide adequate fire protection, the supervisory building authority required the paper roof membrane to be covered with an additional layer of PVC fabric. In the area of the timber ladder-girders, this transparent skin was the sole covering, which meant that the envelope was articulated by a series of bright, arch-like daylight strips. Textile building materials also dominated internally. Visitors descended via a ramp into the main exhibition area, which was covered by a translucent cotton sheet. The tips of the "islands" along the exhibition route extended up through this semitransparent layer and, viewed from above, resembled the rocks in a Japanese garden. The interior was bathed in a soft light that filtered through the translucent skin.

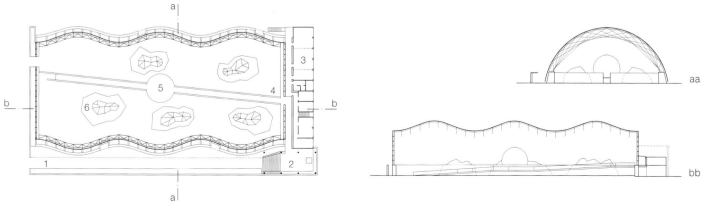

End wall
Section · External elevation
scale 1:20

1 Ø 120/22 mm cardboard tubes; acrylic varnish finish
2 Ø 76 mm cylindrical timber insert
3 Ø 12 mm bolt fixing
4 60/700 mm pine lower chord of curved edge beam
5 membrane; 30 mm plywood
6 EPDM strip
7 wood louvres, painted
8 30/19 mm pine dividing strip, painted
9 elastic seal
10 Ø 12.5 mm stainless-steel tensioning cable
11 Ø 139.8/9.5 mm galvanized steel tubular node
12 30 mm cardboard cellular construction
13 0.89 mm PVC-coated polyester membrane
   0.52 mm five-layer paper membane
14 250/40 mm scaffolding boards
15 steel foundations

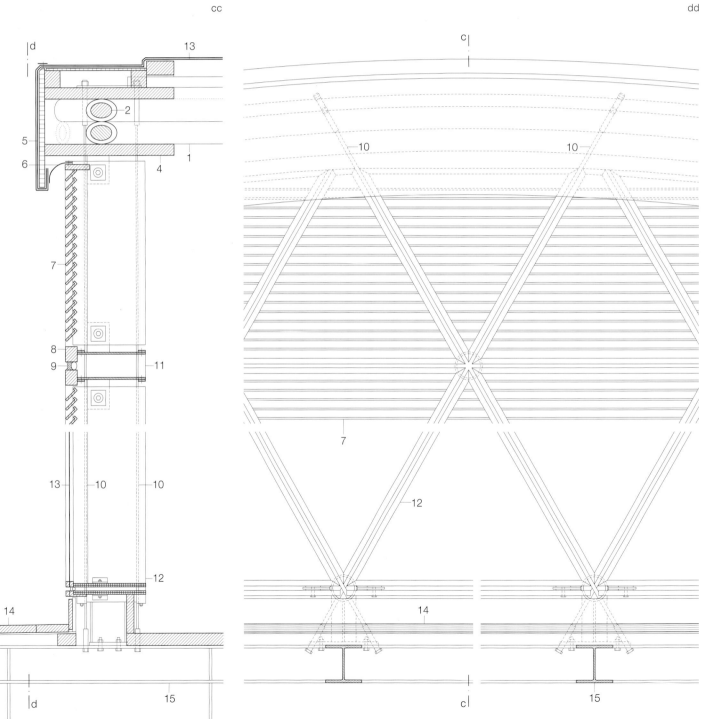

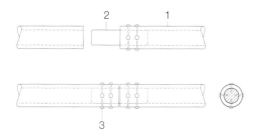

Connection of cardboard tubes
scale 1:20

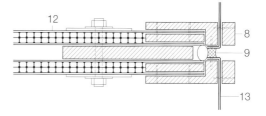

Junction between cellular construction and membrane
scale 1:5

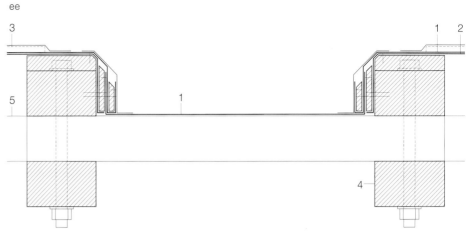

Section through timber ladder-girder   scale 1:5
Foot of timber ladder-girder: structural system
and section   scale 1:50

1 0.89 mm outer membrane:
   PVC-coated polyester fabric, transparent
2 0.52 mm five-layer inner membrane:
   flameproof polythene sheeting,
   non-combustible paper, glass-fibre fabric,
   non-combustible paper,
   flameproof polythene sheeting
3 9/60/1,950 mm horizontal plywood strips
   in membrane sleeves

4 60/75 mm timber arched ladder-girder
   member
5 60/95 mm continuous pine purlin
6 lattice-grid shell:
   Ø 120/22 mm cardboard tubes
7 Ø 6 mm stainless-steel spiral cable
8 foundations: steel construction with scaffolding
   planks, filled with sand
9 steel supporting brackets for ladder girders

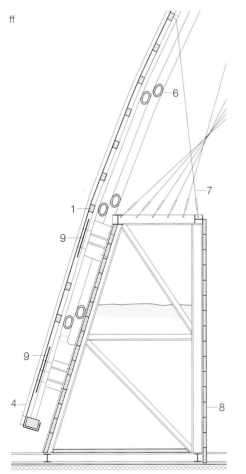

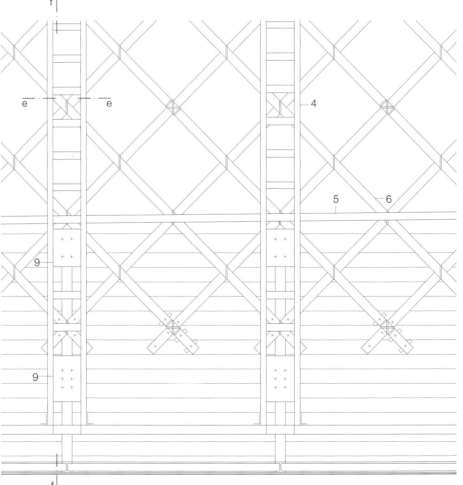

Factory Hall in Bobingen

Architects: Florian Nagler Architekten, Munich

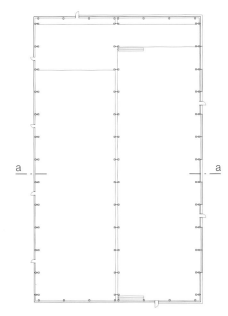

Designed for a timber-processing concern, the hall was erected on a site with a heterogeneous built development. The structure has a simple cubic form, 43 × 76 metres on plan and more than 10 metres high. It is laid out in two bays served by two parallel overhead gantries.

The laminated-timber columns, set out at six-metre centres, are constructed in the form of Vierendeel trusses. Their relatively great depth and the rigid fixing of both chords in the foundations by means of steel plates ensure optimum cross-bracing. The taller chord of the outer columns supports the roof construction. The shorter inner chord bears one of the gantry rails. A central lattice truss transmits the roof loads to the internal row of columns, which also bear part of the loading from the gantries. An elevated access walkway was inserted between the chords of these columns. The roof covering is supported directly by slender laminated-timber beams at two-metre centres. Longitudinal bracing is provided by diagonal, crossed steel members in the long faces of the building, by the three-ply laminated sheeting that functions as roof boarding in certain areas, and by the longitudinal beams and gantry rails. The load-bearing structure is enclosed within a skin of translucent polycarbonate hollow cellular elements that extend over the full height of the building. Internally, the diffused light that enters on all sides lends the hall a pleasant, soft brightness. The vertical polycarbonate elements are rigidly fixed at the base and flexibly restrained at the top to allow for thermal movement in their length. The elements are fixed with metal sections to slender laminated-timber facade rails suspended from steel rods. The fixings are not visible externally.

From the outside, the facade varies in appearance, depending on the angle of view and the lighting conditions. Seen from an oblique angle, it appears as a shiny surface; viewed frontally, it reveals its elegant, slenderly dimensioned structure. At night, the hall is transformed into an illuminated volume.

The large number of gates required, some of which were laid out next to each other, led to the choice of a vertical sliding movement. Together with the emergency exits and smoke-extract openings in the ceiling, these gateways also serve to ventilate the hall. The great thermal storage capacity of the floor slab in smooth-finished steel-fibre-reinforced concrete helps to prevent overheating of the hall in summer.

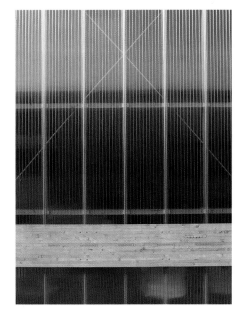

Floor plan
scale 1:1000

Section
scale 1:400

Axonometric of load-bearing structure

126

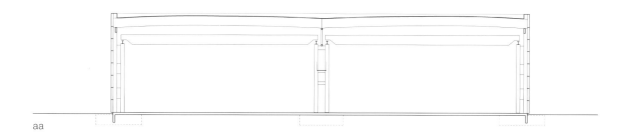

aa

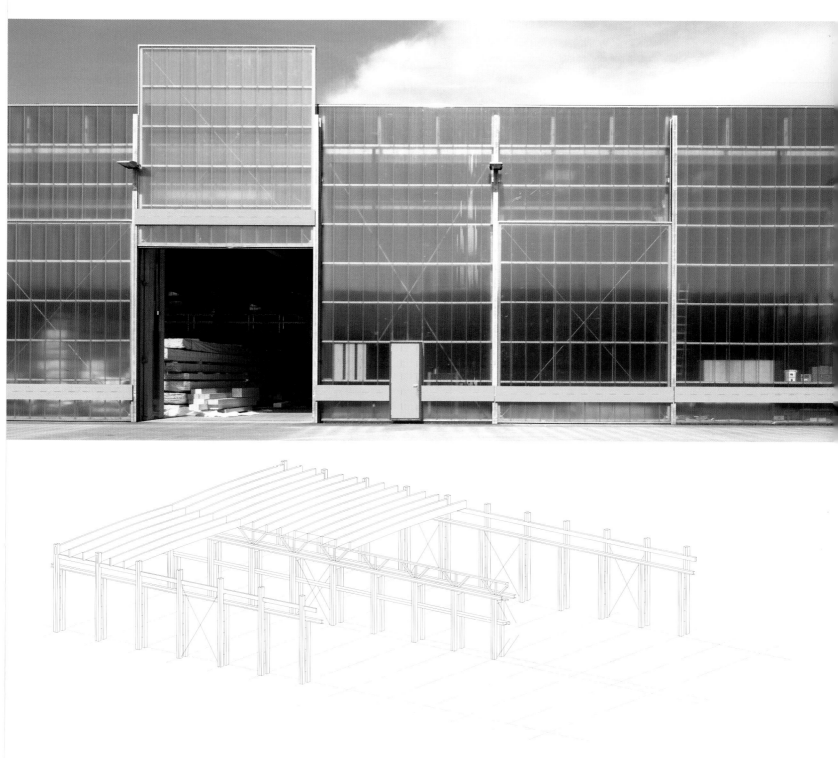

Vertically sliding gate
Horizontal and vertical sections
scale 1:50

1 spotlight
2 330 mm steel I-section
3 motor for raising gate
4 gate hoisting shaft
5 pulley
6 counterweight
7 8 mm solid polycarbonate sheet
8 crash barrier: shuttering panel

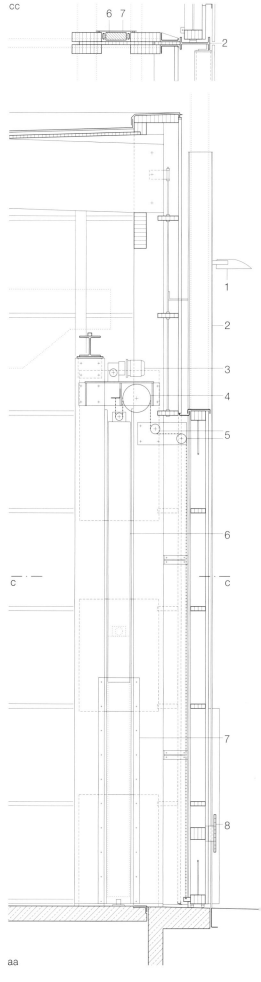

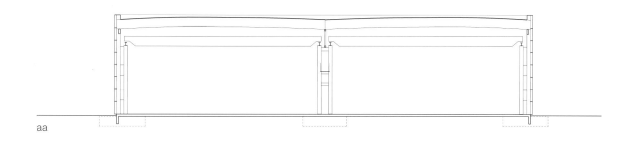

aa

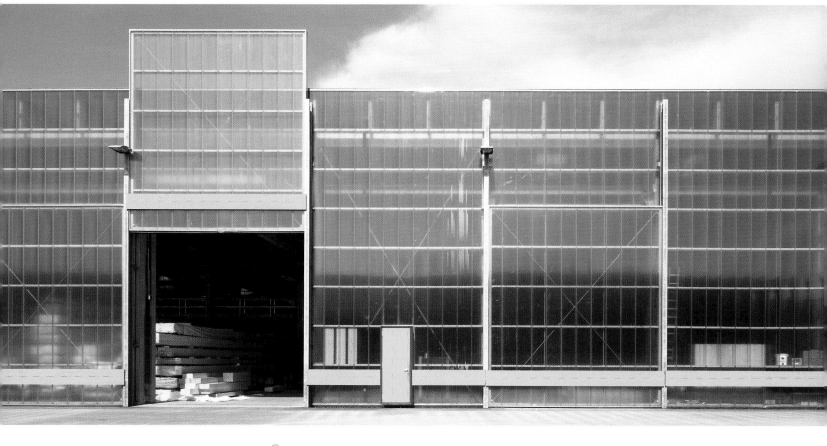

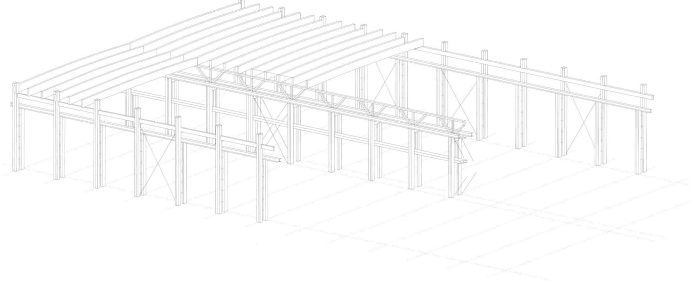

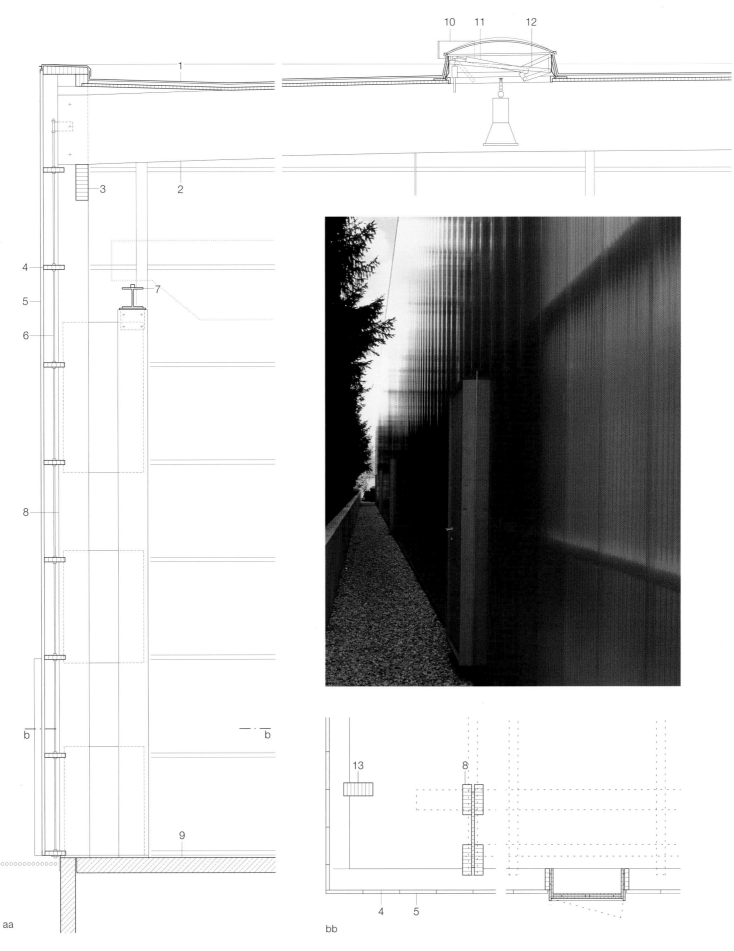

aa

bb

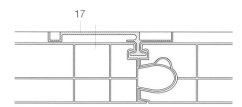

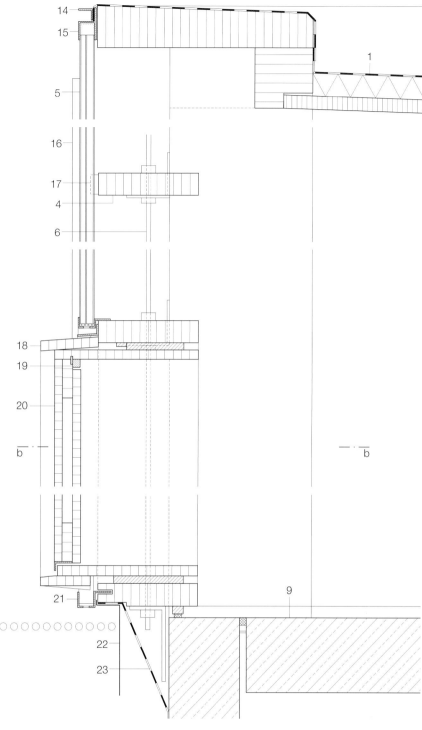

Vertical and horizontal sections   scale 1:50
Vertical and horizontal sectional details   scale 1:10
Detail of joint between polycarbonate elements
scale 1:2.5

  1 roof construction:
     1.3 mm EPDM-rubber sheeting
     50 mm mineral-wool insulation
     35 mm timber boarding or 40 mm three-ply
     laminated sheeting as wind bracing
  2 120/920 mm laminated-softwood roof beam
  3 160/480 mm laminated-softwood beam
  4 60/280 mm laminated-softwood rail
  5 40 mm polycarbonate hollow cellular slab 500 mm
     wide (full height of building); U-value: 1.65 W/m²K
  6 Ø 12 mm steel tube
  7 gantry rail
  8 trussed column: 2× 2× 120/400 mm laminated-
     timber members connected by
     40 mm three-ply laminated sheets
  9 200 mm steel-fibre-reinforced concrete slab
     with smooth finish
 10 wind baffle plates
 11 CO_2 pressure piston
 12 scissors-movement lever
 13 160/400 mm laminated-timber facade post
 14 30/50/5 mm aluminium angle
 15 2 mm aluminium sheet bent to shape
 16 18/18 mm solid polycarbonate member, riveted;
     butt joints offset to those of 24
 17 smooth-pressed aluminium fixing clip
 18 27 mm three-ply laminated sheet
 19 21/21 mm door stop
 20 door: 21 mm three-ply laminated sheet on both
     faces, with 28 mm glued core
 21 smooth-pressed aluminium section
 22 2 mm sheet-aluminium plinth, bent to shape
 23 waterproof sheet to bituminous seal
 24 80/80 mm polycarbonate angle riveted to 5
 25 washer

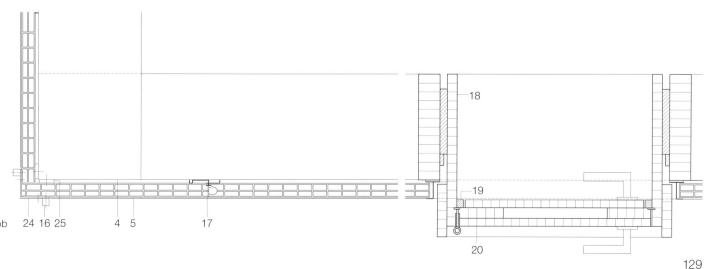

Vertically sliding gate
Horizontal and vertical sections
scale 1:50

1 spotlight
2 330 mm steel I-section
3 motor for raising gate
4 gate hoisting shaft
5 pulley
6 counterweight
7 8 mm solid polycarbonate sheet
8 crash barrier: shuttering panel

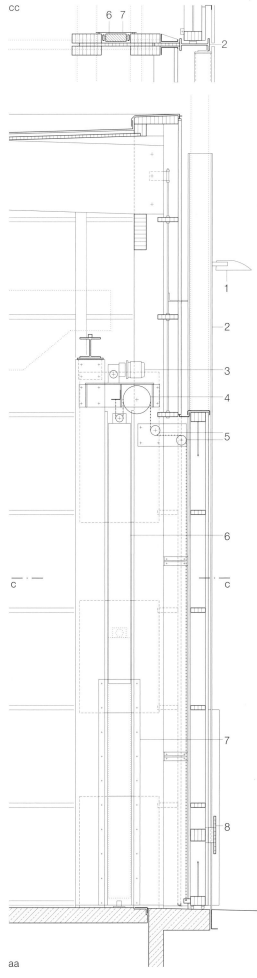

House in Zurndorf

Architects: PPAG Architekten, Vienna

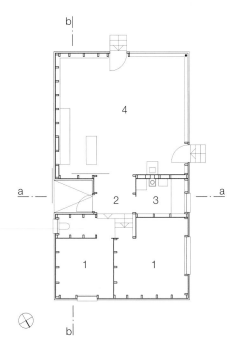

The unusual skin of this house in Austria's tranquil Burgenland region has been likened to that of an elephant. The client's very tight budget obliged the architects to look beyond conventional facade and roof systems. After some research and tests, they came up with a very cost-effective solution – sprayed-on polyurethane foam, as the external insulating layer. The walls are additionally fitted with a moisture-diffusing UV-protecting layer, and on the roof 2–3 mm of polyurethane is used as a seal. Underneath this skin is a load-bearing structure of OSB panels and plywood packing panels (room-side) with a vapour barrier sandwiched in between. Interestingly, although the walls and floors are just 10 to 15 cm thick, they still meet the thermal-insulation requirements of the local building authorities.

The spatial programme and the ground plan are also pared down to the essentials. Arranged on either side of a central services core with solid plinth are the living and sleeping areas. These are timber framed and rest on longitudinal walls with slightly offset heights. In the interior, the dominant features are an abundance of plywood, flush doors and the thick wooden beams of the exposed roof frame. In the end the cost-saving measures left enough surplus for a large, frameless window spanning the corner of the living room, overlooking the surrounding orchard.

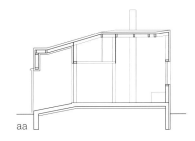

aa

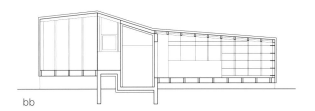

bb

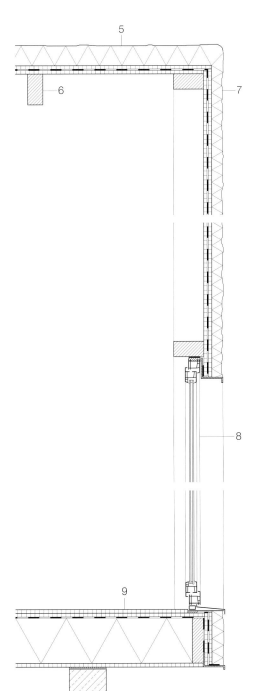

5

6

7

8

9

Floor plan
Sections
scale 1:200

Vertical section
Exit from kitchen
scale 1:20

1 bedroom
2 entrance
3 bathroom
4 lounge
5 roof construction:
   seal/UV protection
   2–3 mm polyurethane coating sprayed onto
   110 mm polyurethane-foam thermal insulation
   19 mm OSB
   vapour barrier
   18 mm plywood
6 solid wooden beam
7 wall construction:
   moisture-diffusing UV-protective coating on
   55 mm polyurethane-foam thermal insulation
   18 mm OSB
   vapour barrier
   18 mm plywood
8 double glazing in plastic frame
9 floor construction:
   18 mm sealed plywood
   24 mm boarding incorporating service ducting
   vapour barrier
   240 mineral-wood thermal insulation between
   solid wooden beams
   18 mm moisture-diffusing wood fibreboard

House near Tokyo

Architects: Shigeru Ban Architects, Tokyo

Reduced to its original function: shelter from wind, rain and cold temperatures – the "Naked House", Shigeru Ban's tenth material and building study, is pure form. An architectonic experiment in the countryside, surrounded by paddy fields, with ramshackle huts and isolated greenhouses as neighbours. Indeed, the long volume of the house with a restrained facade is reminiscent of a greenhouse. The simple, functional structure encloses a single, two-storey high room. Dividing walls, doors, ceilings and stairs – the conventional elements in most houses – simply don't exist in this structure. The bathroom is the only fully enclosed space in the interior; the kitchen, laundry and storage area is merely screened behind curtains. Flexible room-creating furniture, in the shape of container-like crates, takes on the role of individual rooms. The users find their personal spaces for sleeping or retreating in these movable crates, whose "roofs" do double duty as platforms for work or play.

The basic construction of the house consists of slender wood frames which support the roof vaults and the facade. The narrow end faces of the house are mostly transparent and glazed and offer an unfettered view onto the surrounding landscape. Translucent and closed, the synthetic facade of the long faces is perforated only at individual points by ventilation flaps. The project aimed to develop a highly insulated and yet translucent building skin. The search for a suitable insulating material proved to be the greatest challenge. After a series of tests, extruded, white polyethylene fibres were chosen, which are commonly used as a packing material for transporting fruit. The unusual insulating material was hand-coated by members of the architect's studio with a fire-retardant and sealed in 500 sacks. The plastic sacks were quilted to prevent the filling from shifting inside them. The insulation is attached to the wood construction between external skin and internal wall with steel clamps. Two layers of corrugated, fibre-reinforced synthetic panels form the weather membrane of the multi-layer skin. On the inside, the wall construction terminates in a nylon membrane, which is removable for cleaning. The vinyl covering between insulation and membrane prevents condensation on the interior and also serves as an insect screen.

In keeping with traditional Japanese architecture, the synthetic skin allows even, diffuse daylight to penetrate into the interior, a reminder of the paper dividing walls that are typical for this country.

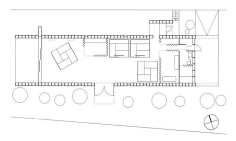

Site plan   scale 1:1000

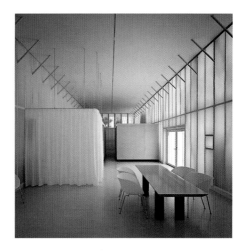

Sections
scale 1:20

1 2× corrugated synthetic panel,
   reinforced with 18 mm glass fibre
2 40/80 mm wood posts
3 9 mm plywood edging board
4 column, 2× 30/280 mm wooden planks
5 translucent insulation, extruded
6 2× 38/89 mm strut
7 synthetic board
8 synthetic membrane
9 steel strut
10 arched girder
11 plasterboard

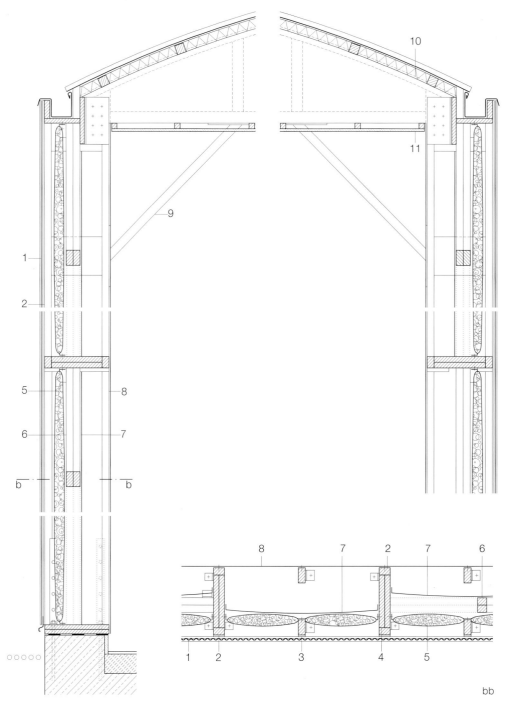

bb

Prada Flagship Store in Tokyo

Architects: Herzog & de Meuron, Basel

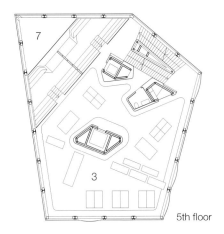

5th floor

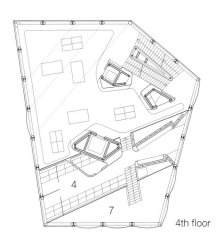

4th floor

Prada's crystalline Epicenter store in the Omotesando fashion area of Tokyo is designed like a giant three-dimensional shop window. The way its interior space is layered and concentrated on the street corner sets it apart from the neighbouring stores. The open area thus created serves as a kind of forecourt, bounded by an artificial wall of tuff stone covered with moss.

The prismatic form of the building arose from the need to make full use of admissible height and distances from other buildings. As a result the store takes on a different outline, depending on where you stand, an effect that is further enhanced by the sculptural design of the envelope itself. Convex, concave and flat panes of glass are fitted into a rhomboid facade grid, the curves and reflections of the glass softening the transition between inside and outside and adding a sensuous note to the overall impression. Passers-by are seduced into stepping inside this spatial sculpture. Inside, too, the structural elements play a big part in the overall impression. The floor slabs are supported by the steel sections in the facade and the three vertical steel cores, while horizontal steel shafts, dubbed the "tubes", take care of bracing. Together these form a rigid cage-like structure which despite the slimness of the sections is designed to withstand earthquakes. The "tubes" also have another function – in the midst of all this transparency they provide enclosed space for changing rooms and tills.

The support frame for the glazing is a diagonal post-and-rail facade. To ensure an effective seal (despite the raking position of the members that results from the rhomboid articulation), the inner faces were additionally wet-sealed with silicone. The requirement for narrow joints without compression strips, and for a certain degree of elasticity in the construction led to the choice of a connection detail with two clamps fixing into opposite edges of the pane. In case of movement due to seismic activity the panes remain in position, while the frame shifts slightly in relation to the edge fixing of the panes. A stainless-steel disc is fixed into the groove of the outer pane, to provide mechanical protection. The curvature of the glass gives it enhanced rigidity. To create this curvature, panes of flat float glass were heated slowly in a trapezoid-shaped frame in an eight-hour process until the centre of the pane depressed by around 150 mm, under its own weight. The panes were then cooled down. This method, i.e. heating and cooling, also achieved partial pre-tensioning. As no sun blinds were planned inside or out, a UV filter was laminated into the panes that are subject to solar radiation, to prevent the goods inside fading in the sun.

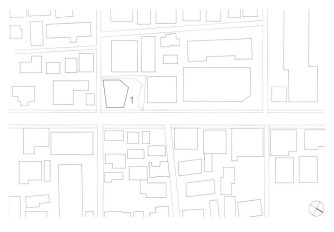

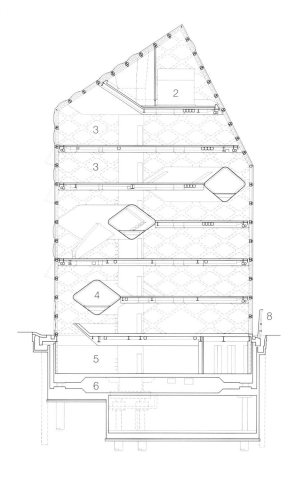

Site plan
scale 1:3000
Plans · Section
scale 1:400

1 Plaza
2 Mechanical services
3 Office
4 "Tube"
5 Café/store
6 Earthquake-resistant foundations
7 Void
8 Wall of tufa stone with moss

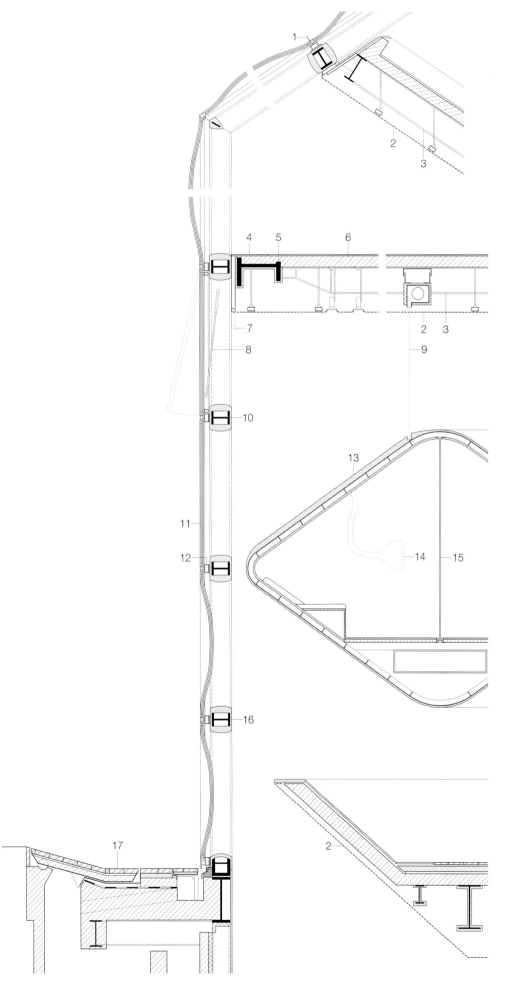

Vertical section through facade
scale 1:50
Details scale 1:5

A Vertical section through ridge
B Horizontal section through corner of building

 1 gutter
 2 perforated sheet aluminium
 3 350/175 mm steel I-section
 4 floor strip along facade:
   2 mm cream epoxy-resin coating
   18 mm screed
   150 mm concrete composite slab
 5 600/400 mm steel bearer and tie member
   between diagonal facade beams
 6 floor construction:
   12 mm carpeting
   10 mm screed
   150 mm concrete composite slab
 7 aluminium smoke-stop spandrel to close
   lower part of rhombus
 8 pneumatic spring to opening flap
 9 extendible smoke curtain
10 load-bearing facade:
   250/180 mm steel I-sections welded on site,
   thicknesses according to loading,
   reinforced at corners of building with solid
   cast-steel members
11 3200/2000 mm rhomboid glazing elements,
   convex or concave:
   12 mm float glass with diamond-cut grooves
   on edges + 16 mm air-filled cavity + 2× 6 mm
   laminated safety glass with UV filter between
   laminations (U=2.6 W/m²K)
12 diagonal aluminium post-and-rail construction
13 "tube" wall:
   25 mm calcium silicate fire-resistant cladding
   internal and external, painted matte cream
   6 mm sheet steel with reinforcing ribs
14 "snorkel" (viewing screen on gooseneck)
15 2× 6 mm laminated float-glass partition to
   changing cabin with liquid-crystal interlayer
16 25 mm (min.) calcium silicate fire-resistant
   layer, painted matte cream
17 floor vent with tufa stone finish as joint for
   seismic structural movement
18 aluminium fixing profile
19 silicone edge profile
20 silicone compression strip
21 silicone wet seal
22 8–20 mm welded sheet-steel supporting
   sections
23 aluminium guide track

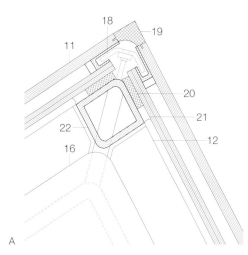

A

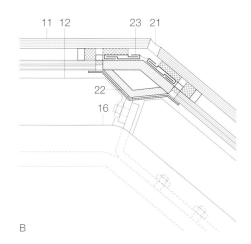

B

Church in Munich

Architects: Allmann Sattler Wappner Architekten, Munich

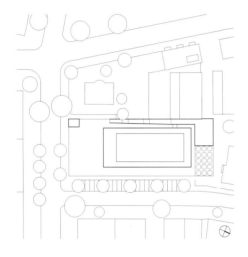

Site plan   scale 1:2000
Plan   scale 1:500

1 Nativity
2 Adoration of the Virgin
3 Veneration of the Five Sacred Wounds
4 Confessional
5 Baptismal font
6 Altar
7 Tabernacle
8 Sacristy

In comparison to the multifunctional community centres that have sprung up in new developments in the past decades, a new urban church building has become a rarity. Yet, just such an opportunity presented itself in the middle of Neuhausen, an established residential district in central Munich. A competition was held in 1995 to replace the Sacred Heart Church, destroyed by fire in the previous year. The adjacent community facilities, untouched by the fire, were to be upgraded at the same time. The new ensemble consists of the church itself – a severe cube, 48 m long, 21 m wide and 16 m high – bordered to the rear by the low sacristy, and the large public square at the front with a freestanding bell tower near the street. The tower is constructed of steel profiles and enveloped in several layers of a metal-fabric mesh, increasing in thickness towards the top so that the structure grows gradually more dense until it reaches its full height at just under 37 m. The bells are suspended in a protective timber cube built inside the steel scaffolding. In plan, the church corresponds to a classic church with a central aisle. On the outside, the volume presents a very unusual aspect: here, the space-within-a-space concept has been translated with great rigour. The external facade, a translucent glass cube that provides the thermal enclosure, houses a timber shrine as the actual liturgical space. The space between the two structures is occupied by the vestibule and a narrow ambulatory with the fourteen Stations of the Cross. The two oversized leafs of the church portal opening onto the forecourt create the impression that the cube has been inserted into the glass skin.

When the hydraulically operated leafs of the main portal are closed, access into the church is provided via two small wicket doors within the huge entrance portal. From the vestibule, the route leads beneath a massive concrete organ loft into the main space, which is flanked by the confessional and the Nativity, and into the impressive nave flooded in soft, filtered light all the way to the altar wall at the end, which is entirely taken up by a shimmering, golden, metal-mesh curtain. The floor slopes imperceptibly down towards the rear. The vertical timber screen, maple louvres that form the internal enclosure, are arranged in such a way that the light increases in intensity towards the altar.

On the outer building skin, the glass facade, transparency is employed in an entirely different manner. Nearly opaque thanks to a white printed glass surface, the glazing is a visual screen around the altar area. Towards the forecourt it grows increasingly translucent as the printed pattern decreases until it reaches full transparency in the vestibule area by means of clear glass panes.

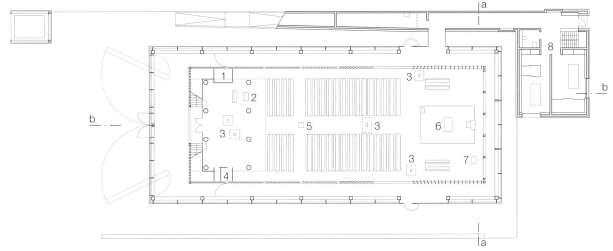
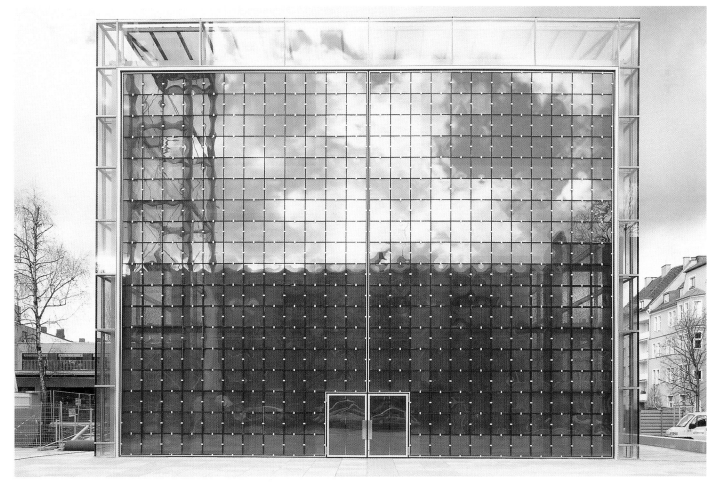

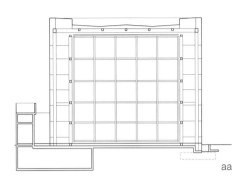

aa

Sections   scale 1:500

The filigree post-and-beam construction of the glass facades is suspended from large steel box-section edge beams, which are supported by steel columns. Glass fins provide wind bracing. The steel beams and posts are not weld-connected, but jointed with invisible screw fasteners. The joints are only fixed by the glazing, which provides the structural support. It consists of insulating glass with flush pressure battens. This unique construction, which creates the uniform smoothness of the outer skin, is made possible by a special glass construction: beginning on the inside with single pane safety glass, followed by an air cavity and laminated safety glass on the outside, whose outermost pane is slightly smaller all around. The pressure battens lie in the widened joints of the uppermost glass layer. For safety reasons, additional plugs were added for the recessed layer. Otherwise, the panels rest on brackets in front of the beams.

The stunning play of light in the interior of the church in daytime is equalled by the nocturnal aspect of the glass volume shining through the timber screen. The deep blue transparent glazing in the large entrance portal is a unique feature, in daytime and at night. The hues of the coated glass panels bathe the entire vestibule in a blue light. The 436 glass panels in the main portal bear images of nails, arranged into a cuneiform script, representing an inscription of Christ's Passion from the Gospel according to St. John. Within the structural-glazing construction, the glass panes are additionally supported by rectangular metal rods as bracing against wind suction. The distinctive metal rods at the centre axis of each pane cover the joints in a unique, silvery pattern.

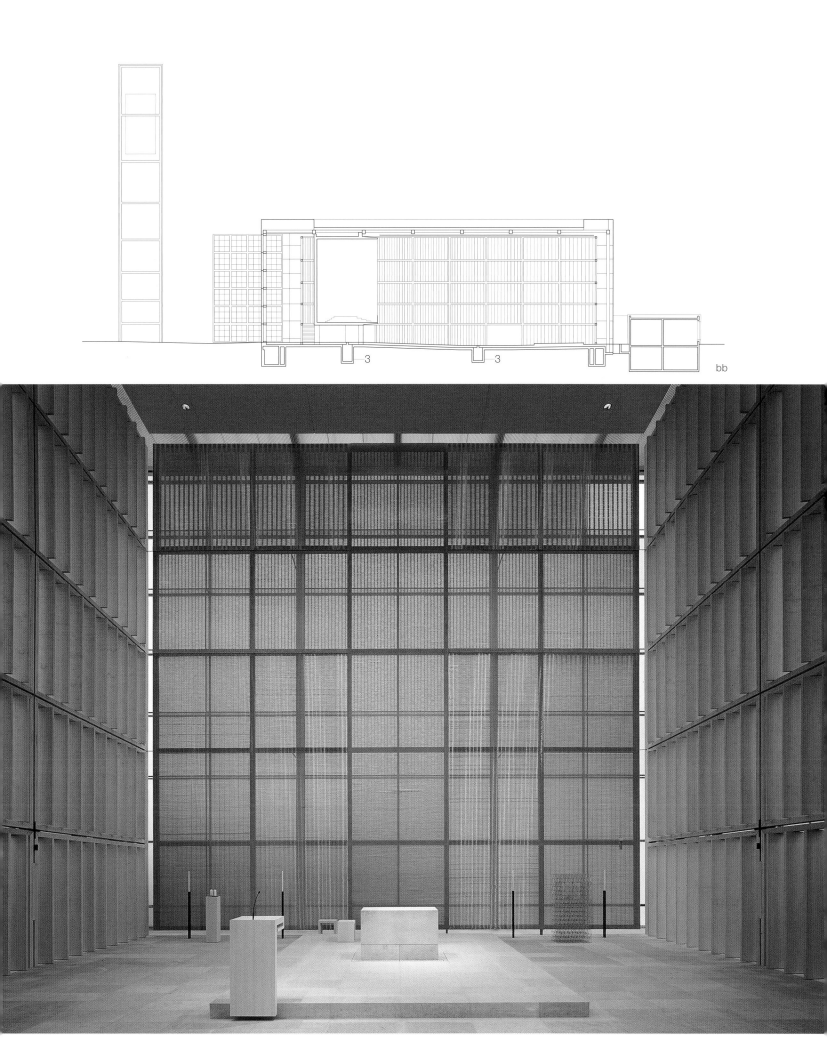

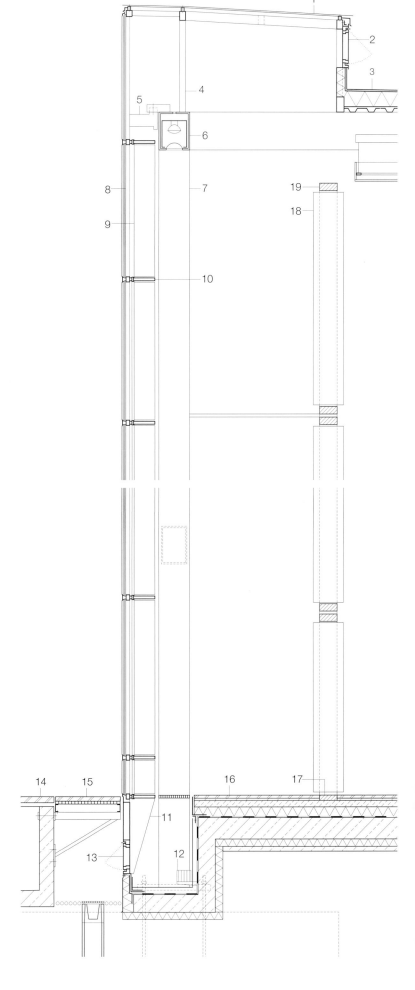

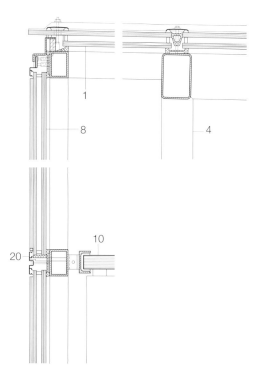

Facade section   scale 1:50
Details   scale 1:10
 1 thermopane roof glazing
 2 vent/smoke extract, aluminium
 3 roof construction:
    plastic waterproof sheeting
    160–240 mm rigid foam insulation laid to falls
    bituminous vapour barrier
    10 mm chipboard
    50 mm trapezoidal sheet
    suspended ceiling, 3× 12.5 mm gypsum
    plasterboard
    15 mm lime-cement plaster with
    integrated cooling loops
 4 80/80/4 mm steel SHS
 5 height-adjustable facade suspension
 6 420/500/20 mm steel RHS edge girder, welded
    with integrated light fixtures
 7 double column, 2× 170/420/60 mm steel RHS
 8 double glazing: 8 mm lam. safety glass + 16 mm
    cavity + 10 mm toughened glass, printed,
    outer pane staggered all round, printed surface
 9 50/70/5 mm steel RHS suspension
10 36/300 mm bracing glass fin
11 steel bracket as bearing for glass fins
12 convector
13 aluminium air inlet flap
14 80 mm sandstone on 50 mm grit bed
15 cover fresh air intake shaft:
    60 mm sandstone panel with ventilation slits
    40 mm grid
    steel I-section bracket 100 mm deep
16 floor construction:
    40 mm sand-lime stone slabs
    30 mm mortar bed
    85 mm heated screed, reinforced with steel fibres
    PE-film separating layer
    120 mm polystyrene rigid foam insulation
    bituminous waterproof sheeting
17 240/50 mm solid maple sill plate
18 maple-veneer wood louvres
    dowel-joined to frame
19 120/240 mm solid maple frame
20 aluminium glazing strip, flush

Horizontal section through corner
of gate   scale 1:20

1 double glazed facade
2 glazing strip, flush
3 glass fin
4 double column
5 170/90/10 mm
   steel angle section
6 gate glazing:

5 mm toughened glass + 20 mm
cavity + 5 mm toughened glass
printed on both sides
755/767 mm pane dimension
7 70/40/8 mm aluminium
   clamp for glazing
8 secondary construction:
   100/60/4 mm steel RHS
9 primary construction:
   280/150 (240 mm) steel RHS

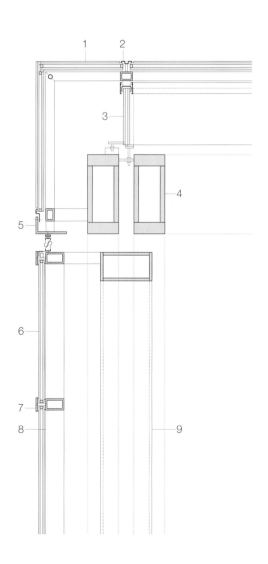

Administration Building in Kronberg

Architects: Schneider + Schumacher, Frankfurt/Main

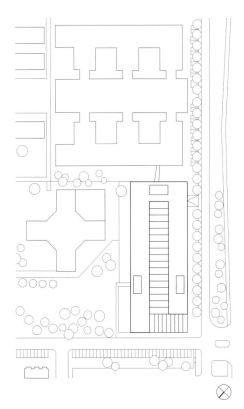

The three-storey building is laid out to a U-shaped plan. The use of prestressed concrete floor slabs meant that it was possible to avoid intermediate columns in the office areas. This allowed a free spatial organization according to user needs; in other words, in the form of single-cell, combination or open-plan offices. Partitions can be erected anywhere they are required. The entire mechanical services (lighting, heating and cooling runs) are housed in the solid slabs, which also provide thermal storage mass. The heating and cooling system consists of thin capillary tubes laid in the plaster, while the media networks were installed in the double-floor construction. The limited scope for controlling temperatures via the ceilings imposed special demands on the facade. Basically, a storey-height box-type window was developed. The outer layer, consisting of 12 mm toughened safety glass, reduces the heat losses during cold weather and also protects the perforated louvre sunblinds, which are housed in the intermediate space. By opening this outer skin, overheating through insolation can be prevented. The blinds are thus an ideal form of external sunshading for the inner facade skin. This layer consists of an insulating double-glazed element to every bay of the facade with a narrow, non-transparent, thermally insulated ventilation flap. The main element can be opened only for cleaning purposes. The ventilation flap is fitted with a magnetic seal of the kind found in refrigerators. A central computer controls the operation of the outer facade skin and the sunshading.
The inner facade skin is manually operated. Users can also activate the blinds by pressing a button and can open an element in the outer facade in conjunction with the internal ventilation flaps. If a user makes the wrong decision, the system reacts accordingly. This represents a good means of combining energy-efficient computer controls with individual needs. In addition to its technical features, the facade also possesses its own special aesthetic. Depending on whether the casements are open or closed and on the angle of view, it may appear completely smooth and reflecting, or transparent with a scale-like structure. This scope for variability is an attractive element of the design that relativizes any sense of austerity the building might seem to radiate.
The central hall forms a buffer zone between internal and external space. It is covered with an air-cushion roof that can be automatically opened. This reduces the external surface area through which heat can escape. The hall is ventilated via a floor duct. The air inlets are laid out along a pool of water that ensures better air quality. Each bay of the offices oriented to the hall has a fixed, double-glazed element and a narrow, non-transparent ventilation flap.

Site plan
scale 1:2500

Longitudinal section
Ground floor plan
scale 1:750

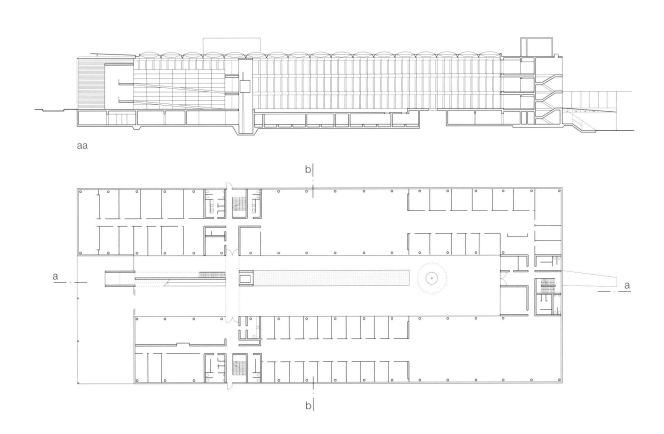

aa

b

a ────   ──── a

b

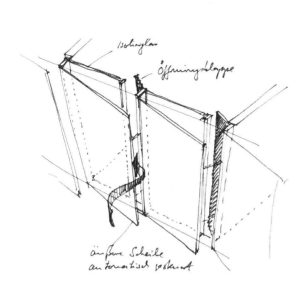

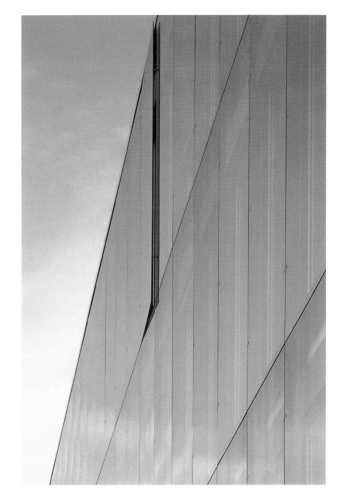

Corner of outer facade:
horizontal section
scale 1:20
(see p. 154 for key)

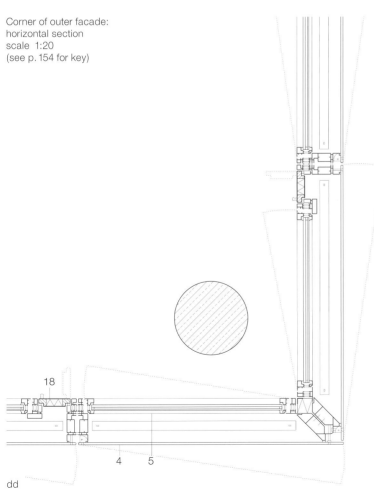

18

4   5

dd

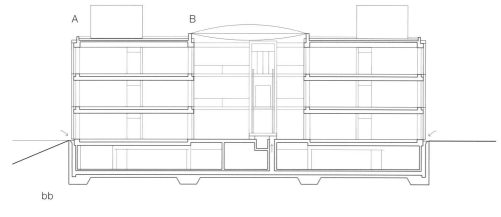

bb

Cross-section
scale 1:400

External and courtyard facades:
vertical sections
Courtyard facade:
horizontal section
scale 1:20

External facade window details:
horizontal and vertical sections
scale 1:5

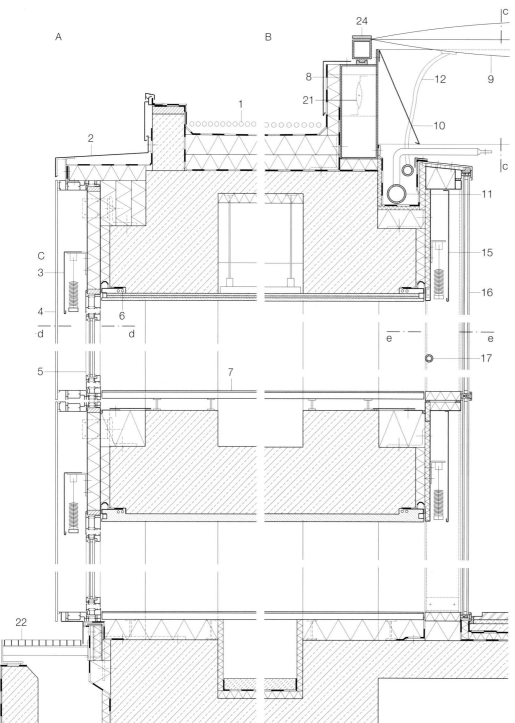

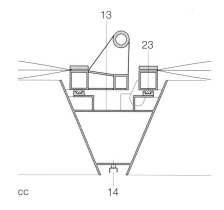

cc

1 roof construction:
    50 mm layer of gravel
    2 mm plastic roof sealing layer
    110–35 mm rock-wool insulation to falls
    0.25 mm polythene sheet vapour barrier
    priming coat
    120 mm reinforced concrete roof slab
    and downstand beams
    50 mm rock-wool thermal insulation
    2× 12.5 mm plasterboard
    20 mm plaster with integrated
    heating/cooling mat
2 2 mm stainless-steel flashing
3 2 mm sheet-aluminium casing
4 12 mm external glazing layer
5 extruded aluminium casement and frame,
    thermally divided; glazing: 6 mm + 14 mm
    cavity + 8 mm laminated safety glass
6 Ø 20 mm water pipe for
    heating/cooling soffit
7 floor construction:
    carpeting on 40 mm double-layer floor slabs
    260 mm void
    dust-protection layer
    360 mm prestressed reinf. conc. floor slab
    40 mm plaster with integrated heating/
    cooling mat (Ø 2 mm micro water tubes)
8 200/500 mm welded steel section with
    ventilation opening to every bay
9 three-layer transparent membrane cushion
10 2 mm sheet-steel masking strip
11 main run for sprinkler installation
12 air supply to membrane cushion
13 drainage channel
14 power rail
15 2 mm sheet-aluminium casing
16 glazing (10 mm + 16 mm cavity + 10 mm)
17 Ø 30 mm stainless-steel tube
18 ventilation flap: sheet aluminium on both
    faces with seal and magnetic fastener
19 pressure equalization slits
20 motor-operated stainless-steel chain
21 louvre flaps for hall ventilation when
    membrane roof closed
22 grating over air-supply duct to hall
23 friction-fixed sealing strips
24 membrane clamping strip

154

Both the external and the courtyard faces of the building are in a double-skin form of construction.
In the case of the external facade, the inner skin consists of a layer of double insulating glazing; the outer skin is in single glazing (details A and C).
On the courtyard side, the office facades consist of a skin of double insulating glazing. The second layer of the double-skin construction here is formed by the membrane roof. The internal courtyard provides a functional buffer zone (detail B and photo).

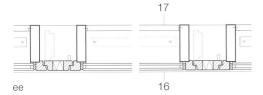

ee   16

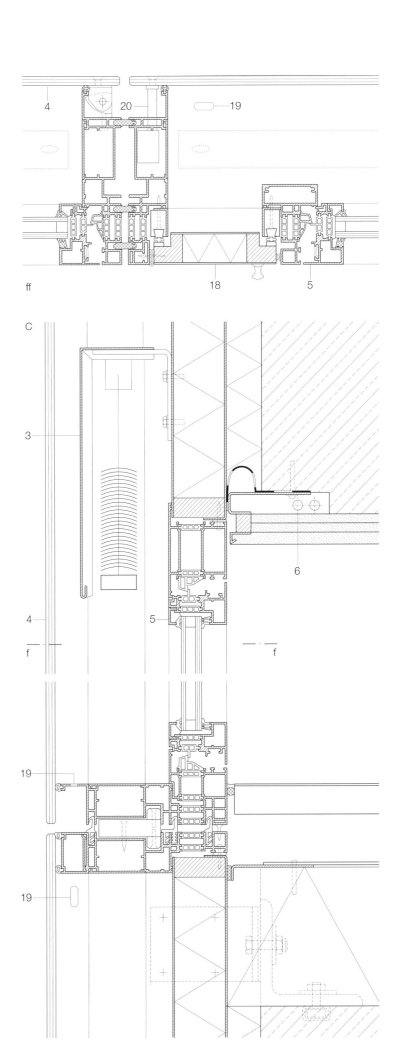

155

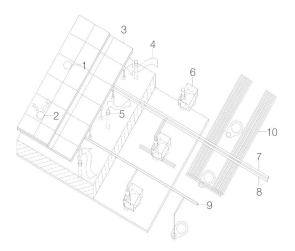

Floor construction system
Isometric

1 electrical, computer and telephone
  connections via floor tanks
2 air supply via the floor
3 double-floor construction with
  carpet-tile finish
4 subfloor void used as air-supply duct
5 inlet sleeve for service installation unit
6 built-in unit for lighting, sprinkler and
  heating valves
7 cold-water supply
8 hot-water supply
9 sprinkler supply
10 plastic micro-tubes within plaster forming
  heating/cooling mats

Trade-Fair Tower in Hanover

Architects: Herzog + Partner, Munich

With a height of 85 m (excluding roof installations for ventilation), the new trade-fair tower is the tallest building in Hanover. Its soaring height not only underscores the importance of the fair for the city; it also creates a landmark for the trade-fair grounds between the northern site entrance and the northern end of the large green adjoining space. To maintain visual links between these important open spaces despite the limited available area, the tower was laid out on the diagonal. By locating the two access "cores" outside the building, it was possible to create a transparent entrance hall. The square plan of the tower, with office areas of roughly 400 m² on each of the 17 upper floors, allows for a division into as many as 20 workplaces in open-plan, combination- or cell form, with each workplace enjoying equal window access. The external cores, situated at opposite corners of the building, have clay-tile facades and provide shading to the glazed south and east faces of the office tower, a feature that is especially important for preventing excessive heat loads in summer and glare. Heating and cooling are based primarily on the thermal activation of the solid volumes of the building, including the unclad floor slabs, which serve as storage mass for the heating and cooling installation integrated into the screed. Internal heat sources (occupants, equipment, lamps, etc.) are more or less sufficient to heat the building. Unwanted thermal gains from insolation in summer are removed directly – without being allowed to penetrate into the offices – by the large volume of air flowing between the inner and outer facade layers. Movable ventilation louvres in the external steel and glass facade allow fresh air to flow into the corridor. Flint glass was used in the outer skin to ensure greater transparency and to maintain visual contact with the outside without changes in colour. Room-high sliding casements in the inner timber skin allow the offices to be ventilated individually. When the windows are closed, outlets at the foot of the casements admit air from a small duct. Exhaust air is collected via a central system of conduits with the help of the natural upward flow and is drawn out at the roof. The ventilation system is activated largely by natural forces.

Section · Plans
scale 1:750

Principle of natural air flow from outside to inside through corridor facade

A Winter
B Transitional season
C Summer

+   Wind pressure
–   Wind suction
—o   Facade opening
    Temperature sensor
▶   Outside air, evacuated air
▶   Air flow in
      corridor facade
>>> Fresh air, exhaust air
●▭ Exhaust-air shaft

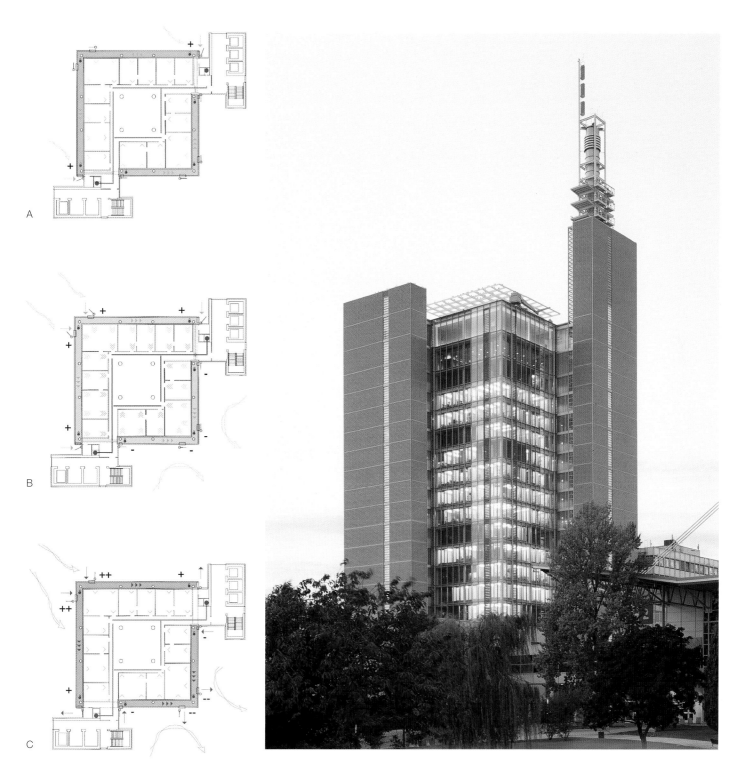

A

B

C

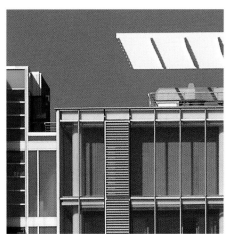

Sectional details   scale 1:10

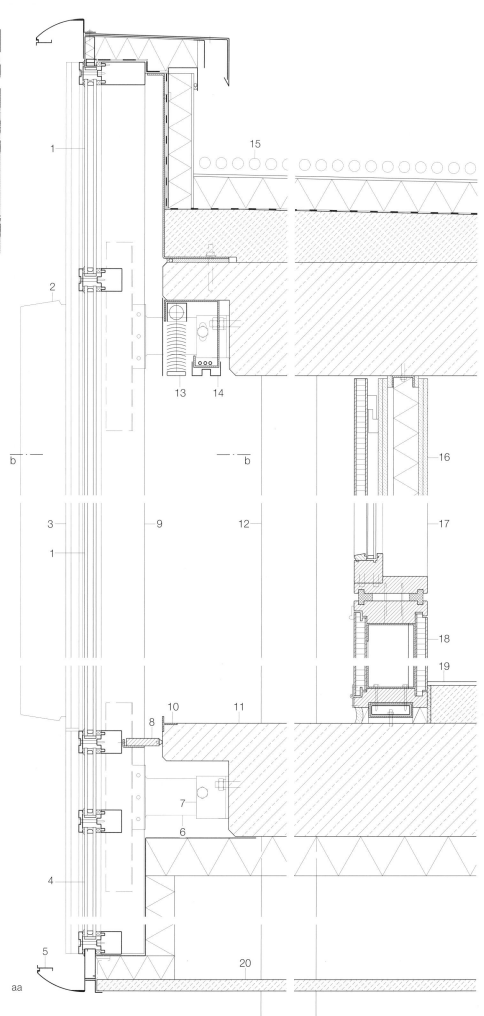

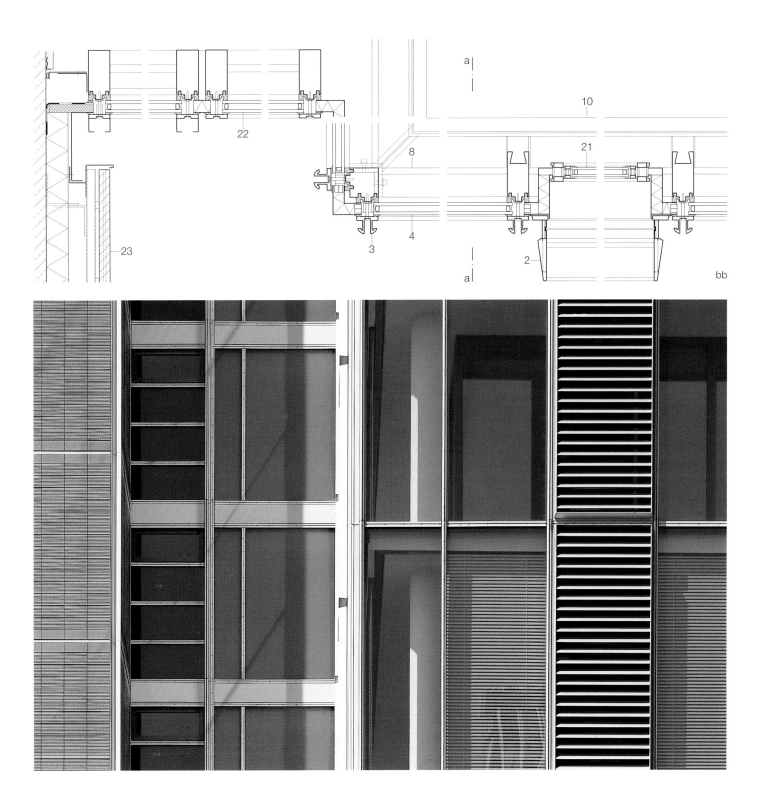

1 steel and flint glass outer facade
(8 + 16 + 8 mm)
(U = 1.1 W/m²K)
2 aluminium ventilating element
with protective louvres
3 cover strip as guide track for travelling
cradle
4 steel and glass facade (8 + 16 + 8 mm);
(U = 1.1 W/m²K); outer pane printed white
5 aluminium section with drainage opening
6 coated cast-aluminium element
7 100/100/10 mm galvanized steel angle,
painted white; bolt fixed
8 20 mm hardwood smoke-tight closing strip
9 facade post with fixing groove
10 40/40/4 mm steel T-section edge strip

11 300 mm reinforced concrete floor,
surface coated
12 Ø 500 mm reinforced concrete column
13 aluminium louvre sunblind
14 cable duct with sheet-aluminium cover
15 roof construction: layer of coarse gravel
80 mm rigid-foam insulation
2 mm roof sealing layer
120–20 mm concrete finished to falls
300 mm reinforced concrete slab
16 veneered plywood on plasterboard stud wall
(services storey only)
17 wood and glass inner facade:
hemlock with high-build varnish;
double glazing (4 + 16 + 6 mm), inner pane
in toughened glass (U = 1.1 W/m²K)

18 air-supply duct in hemlock with inspection
opening, and air inlet in room
19 office flooring:
carpeting 100 mm monolithic screed with
electrical installation and runs for cooling
structural slab
20 30 mm glass-fibre-reinforced concrete soffit
over entrance hall
21 ventilating glass louvres to corridor
22 corridor glazing (8 + 16 + 8 mm),
inner pane in laminated safety glass
23 lift core facade:
30 mm natural-colour clay tiles with
grooved surface
40 mm cavity; 60 mm rigid-foam insulation
reinforced concrete wall

1 aluminium ventilating element with protective
  louvre construction
2 cable duct with sheet-aluminium cover
3 glass ventilating louvres to corridor
4 Ø 500 mm reinforced concrete column
5 hemlock inner facade element with high-build
  varnish
6 fixed glazing (4 + 16 + 6 mm) (U = 1.1 W/m²K)
7 natural ventilation via sliding windows
8 mechanical ventilation via skirting duct
  with air inlet
9 inspection opening:
  35 mm hemlock-veneered plywood panel
10 35 mm hemlock-veneered plywood lining
11 fabric blind
12 carpeting
  100 mm monolithic screed with electrical
  installation and runs for heating structural
  slab; 300 mm reinforced concrete floor slab

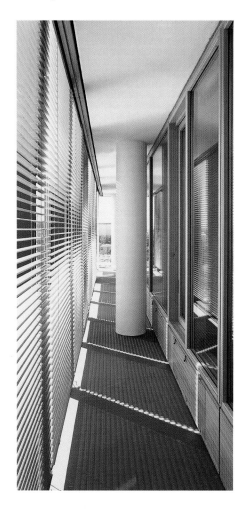

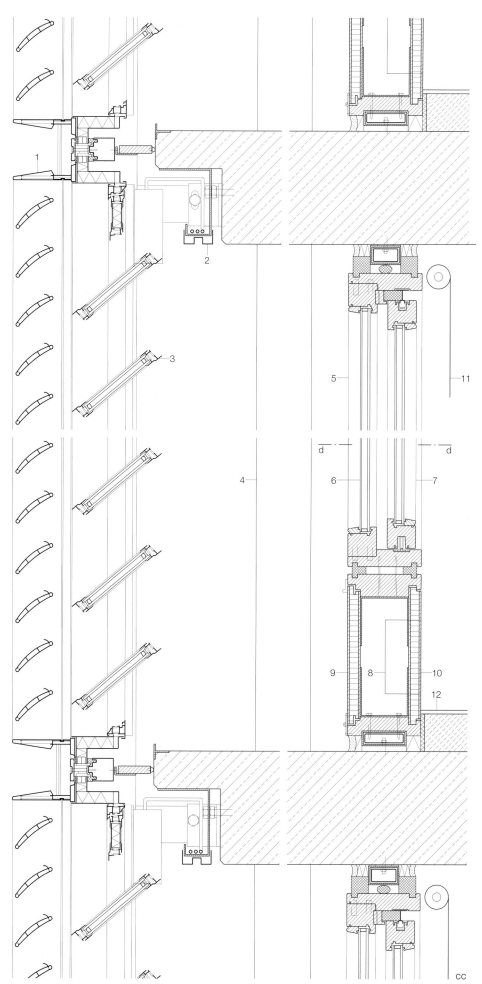

Diagrams   scale 1:200
Sectional details through two-layer
facade   scale 1:10

Thermoactive floor slab   Ventilation

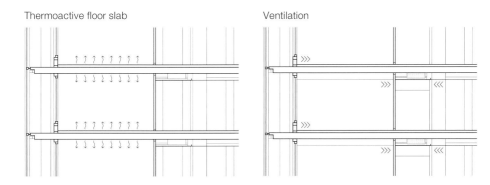

Winter
· flow temperature of pipes in screed: ca. 23 °C
  for heating; room temperature ca. 20 °C
· warm air supplied mechanically via skirting duct;
  cool air supplied naturally via window ventilation

Summer
· flow temperature of pipes in screed: ca. 21 °C
  for cooling; room temperature ca. 26 °C
· cool air supplied mechanically via skirting duct;
  warm air supplied naturally via window
  ventilation

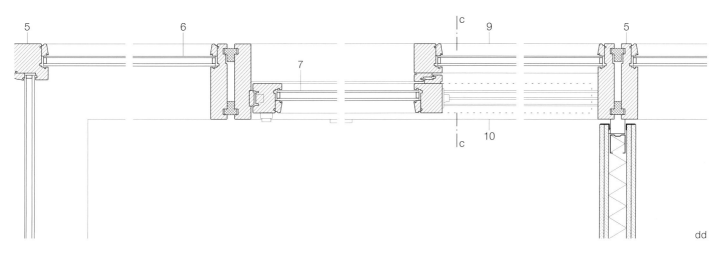

Administration Building in Wiesbaden

Architects: Herzog + Partner, Munich

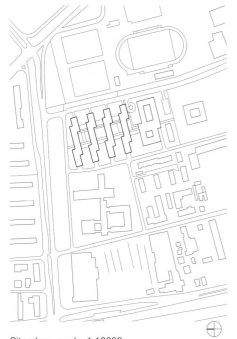

Site plan   scale 1:10000
Section through office slab   scale 1:500
Vertical section through
north facade   scale 1:20

The new administration building of the supplementary insurance company is located in convenient proximity to Wiesbaden's central railway station. Continuous and hence profitable use of the building is guaranteed by the fact that large sections of the building can be leased to the city of Wiesbaden. The four slender volumes of the complex are arranged to maintain the east-west wind flow, important for the urban climate. All five buildings are linked by dual access on the longitudinal sides on the north-south axes. Each volume contains two vertical access cores, placed on these axes, which are directly accessible from the street level, allowing for individual use or leasing arrangements for each office area.

The office slabs are realized as a reinforced-concrete skeleton construction with bracing panes and structural cores. The flat ceiling slabs are in dimensions that do not require binding beams. This allows for tremendous flexibility in terms of the internal division: the areas can be used as individual, group or combination offices and as open-plan offices. The complex is above all distinguished for its intelligent facade concept, which not only allows for differentiated lighting, but also for flexible ventilation options and a variety of energy-related features. Curved sunscreen- and light-deflecting elements in aluminium mark the design of the south elevation. The elements on the insulated facade are automatically adjusted to maintain in the interior office spaces appropriate for computer screens. On the outside, the varying positioning of the elements creates a lively face, which changes according to weather conditions. The north side of the office slabs also features light-deflecting elements. On both sides, a post-and-beam facade with triple insulated glazing lies behind these elements. Excellent energy consumption values are achieved in combination with adjustable heating and cooling of building components, ensuring a good internal climate. Timber ventilation flaps are attached laterally in the area of the facade elements. These can be operated manually. Integrated plastic flaps allow fresh air, which is prewarmed in an integrated convector, to flow into the interior spaces. This system ensures good ventilation even when the windows are closed, contributing to the flexibility and user-friendliness of the building.

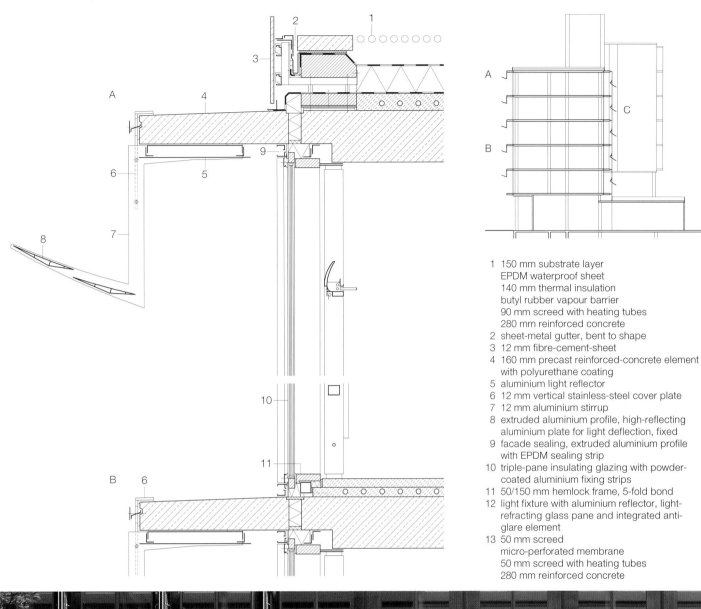

1 150 mm substrate layer
    EPDM waterproof sheet
    140 mm thermal insulation
    butyl rubber vapour barrier
    90 mm screed with heating tubes
    280 mm reinforced concrete
2 sheet-metal gutter, bent to shape
3 12 mm fibre-cement-sheet
4 160 mm precast reinforced-concrete element
    with polyurethane coating
5 aluminium light reflector
6 12 mm vertical stainless-steel cover plate
7 12 mm aluminium stirrup
8 extruded aluminium profile, high-reflecting
    aluminium plate for light deflection, fixed
9 facade sealing, extruded aluminium profile
    with EPDM sealing strip
10 triple-pane insulating glazing with powder-
    coated aluminium fixing strips
11 50/150 mm hemlock frame, 5-fold bond
12 light fixture with aluminium reflector, light-
    refracting glass pane and integrated anti-
    glare element
13 50 mm screed
    micro-perforated membrane
    50 mm screed with heating tubes
    280 mm reinforced concrete

Vertical section through south facade
scale 1:20

1 100/12 stainless-steel profile,
   glass-bead-blasted finish
2 powder-coated aluminium stirrup
3 extruded aluminium profiles,
   high-reflecting aluminium sheet for
   indirect light redirection
4 extruded aluminium profiles,
   high-reflecting aluminium sheet for
   direct light redirection
5 spindle hoisting motor
6 stainless-steel tube for cabling
7 precast reinforced-concrete element
   with polyurethane coating
8 aluminium light reflector
9 facade sealing, extruded aluminium
   profile with EPDM sealing strip
10 50/150 mm hemlock frame,
   5-fold bond
11 triple-pane insulating glazing with
   powder-coated aluminium fixing
   strips
12 light fixture with aluminium reflector,
   light-refracting glass pane and
   integrated anti-glare element
13 floor construction:
   50 mm screed
   micro-perforated membrane
   50 mm screed with heating tubes
   280 mm reinforced concrete

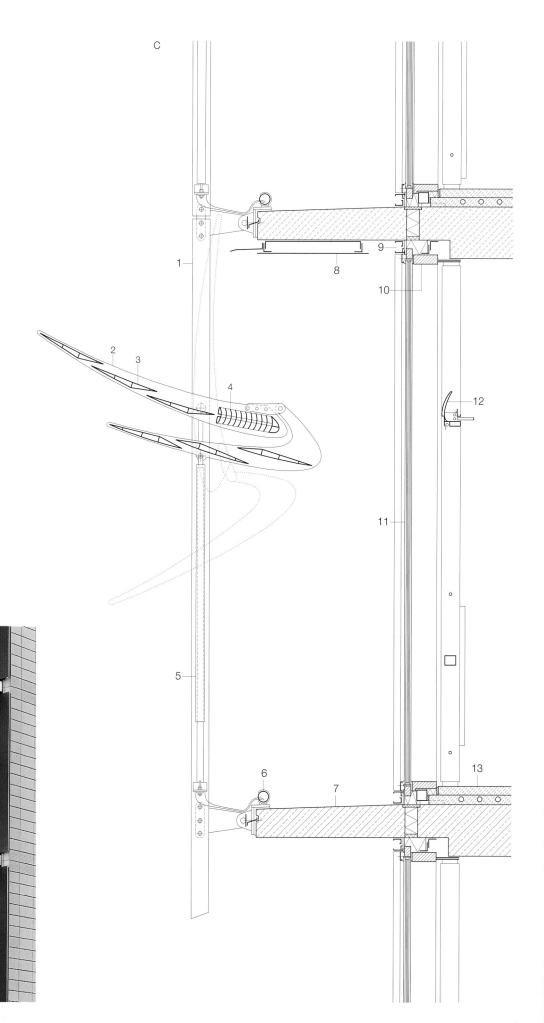

Sections through internal facade
scale 1:20

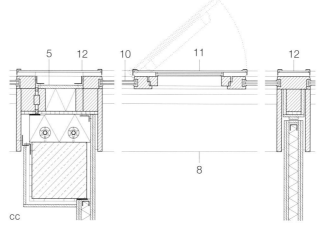

cc

Federal Environment Agency in Dessau

Architects: sauerbruch hutton, Berlin
Matthias Sauerbruch, Louisa Hutton
Juan Lucas Young, Jens Ludloff

Site plan   scale 1:5000
Floor plan · Sections   scale 1:2000

1 Forum
2 Lecture hall
3 Exhibition
4 Library (new building)
5 Old Wörlitz station
6 Atrium
7 Reception, meeting rooms
8 Connecting bridge

The Federal Environment Agency's new home in Dessau is a model project in innovative, energy-efficient architecture. 460 metres long from one end to the other, and providing workplaces for 800 people, the development traces a dynamic and colourful loop on this inner-city former railway site. In size and length this administration building sets itself apart from the surrounding heterogeneous, small-scale urban fabric. The curves of the facade, articulated in response to the differing situations around the site, and the doubling back of the loop, generate interesting spatial qualities inside and outside.

At one end a semi-circular forum with glass facade opens out to the surroundings; public events and exhibitions are held here. Behind it is the start of the landscaped inner courtyard, the space between the sides of the loop covered by an all-glass roof with integrated solar shading. On the outside, the facade is inspired in material and colour design by the idea of a continuous strip: 33 chromatically graded colours, from seven colour groups, are used around its circumference. Horizontal bands of larchwood parapet cladding wrap around the loop, between them lines of recessed windows interspersed with flush, colour-printed glass panels. Powder-coated steel sheet and stained aluminium louvres are used as cladding on the window reveals. Night-time ventilation of the offices is taken care of by means of automatically operating flaps behind opaque glass. By providing daylight and fresh air for the inward-facing offices, the atrium and forum also play a role in minimising energy consumption. Exhaust air passes out of the building through the folded plate roof running down the centre of the building. Further energy reductions, almost to the level of a passive-energy house, are achieved by making use of highly insulated walls, photovoltaic systems to generate power, and a large geothermal heat-exchange installation. Appropriately for the tenant of the building, the result is a successful blend of energy-efficient building with contemporary architectural design.

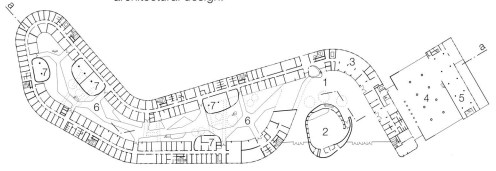

Ground floor

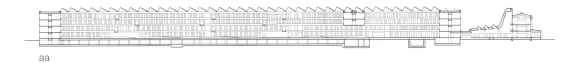

aa

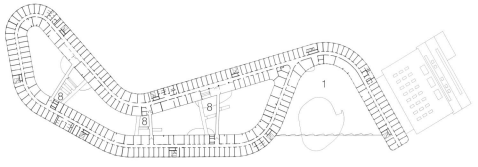

3rd floor

Sections through internal facade
scale 1:20

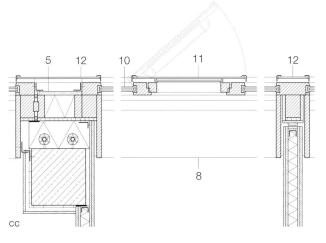

cc

170

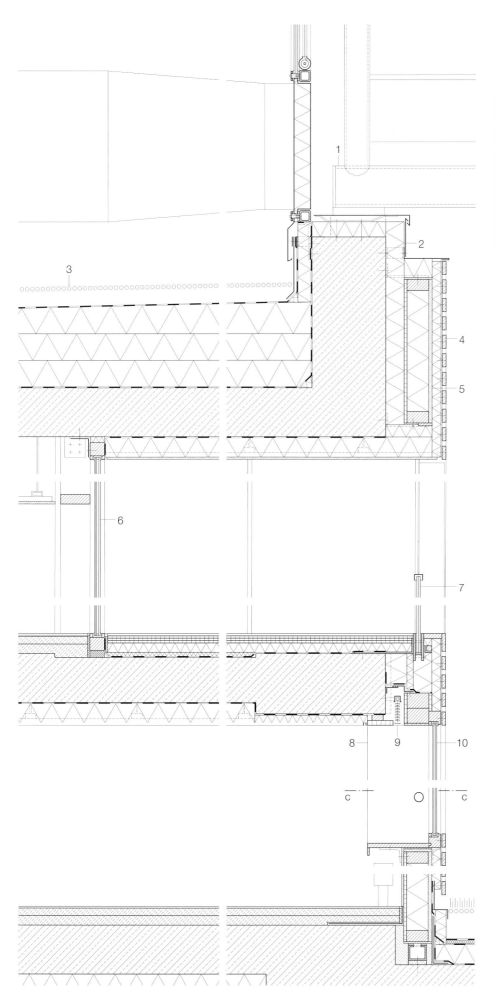

1 trussed girder of 219 mm dia./20 mm and
140 mm dia./12.5 mm steel tubes
2 2 mm sheet aluminium
50 mm mineral-wool thermal insulation
400 mm reinforced concrete
3 100 mm layer of gravel
two layers of 2 mm waterproof membrane
460 mm (max.) thermal insulation
sealing layer, 1.5 mm vapour barrier
260 mm reinforced concrete
4 20/70 mm larch strips on
30/50 mm wood battens
50 mm melamine-foam sound insulation
5 panel: 19 mm fibrous plasterboard
120/60 mm laminated timber frame
120 mm cellulose thermal insulation
16 mm OSB
6 double glazing in larch frame (U=1.2 W/m²K):
6 mm toughened glass + 16 mm cavity +
8 mm lam. safety glass
7 22 mm lam. safety glass balustrade
30/45/5 mm stainless-steel channel handrail
8 window reveal, 340/25 mm larch-veneered
composite wood board
9 25 mm louvred sunblind
10 double glazing in glazed larch frame
(U=1.2 W/m²K):
6 + 4 mm float glass + 16 mm cavity
11 stepped insulating glass in glazed larch
frame (U=1.2 W/m²K):
6 mm float glass with colour film on inside +
14 mm cavity + 4 mm float glass
12 8 mm toughened glass fascia with coloured
screen printing on the outside clamping strip

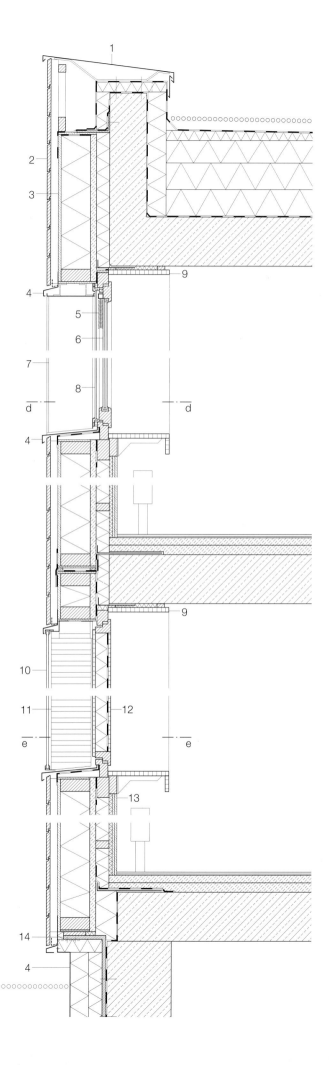

Sections through external facade
scale 1:20

1 cover plate:
  0.8 mm tin-plated sheet-copper
  two layers of bituminous seal
  72 mm mineral-fibre insulation
  vapour barrier
  200/650 mm reinforced concrete
2 20/150 mm larch strip
  40/40 mm wooden battens
  40 mm ventilated cavity
3 panel:
  15 mm fibrous plasterboard
  100/160 mm lam. timber studding
  160 mm cellulose-fibre
  29 mm cement and wood-fibre
  board
4 1 mm tin-plated sheet-copper
  drip
5 25 mm louvred sunblind
6 double glazing in wood frame
  glaze-finished larch,
  (U=0.8 W/m²K)
  2× 4 mm toughened glass +
  16 mm cavity

7 1.5 mm powder-coated steel
  sheet
8 8 mm toughened glass fascia
9 340/25 mm larch-veneered
  composite wood-board surround, with glazed finish
10 10 mm colour-enamelled toughened glass in 20 mm alum.
  channel frame
  52 mm ventilated cavity
11 aluminium ventilation grille,
  painted
12 electrically operated ventilation
  flap, 14 mm coated plywood
  vapour barrier, 70 mm cellulose
  14 mm larch-veneered plywood
13 2× 12.5 mm fibrous plasterboard
  90 mm cellulose insulation
  27 mm spring strips
  63 mm wood bearers
14 support, 240/500/20 mm stainless-steel angle
15 cladding, 23 mm larch-veneered
  composite
  wood board with a glazed finish
  40 mm cellulose insulation board

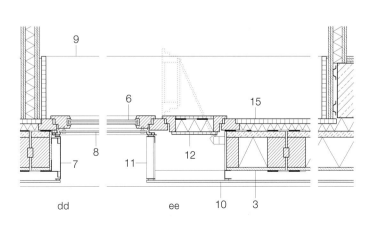

Museum of Hiroshige Ando in Batoh

Architects: Kengo Kuma and Associates, Tokyo

The wood louvres surround the long building volume like a veil. The trees in the surroundings are reflected in the facade, hinting at the glazing behind the cedar planks. The subtle skin contracts the building volume, its playful treatment of transparency, light and material elicits associations with the phenomenon of cloud formation – an accumulation of tiny droplets of water transformed into a visible, constantly shifting appearance solely by their density.

The museum is dedicated to Ando Hiroshige, a representative of the "Ukiyoe" style, famous in Japanese art history. The artist's works depict natural phenomena such as light, wind, rain and fog in an abstract manner. The method of capturing such ephemeral and complex phenomena in pictorial form has been applied to the design of the building. Set into a wooded environment, the mass of dense and uniformly arranged individual pieces of wood achieves the archetypal form of a house. The shape of the volumes contained within this transparent building skin is difficult to grasp, as the visual appearance of the spatial outlines shifts according to angle of light and mood. The timber screen laid openly across steel profiles fronts unframed glass panes, insulated concrete walls, sheet metal roofs, skylights and open passages. The degree of transparency and colour saturation shifts constantly depending on the angle of the sun and the weather, which transform the cedar skin into a transparent filter. In the interior, too, the playful treatment of glass surfaces, traditional paper room dividers and solid walls is an attractive ever-changing presence despite the great number of fully enclosed rooms.

Plan scale 1:1000

1 Parking area
2 Restaurant
3 Shop
4 Outdoor passage
5 Approach
6 Wind lobby
7 Hall
8 Training room
9 Exhibition
10 Office
11 Conference room
12 Machine room

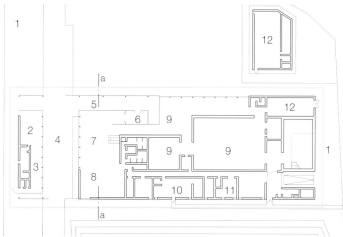

1 17.3 mm dia. galvanized steel tube
2 30/60 mm cedar battens
3 steel angle
4 50/70/6 mm steel angle
5 400/200/10 mm steel I-beam roof girder
6 bearing wood batten steel Z-section
7 10 mm dia. threaded rod
8 corrugated wire glass on steel sections
9 transverse girder, 400/200/10 mm steel
   I-section
10 toughened-glass skylight strip
11 ridge connection, steel stay

12 ridge girder, 160/80/5 mm steel I-section
13 suspended ceiling, 30/60 mm cedar battens
14 steel-angle glass fastener
15 toughened glass wall
16 floor track, steel profile
17 1200/240 mm natural stone slabs
18 10/40 mm galvanized steel flat
19 200 mm steel SHS
20 roof construction:
   30/60 mm cedar battens on steel sections
   galvanized sheet-metal
   standing-seam roof

   bituminous roofing layer
   35 mm rigid-foam insulation
   20 mm cement-bound hard particle board
21 wall construction:
   30/60 mm cedar battens on steel sections
   galvanized sheet-metal standing-seam
   elements
   bituminous insulating layer
   30 mm rigid-foam insulation
   18 mm cement-bound hard particle board
   200 mm reinforced-concrete wall
   gypsum board, painted

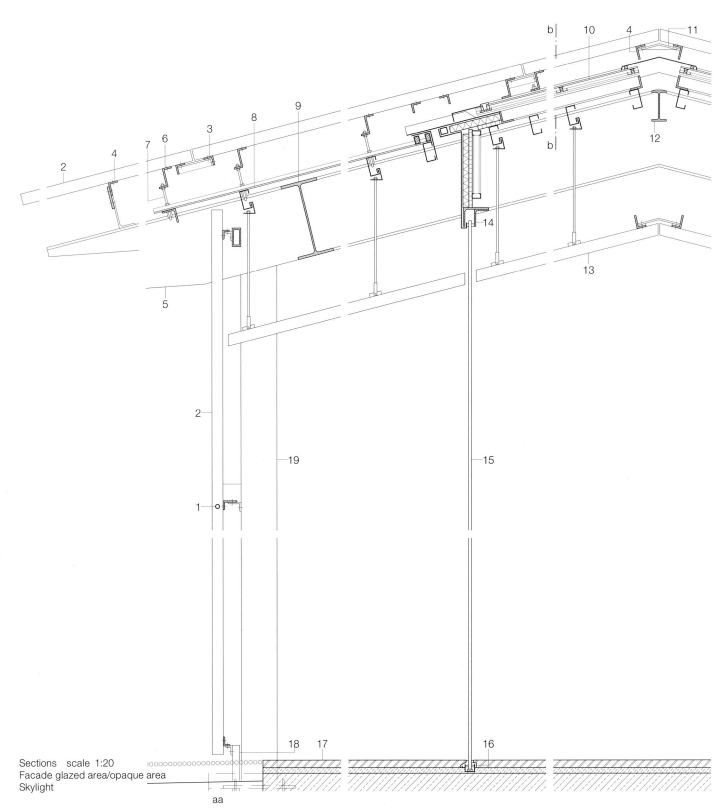

Sections   scale 1:20
Facade glazed area/opaque area
Skylight

176

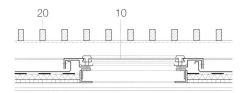

20   10

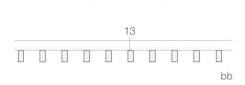

13

bb

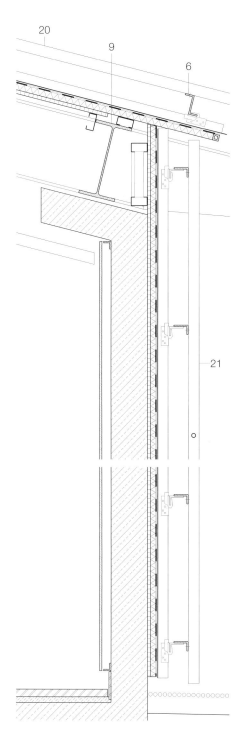

20

9

6

21

Passenger Shipping Terminal in Yokohama

Architects: Foreign Office Architects, London
Farshid Moussavi, Alejandro Zaera Polo

The international competition brief for Yokohama harbour specified a passenger shipping terminal that should also be accessible to the general public. The architects proposed the concept of a city gateway, interpreted in the form of a building with a roof surface inspired by the city's parks. Instead of taking up and reinforcing the linear structure of the existing pier, they based their design on a flow diagram of the movement of incoming and outgoing passengers. Pathways loop around inside the terminal while the building envelope itself traces a series of angles and curves. This lively form generates variously shaped interior spaces and opens up slits and trenches in the upper surface to function as entrances and exits. Inside and outside space, roof surfaces and interior levels, form a single smooth continuum. All floors are of untreated hardwood (ipé), like a giant ship's deck, the uppermost level doubling also as a public viewing platform and plaza, as well as providing passenger access and acting as a gateway for visitors.

Following investigation of various hybrid mesh and honeycomb structures, a steel folded-plate structure was chosen for the load-bearing structure, its powerful shapes creating a distinctive atmosphere in the main interior spaces. The rows of steel-plate space frames span up to 30 metres column-free and can absorb the kind of seismic forces experienced in Japan without damage. Although the overall form of the roof is complex, the number of repeating elements within it was maximised through careful arrangement of the segments, thus reducing the number of different types of connection required. Large parts of the structure were prefabricated and delivered to the site by boat. All the secondary elements, such as the raised timber decks and the handrails are attached to the main structure with connecting details that were easy to adapt to the complex building geometry at the various points. The long sides and the folds in the roof surface are fully glazed, the profiles minimised and positioned to maintain maximum transparency; the spacious wooden deck continues uninterrupted from end to end, interior and exterior space merging seamlessly into each other.

Site plan
scale 1:30000
Section · Top view of roof
scale 1:2500

178

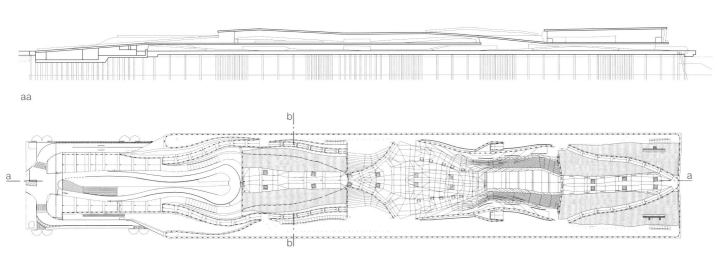

aa

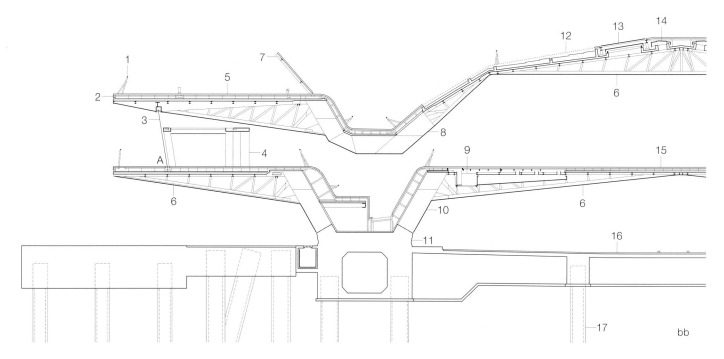

Cross section
scale 1:250

1 handrail
  stainless-steel profile
2 edging
  stainless-steel mesh
3 19 mm toughened glass
4 shop glazing
5 exterior timber deck:
  30 mm ipé wood
  60/60 mm wood bearers
  900 mm cavity
  25 mm thermal insulation
  polyurethane sealing layer
  reinforced-concrete floor
6 steel support structure
  with fire-resistant coating
7 200/200 mm steel I-section
  covered with 30 mm ipé boards
8 box girder
  welded from steel plate

9 services duct
10 longitudinal member welded
   from steel plate
11 reinforced concrete
12 planted roof:
   turf
   100–150 mm soil substrate
   height equalization
   rigid polystyrene foam
   50 mm rigid-foam drainage slab
   polythene sheeting
   polyurethane sealing layer
   on reinforced concrete floor
13 smoke-extract flap
14 ventilation aperture
15 interior timber deck:
   20 mm ipé wood
   60/45 mm wood bearers
   900 mm cavity
   15 mm fire-resistant panels
16 50 mm asphalt covering
17 reinforced-concrete foundation pile

Library in Delft

Architects: mecanoo architecten, Delft

The library has been conceived as a continuation of existing topography to avoid entering into visual competition with a dominant concrete structure from the 1960s. It pushes itself wedge-like beneath the surface of the lawn; its planted shell – on a concrete slab supported by concrete pillars – rises on an incline from the ground level and creates a public space, an ideal seating and sunbathing area: skin and landscape merge seamlessly. A central main access, whose incline is less steep, leads into the interior of the building in the form of a cone-shaped funnel.

From its highest point above the fifth floor, the rooftop landscape falls gently towards the eastern edge, supported by a series of slender columns. The angled facade construction is a recessed glass front that surrounds the library on three sides. The verdant ceiling slab is penetrated by a light cone, which allows natural light to fall into the central hall. Technical roof installations are unnecessary, since the groundwater is utilized as an energy source for climate control inside the building. The storage mass of the concrete roof slab and rainwater evaporation from the planted layer act to support the cooling. The double-facade construction also supports the natural ventilation and cooling of the interior. Air enters the intermediate space at the base and is vented at ceiling level.

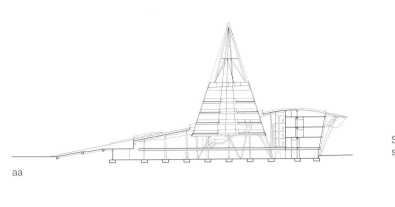

aa

Section · Plan
scale 1:1250

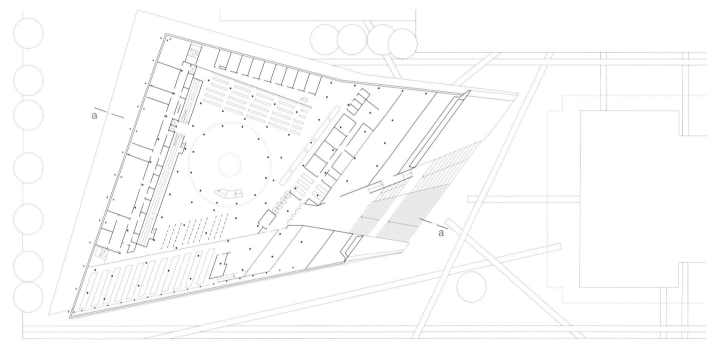

a

a

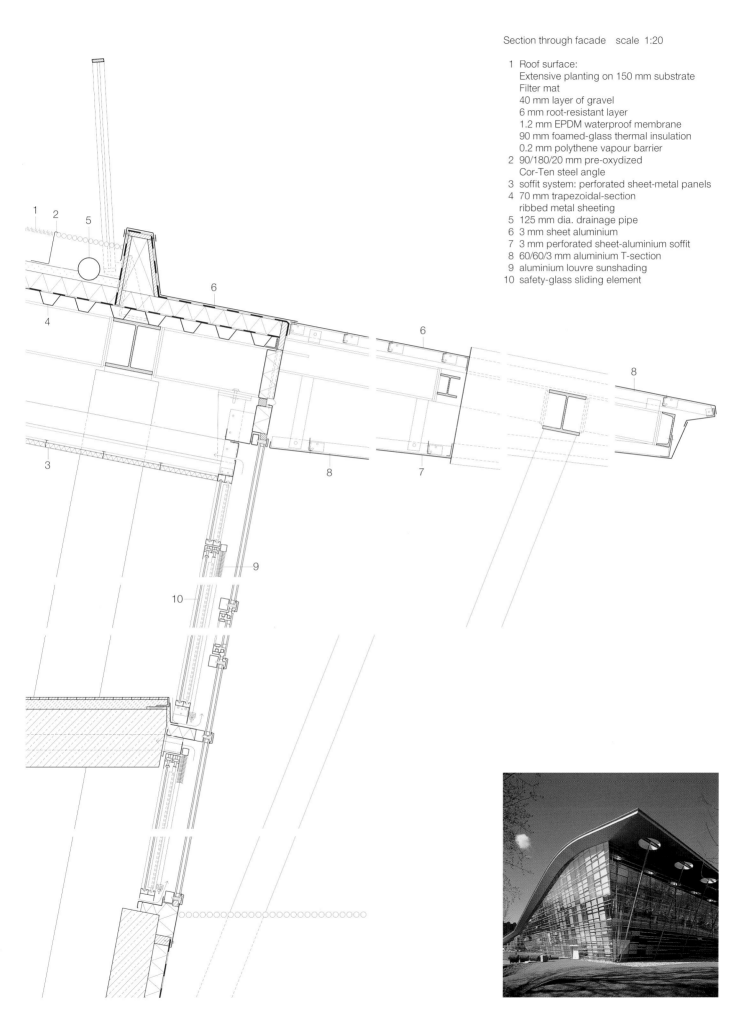

Section through facade   scale 1:20

1 Roof surface:
  Extensive planting on 150 mm substrate
  Filter mat
  40 mm layer of gravel
  6 mm root-resistant layer
  1.2 mm EPDM waterproof membrane
  90 mm foamed-glass thermal insulation
  0.2 mm polythene vapour barrier
2 90/180/20 mm pre-oxydized
  Cor-Ten steel angle
3 soffit system: perforated sheet-metal panels
4 70 mm trapezoidal-section
  ribbed metal sheeting
5 125 mm dia. drainage pipe
6 3 mm sheet aluminium
7 3 mm perforated sheet-aluminium soffit
8 60/60/3 mm aluminium T-section
9 aluminium louvre sunshading
10 safety-glass sliding element

185

Extension of Villa Garbald in Castasegna

Architects: Miller & Maranta, Basle

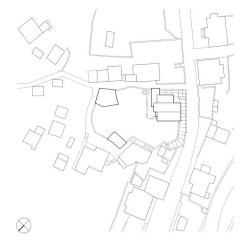

Castasegna is a small Swiss community on the border of Italy. One would hardly expect to find the southernmost building designed by Gottfried Semper there – a villa erected for the customs director Agostino Garbald. Today, the house is filled with new life, thanks to Garbald's deceased son, Andrea, who established a seminar centre for the arts, crafts and science in an endowment he laid down in his will. The University of Technology (ETH) in Zurich participated in financing the scheme and now uses the facilities together with the population of the surrounding area. Dating from the end of the 19th century, the villa has been carefully rehabilitated. At the northern end of the site, a former barn has made way for a new housing structure. Inspired by the north Italian bird catching towers known as *"roccoli"*, the new block rises up from the garden wall. An independent, non-rectlinear building was created, the coloration, surface qualities and manner of which help to integrate it subtly into its surroundings.

The outer walls of this *"roccolo"* are in exposed concrete. To bring out the aggregate, which was obtained from the river valley, and to enliven the surface texture, the concrete was sprayed with a high-pressure jet of water after the formwork was removed. The square openings distributed irregularly over the various faces of the block are shaded by larch shutters that can be pivoted upwards and outwards. Moss is slowly overgrowing the concrete, and the shutters are turning grey, so that the building will merge with the surrounding fabric of the village in the course of time. The structure is insulated internally with foamed glass.

Access to the entrance hall of this dwelling block is from the south. A large opening in the adjoining lounge faces on to the garden. The different storeys are offset in level, and the rooms, which alternate with seating recesses, are laid out about the central staircase. Having reached the room with a fireplace at the top, guests are rewarded with a grand panoramic view of the valley. Semper himself was unable to enjoy the outlook: he never visited Castasegna.

Site plan
scale 1:2000
Section
Layout plan at ground
floor level
scale 1:500

1 Entrance hall
2 Lounge
3 Room
4 Room with fireplace

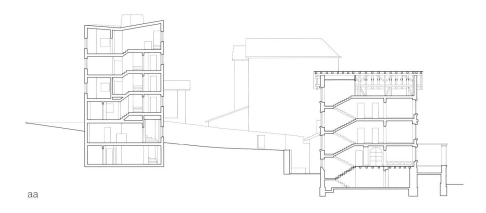

aa

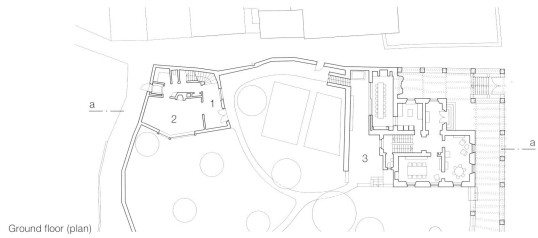

a

a

1

2

3

Ground floor (plan)

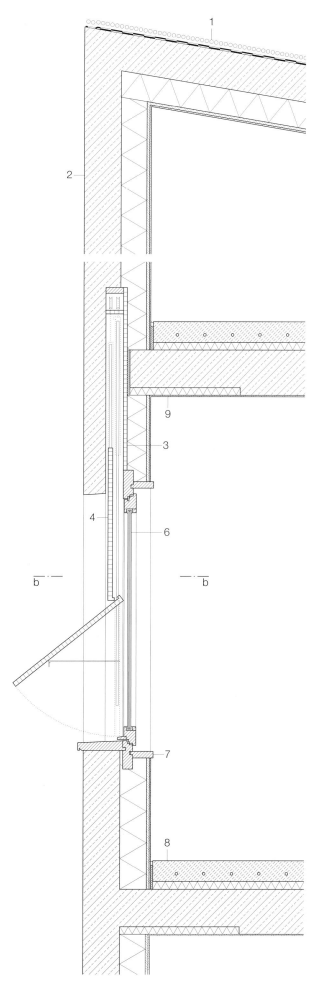

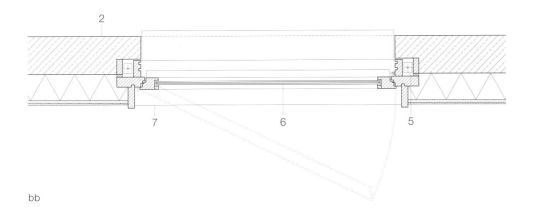

bb

Sections through new building
scale 1:20

1 roof construction:
10 mm layer of gravel in adhesive over
full area
two-layer bituminous seal
200 mm reinforced concrete roof
140 mm foamed-glass insulation
15 mm plasterboard
5 mm gypsum plaster
2 wall construction:
200 mm exposed concrete wall,
high-pressure sprayed
140 mm foamed-glass insulation
15 mm plasterboard
5 mm gypsum plaster
3 24 mm waterproof composite-wood
board
4 sliding shutter:
24 mm three-ply laminated larch sheeting
in metal guide tracks at sides
5 counterweight for shutter in wall recess
6 100/60 mm larch casement frame with
double glazing (U = 1.1 W/m²K):
2× 4 mm float glass + 16 mm cavity
7 35 mm larch window sill
8 floor construction:
110 mm granolithic screed with underfloor heating
40 mm impact-sound insulation
240 mm reinforced concrete floor
9 5 mm gypsum plaster

189

Academy of Music in Santiago de Compostela

Architects: Antón García-Abril, Madrid
Javier Cuesta

From a distance the Academy of Music looks like a giant block of stone set in Vista Alegre Park, near the centre of this town of pilgrimage. On closer inspection horizontal courses become visible, thick rough-hewn slabs of granite, punctuated by an irregular array of window slits. This rough texture enlivens the facade and gives rise to interesting light effects. But it is more than just a design feature: the markings were created when the blocks were bored out of the local quarry. As no further surface treatment was applied, it turned out to be a lasting and cost-effective solution, and one that tells the story of its extraction. Hidden behind this facade is the actual load-bearing structure of the building, a steel frame made of roll-formed and box profiles. Internally, a continuous vertical axis, narrowing towards the top, links all storeys and brings daylight into the interior. On the lower ground floor the space opens out into a broad foyer leading to the outside. This airy plinth seems at odds with the weighty cube above; seen from other angles the building merges seamlessly into the surrounding meadow. Granite is also the dominant material in the communication zones inside, but here used with a smooth, sawn surface. Arranged around this central space are practice rooms and offices, the concert hall and other rooms with acoustic specifications being located in the lower ground floor. The larger spaces at the bottom of the building give way to layouts divided into smaller units towards the top.

Floor plans • Sections scale 1:500	1 Seminar room	7 Balcony
	2 Main entrance	8 Rehearsal space for
	3 Office	chamber ensembles
A Lower ground floor	4 Void	9 Library
B Upper ground floor	5 Void over concert	10 Tutor's office
C 1st floor	hall	11 Individual practice
D 2nd floor	6 Foyer	rooms

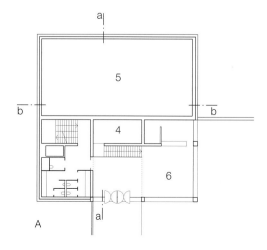

A

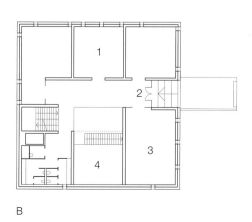

B

aa

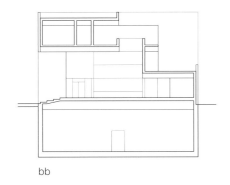

bb

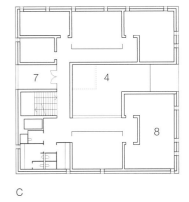

C

D

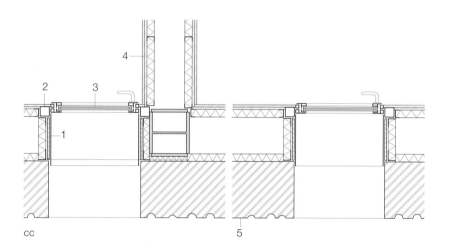

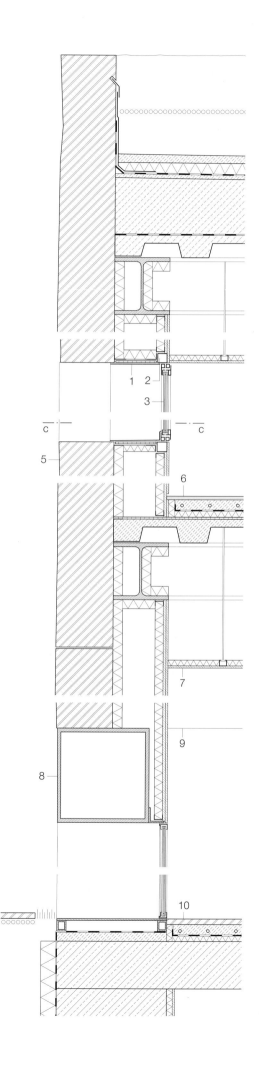

Horizontal section
Vertical section
scale 1:20

1 window reveal, 1.6 mm sheet-aluminium
  19 mm cement-bonded chipboard
  thermal insulation, 40 mm polyurethane
  foam
2 50/50/2 mm steel SHS
3 double glazing (6 + 6 + 4 mm)
  in aluminium frame
4 partition construction:
  2× 13 mm plasterboard,
  painted matte white
  40 mm rock-wool acoustic insulation
  between steel channels
  void/services space
5 wall construction:
  300 mm Mondariz granite blocks;
  courses 1750 mm high
  40 mm polyurethane-foam thermal
  insulation

190 mm void/services space
40 mm rock-wool thermal / acoustic
insulation between steel channels
2× 13 mm plasterboard,
painted matte white
6 22 mm solid oak flooring
7 suspended soffit:
  13 mm plasterboard,
  painted matte white
  40 mm rock-wool thermal/acoustic
  insulation between steel channels
8 steel-plate hollow beam with
  steel-plate stiffening
9 wall cladding in foyer:
  30/875/1750 mm Mondariz
  granite slabs
10 floor in foyer:
  20/875/875 mm Mondariz granite slabs

Documentation Centre in Hinzert

Client:
Land Rheinland-Pfalz, Landesbetrieb Liegenschafts- und Baubetreuung NL Trier, Landeszentrale für politische Bildung
Architects:
Wandel Hoefer Lorch + Hirsch, Saarbrücken
Project team:
Wolfgang Lorch, Nikolaus Hirsch, Andrea Wandel, Christine Biesel, Alexander Keuper
Structural engineers:
Schweitzer Ingenieure, Saarbrücken
Completion: 2005

Prof. Wolfgang Lorch,
Born 1960 in Nürtingen am Neckar; 2001–03 professorship at the Hochschule für Technik Stuttgart; since 2003 Professor of Building Design and Construction at the Technical University of Darmstadt.

Nikolaus Hirsch,
Born1964; studied at the Technical University of Darmstadt; since 2000 Unit Master at the AA London; since 2005 visiting professor at the University of Pennsylvania.

Andrea Wandel,
Born 1963 in Saarbrücken; studied architecture at the Technical University of Kaiserslautern, Technical University of Darmstadt.

House in Dornbirn

Client:
Siegfried Innauer
Architects:
Oskar Leo Kaufmann + Albert Rüf, Dornbirn
Team:
Sacha Vaucher
Structural engineers:
Norbert Gsteu, Feldkirch
Facade:
Hagn & Leone, Dornbirn
Completion: 2002

Oskar Leo Kaufmann
Born 1969 in Bregenz; 1995 diploma from the Technical University of Vienna; 1996 founded the Kaufmann 96 practice with Johannes Kaufmann; since 2001 Oskar Leo Kaufmann ZT GmbH; 2005 with Albert Rüf renamed the practice Oskar Leo Kaufmann / Albert Rüf ZT GmbH.

Albert Rüf
Born 1968 in Au; since 2005 in partnership with Oskar Leo Kaufmann in Oskar Leo Kaufmann / Albert Rüf ZT GmbH.

www.olkruf.com

Cycling Stadium in Berlin

Client:
OSB Sportstätten GmbH, Berlin
Architects:
Dominique Perrault, Paris
Reichert, Pranschke, Maluche, Munich
Schmidt-Schicketanz und Partner, Munich
Project architects:
Wolfgang Keuthage (cycling stadium),
Hella Rolfes (Swimming pool), Gebhard Weißenhorn (competition and commission)
Peter Edward (supervision)
Structural engineers:
Ove Arup und Partner, London/Berlin
Completion: 1998

Dominique Perrault
Born 1953 in Clermont-Ferrand; independent architecture office since 1981.

www.perraultarchitecte.com
www.rpm-architekten.de

Service Centre in Munich

Client:
Landeshauptstadt München, Baureferat München
Architects:
Staab Architekten, Berlin
Volker Staab, Alfred Nieuwenhuizen
Team:
Alexander Böhme, Madina von Arnim, Birgit Knicker, Helga Blocksdorf
Structural engineers:
CBP Cronauer Beratung und Planung, Munich
Facade:
KM Europa Metal AG, Osnabrück
Completion: 2004

Volker Staab
Born 1957 in Heidelberg; 1983 diploma from the ETH Zürich; since 1996 joint practice with Alfred Nieuwenhuizen; since 2002 various teaching posts; 2005 member of the Akademie der Künste Berlin.

Alfred Nieuwenhuizen
Born 1953 in Bocholt; 1984 diploma from the RWTH Aachen; since 1996 joint practice with Volker Staab.

www.staab-architekten.com

Museum Liner in Appenzell

Client:
Carl Liner Foundation, Father and Son
Architects:
Gigon / Guyer, Zurich
Annette Gigon, Mike Guyer
Staff:
Urs Birchmeier, Daniel Kaufmann
Structural engineers:
Aerni +Aerni, Zurich
Completion: 1998

Annette Gigon
Born 1959 in Herisau, Switzerland; independent architecture office since 1987; since 1989 in partnership with Mike Guyer.

Mike Guyer
Born 1958 in Ohio, USA; since 1987 teaching and independent architecture office; since 1989 in partnership with Annette Gigon.

www.gigon-guyer.ch

Administration Building in Heilbronn

Client:
Südwestmetall, Stuttgart
Architekt:
Dominik Dreiner, Gaggenau
Team:
Roger Gerber (project manager), Jochen Hien, Bianca Wildrich
Structural engineers:
Werner Sobek Ingenieure, Stuttgart
Facade design:
R + R Fuchs, Munich
Facade construction:
Klass Metall, Offenburg
Completion: 2004

Dominik Dreiner
Born 1966 in Rastatt; trained as a carpenter; studied architecture in Konstanz; founded the architectural practice of Dominik Dreiner 1998 in Gaggenau following periods abroad in Europe, Canada and the US.

www.dominikdreiner.de

Glasgow Science Centre

Client:
Glasgow Science Centre Limited
Architects:
Building Design Partnership, Glasgow
Project architects:
Colin Allan, Andrea Borland, David Craig, Neil Crawford, Mark Dennis, Peter Dunne, Alistair Elder (facade) Sandy Ferguson, Fraser Harle, Sandy Hendry, Andy McCrory, Gareth Maguire, Marnie Macdonald, Andrew Morrison, Paul Smith, Keith Stephen, Andrew Stupart
Structural engineers:
WA Fairhurst, Glasgow
Facade:
Mero System GmbH, Würzburg
Completion: 2000

BDP
Founded in 1961.

Colin C. Allan
Born 1953; independent architect since 1979; since 1983 with BDP and since 1997 as managing director.

www.bdp.co.uk

Pavilion in Amsterdam

Client:
Woningcorporatie Het Oosten
Architects:
Steven Holl Architects, New York
Rappange & Partners, Amsterdam
Project architects:
Steven Holl, Justin Korhammer, Bart Kwant, Bert Wever
Structural engineers:
van Rossum, Amsterdam
Lighting design:
L'Obervatoire international, New York
Completion: 2000

Steven Holl
Born 1947 in Bremerton, Washington;
Foundation of independent architecture office in 1976; since 1981 teacher, lecturer and visiting professor at various universities

www.stevenholl.com

Micro-Compact Home in Munich

Client:
Studentenstadt München e.V.
Architects:
Horden Cherry Lee, London
Haack + Höpfner, Munich,
Team: T. Dietsch, S. Koch
Structural engineers:
Brengelmann Ingenieure, Munich
Concept i-home:
Prof. Richard Horden, Technical
University of Munich, Lehrstuhl für
Gebäudelehre und Produktent-
wicklung
Supervisors: L. Haack, W. Klasz
Studenten: V. Blacker-Sturm,
V. Gruber, C. Hainzlmeier, S. Koch,
B. Matern, D. Oswald, M. Penev,
W. Seidler, T. Tuhkanen
Completion: 2005

Richard Horden
Born 1944; since1996 professor at
the Technical University of Munich;
since 1999 Horden Cherry Lee
Architects, London.

Lydia Haack
Born 1965 in Hof/Saale; since 1996
Lydia Haack + John Höpfner
Architekten BDA, Munich.

John Höpfner
Born 1963 in Munich; since 1996
Lydia Haack + John Höpfner
Architekten BDA, Munich.

www.hcla.co.uk
www.haackhoepfner.com

A Summer Space

Client:
Student project at the TU Berlin,
Institute of Design, Construction
and Urban Planning,
Chair Prof. Dietrich Fink
Design:
Michael Johl, Radoslaw C. Jozwiak
Cosmas Ph. Th. Ruppel
Supervision:
Andrew Alberts, Katharina
Feldhusen, Oliver Heckmann,
Regine Siegel
Staff, execution:
El-Agha, Bergenthal,
Arndt, Dzendzel, Eynern, Fink,
Isrusch, de Grossi, Hermann,
Hess, Melenk, Mikkelsan, Pavic,
Radunski, Raizberg, Türk
Completion: 2000

Michael Johl
Born 1975 in Flensburg;
Trained carpenter.

Radoslaw Cezary Jozwiak
Born 1978 in Kovary, Poland.

Cosmas Ph. Th. Ruppel
Born 1977 in Bochum.

Allianz Arena in Munich

Client:
Allianz Arena München-Stadion
GmbH
Architects:
Herzog & de Meuron, Basel
Jacques Herzog, Pierre de Meuron,
Robert Hösl, Harry Gugger,
Tim Hupe
Structural engineers:
Arup, Manchester
Sailer Stepan Partner, Munich
Kling Consult, Krumbach
Walter Mory Maier, Basel
IB Haringer, Munich
Completion: 2005

Jacques Herzog
Born 1950 in Basel; since 1978 in
partnership with Pierre de Meuron;
since 1999 professor at the ETH
Zürich, ETH-Studio Basel; since
2002 Institut Stadt der Gegenwart.

Pierre de Meuron
Born 1950; since 1978 in partner-
ship with Jacques Herzog; since
1999 professor at the ETH Zürich,
ETH-Studio Basel; since 2002
Institut Stadt der Gegenwart.

Factory Hall in Bobingen

Client:
Kaufmann Holz AG, Bobingen
Architects:
Florian Nagler Architekten, Munich
Staff:
Stefan Lambertz, Matthias Müller,
Barbara Nagler
Structural engineers:
Merz Kaufmann Partner, Dornbirn
Konrad Merz, Gordian Kley,
Hansueli Bühlmann
Completion: 1999

Florian Nagler
Born 1967 in Munich;
apprenticeship as a carpenter;
independent architecture office
since 1996; 2002 visiting professor
at the Royal Danish Academy in
Copenhagen; 2005–06 visiting
professor at the Hochschule für
Technik Stuttgart.

www.nagler-architekten.de

Selfridges Department Store in Birmingham

Client:
Selfridges, London
Architects:
Future Systems, London
Structural engineers:
Arup, London
Facade design:
Arup, London
Completion: 2003

Jan Kaplicky
Born 1937; 1962 diploma from the
College of Applied Arts &
Architecture, Prague; since 1964
independent architect; since 1979
Future Systems in London.

Amanda Levete
Born 1955; 1982 diploma from the
Architectural Association, London;
since 1989 Future Systems in
London.

www.future-systems.com

Eden Project near St. Austell

Client:
Eden Project, Cornwall
Architects:
Nicholas Grimshaw & Partners,
London
Project architect:
Andrew Whalley
Staff:
Jolyon Brewis, Michael Pawlyn,
Perry Hooper, William Horgan,
Oliver Konrath
Structural engineers:
Anthony Hunt, Cirencester
Completion: 2000

Nicholas Grimshaw
Since 1965 active as an independent architect; from 1980 onwards
Nicholas Grimshaw & Partners;
guest lectures at international
universities.

www.ngrimshaw.co.uk
www.edenproject.com

Japanese Pavilion in Hanover

Client:
JETRO Japan External Trade
Organization, Berlin
Architects:
Shigeru Ban Architects, Tokyo
Staff:
Nobutaka Hiraga, Shigeru Hiraki,
Jun Yashiki
Structural engineers:
Büro Happold, Berlin
Structural consultant:
Frei Otto, Warmbronn
Completion: 2000

Shigeru Ban
Born 1957 in Tokyo;
independent architect since 1985;
2000 visiting professor in New York,
since 2001 professor in Tokyo.

www.shigerubanarchitects.com

House in Zurndorf

Client:
Bettina Stimeder
Architects:
PPAG Architekten, Vienna
Anna Popelka, Georg Poduschka
Team:
Sandra Janser, Corinna Toell,
Klaus Moldan
Structural engineers:
M-Baugesellschaft, Wieselburg
Completion: 2005

Anna Popelka
1987 diploma from the Technical
University of Graz; since 1995
PPAG Popelka Poduschka
Architekten.

Georg Poduschka
1986–94 studied at the Technical
University of Graz and at the Ecole
d'Architecture Paris-Tolbiac; since
1995 PPAG Popelka Poduschka
Architekten.

www.ppag.at

House near Tokyo

Client:
private
Architects:
Shigeru Ban Architects, Tokyo
Project architects:
Shigeru Ban, Anne Scheou,
Mamiko Ishida
Structural engineers:
Hoshino Architects and Engineers
Completion: 2000

Shigeru Ban
Born 1957 in Tokyo;
independent architect since 1985;
2000 visiting professor in New York,
since 2001 professor in Tokyo.

www.shigerubanarchitects.com

Church in Munich

Client:
Catholic Church Foundation of the
Sacred Heart,
represented by the bishopric of
Munich
Architects:
Allmann Sattler Wappner
Architekten, Munich
Markus Allmann, Amandus Sattler,
Ludwig Wappner
Staff:
Karin Hengher, Susanne Rath,
Annette Gall, Michael Frank
Structural engineers:
Ingenieursgesellschaft mbH Hagl,
Munich
Facade construction:
Brandl Metallbau, Eitensheim
Completion: 2000

Markus Allmann
Born 1959 in Ludwigshafen/
Rhine; 1987 co-founder of
Allmann Sattler, Architekten.

Amandus Sattler
Born 1957 in Marktredwitz;
1987 co-founder of
Allmann Sattler, Architekten.

Ludwig Wappner
Born 1957 in Hösbach;
since 1993 partnership with Allmann
Sattler Wappner Architekten.

www.allmannsattlerwappner.de
www.herzjesu-muenchen.de

Trade-Fair Tower in Hanover

Client:
Deutsche Messe AG, Hanover
Architects:
Herzog + Partner, Munich
Thomas Herzog,
Hanns Jörg Schrade
Project architect:
Roland Schneider
Staff:
Nico Kienzl, Christian Schätzke,
Thomas Straub, Brigitte Tacke,
Stephanie Zierl
Structural engineers:
Sailer Stepan und Partner,
Hanover
Facade construction:
Seufert-Niklaus, Bastheim (wood)
Magnus Müller, Butzbach (metal)
Trauco Spezialbau (brick)
Completion: 1999

Thomas Herzog
Born 1941 in Munich; independent
office since 1971; since 1974
professor – since 1993 at the
Technical University Munich.

Hanns Jörg Schrade
Born 1951 in Stuttgart; since 1994
partnership with Thomas Herzog.

www.herzog-und-partner.de

Federal Environment Agency in Dessau

Client:
Bundesrepublik Deutschland,
Bundesministerium für Verkehr,
Bau- und Wohnwesen Berlin
Architects:
sauerbruch hutton, Berlin, Matthias
Sauerbruch, Louisa Hutton,
Juan Lucas Young, Jens Ludloff
Project management:
Andrew Kiel, René Lotz
Structural engineers:
Krebs und Kiefer, Berlin
Energy concept, building services:
Zibell Willner & Partner, Köln/Berlin
Completion: 2005

Matthias Sauerbruch
Born 1955 in Konstanz; since 1989
joint practice with Louisa Hutton;
from 1995 professor at various
universities.

Louisa Hutton
Born 1957 in Norwich; from 1989
partnership with Matthias Sauerbruch; 2005 visiting professor.

Juan Lucas Young
Born 1963 in Buenos Aires; since
1999 partner at sauerbruch hutton.

Jens Ludloff
Born 1964 in Haan; since 1999
partner at sauerbruch hutton.

www.sauerbruchhutton.com

Prada Flagship Store in Tokyo

Client:
Prada Japan Co., Tokio
Architects:
Herzog & de Meuron, Basel
Staff:.
Stefan Marbach, Reto Pedrocchi,
Wolfgang Hardt, Hiroshi Kikuchi,
Yuko Himeno, Shinya Okuda,
Daniel Pokora, Mathis Tinner, Luca
Andrisani, Andreas Fries, Georg
Schmid
Structural engineers:
Takenaka Corporation, Tokio
WGG Schnetzer Puskas, Basel
Facade design:
Emmer Pfenninger Partner AG,
CH-Münchenstein
Completion: 2003

Jacques Herzog
Born 1950 in Basel; since 1978 in
partnership with Pierre de Meuron;
since 1999 professor at the ETH
Zürich, ETH-Studio Basel; since
2002 Institut Stadt der Gegenwart.

Pierre de Meuron
Born 1950; since 1978 in partner-
ship with Jacques Herzog; since
1999 professor at the ETH Zürich,
ETH-Studio Basel; since 2002
Institut Stadt der Gegenwart.

Administration Building in Kronberg

Client:
Braun AG, Kronberg
Architects:
Schneider + Schumacher,
Frankfurt/Main
Till Schneider,
Michael Schumacher
Project architect:
Stefano Turri
Staff:
Thomas Zürcher, Diane Wagner,
Britta Heiner, Torsten Schult,
Karoline Dina Sievers, Niko
Alexopoulos, Stefan Goeddertz
Structural engineers:
Bollinger + Grohmann,
Frankfurt/Main
Building services:
Ove Aup, Berlin
Completion: 2000

Till Schneider
Born 1959 in Koblenz;
since 1989 partnership with
Michael Schumacher.

Michael Schumacher
Born 1957 in Krefeld; since 1989
partnership with Till Schneider;
1999 visiting professor in Frankfurt/
Main.

www.schneider-schumacher.com

Administration Building in Wiesbaden

Client:
Zusatzversorgungskasse des
Baugewerbes VVaG
Architects:
Herzog + Partner, Munich
Thomas Herzog,
Hanns Jörg Schrade
Project architect:
Klaus Beslmüller
Staff:
Fissan (Facade planning),
Schmid (Planning supervision),
Bathke, Berg, Braun, Bürklein,
Dicke, Donath, Frazzlca, Geisel,
Grüner, Hefele, Heinlin, Kal-
tenbach, Kaufmann, Madeddu,
Schankula, Scholze, Sinning,
Stocker, Volz, Wiegel, Zengler
Energy concept:
Kaiser Consult
Prof. Dr. Eng. Hausladen
Prof. Dr. Eng. Oesterle, DS-Plan
Lighting planning:
Bartenbach Lichtlabor
Completion: 2001

Biographies, see previous project.

www.herzog-und-partner.de

Museum of Hiroshige Ando in Batoh

Client:
Bato machi
Architects:
Kengo Kuma and Associates,
Tokyo
Ando Architecture Design Office
Staff:
Shoji Oshio, Susumu Yasukouchi,
Toshio Yada, Hiroshi Nakamura,
Yoshinori Sakano, Takeshi Goto,
Ryusuke Fujieda design team,
Ando Architects - Masami Nakatsu,
Takashi Shibata
Structural engineers:
Aoki Structural Engineers
Completion: 2000

Kengo Kuma
Born 1954 in Kanagawa
Prefecture; independent since
1987;
since 1990 Kengo Kuma and
Associates; professor at Keio
University 1998 and 1999.

www.kkaa.co.jp

Passenger Shipping Terminal in Yokohama

Client:
Port & Harbour Bureau, Yokohama
Architects:
Foreign Office Architects, London
Farshid Moussavi, Alejandro Zaera
Polo
Team (construction):
Shokan Endo, Kazutoshi Imanaga,
Kensuke Kishikawa, Yasuhisa
Kikushi, Izumi Kobayashi, Kenichi
Matsuzawa, Tomofumi Nagayama,
Xavier Ortiz, Lluis Viu Rebes,
Keisuke Tamura
Structural engineers:
Structure Design Group, London
Arup, London
Completion: 2002

Farshid Moussavi
1992 founded Foreign Office
Architects in London; since 2006
professor at the Harvard University
Graduate School of Design.

Alejandro Zaera Polo
1992 founded Foreign Office
Architects in London; 2002–06
dean of the Berlage Institute in
Rotterdam.

www.f-o-a.net

Library in Delft

Client:
ING Vastgoed Ontwikkeling b.v.,
Den Haag
TU Delft Vastgoedbeheer, Delft
ING Vastgoed Ontwikkeling b.v.,
Den Haag
Architects:
mecanoo architecten, Delft
Project architects:
Francine Houben, Chris de Weijer
Structural engineers:
ABT adviesbureau voor bouw-
techniek b.v., Delft
Completion: 1997

Francine Houben
Born 1955 in Sittard,
the Netherlands; 1984 founding
member of mecanoo;
professor at Mendrisio and Delft.

www.mecanoo.nl

Extension of Villa Garbald in Castasegna

Client:
n.n.
Architect:
Miller & Maranta, Basel
Team:
Jean-Luc von Aarburg (project man-
ager), Sabine Rosenthaler, Tanja
Schmid, Julia Rösch, Urs Meng
(construction manager)
Structural engineers:
Conzett/Bronzini/Gartmann, Chur
Completion: 2004

Quintus Miller
Born 1961 in Aarau;
1987 diploma from the ETH Zürich;
2000–2001 visiting professor at the
ETH Lausanne; since 2004 member
of the Buildings Commission of the
City of Lucerne; since 2005 member
of the Historical Buildings Commission of the City of Zürich.

Paola Maranta
Born 1959 in Chur; 1986 diploma
from the ETH Zürich; 1990 Master
of Business Administration at the
Institute for Management Development in Lausanne; 2000–2001
visiting professor at the ETH
Lausanne.

1994 founded the architectural
practice of Miller & Maranta.

www.millermaranta.ch

Academy of Music in Santiago de Compostela

Client:
Consorcio de la Ciudad de
Santiago, Santiago de Compostela
Architects:
Antón García-Abril, Madrid
Javier Cuesta (construction)
Team:
Ensamble Studio: Bernardo
Angelini, Eduardo Martín Asuncíon,
Arantxa Osés, Débora Mesa,
Andrés Toledo, Guillermo Sevillano
Structural engineers:
Antonio Reboreda, Vigo
Completion: 2002

Antón García-Abril
Born 1969 in Madrid; 1995 diploma,
2000 doctorate from the ETSA
Madrid; 1995 founded the practice
Antón García-Abril Ruiz; 2000
founded the practice Ensamble
Studio; 1997–2006 numerous
teaching commissions at various
universities.

Javier Cuesta Rodríguez-Torices
Born 1973 in Madrid; 1995 diploma
from the EUAT Madrid; 2000
Ensamble Studio.

www.ensamble.info

Authors

Christian Schittich (editor)

Born 1956
Studied architecture at University of Technology, Munich,
followed by seven years' office experience and work as
journalist,
from 1991 editorial board of DETAIL, Review of Architecture,
from 1992 responsible editor,
since 1998 editor-in-chief.
Author and editor of numerous textbooks and articles.

Werner Lang

Born 1961
Studies in architecture at Technical University Munich,
Architectural Association, London and at the University of
California, Los Angeles
B.A. 1988
M.A. Architecture (UCLA) 1990
1990 bis 1994 architectural practice of Kurt Ackermann +
Partner
1994 to 2001 assistant at Technical University, Munich
Promotion 2000
2001 architectural practice of Werner Lang in Munich
since 2006 Lang Hugger Rampp Architekten.

Roland Krippner

Born 1960
Trained machinist
Studies in architecture at the Polytechnic Kassel
1993 to 1995, independent practice
since 1995 staff member in the science department at the
Technical University, Munich,
Dept. of Building Technology, doctorate in 2004
Publications and contributions since 1994
Lecturer at Salzburg University of Applied Sciences and the
University of Kassel.

Illustration credits

The authors and editor wish to extend their sincere thanks to all those who helped to realize this book by making illustrations available. All drawings contained in this volume have been specially prepared in-house. Photos without credits are form the architects' own archives or the archives of "DETAIL, Review of Architecture". Despite intense efforts, it was not possible to identify the copyright owners of certain photos and illustrations. Their rights remain unaffected, however, and we request them to contact us.

from photographers, photo archives and image agencies:

- Allianz Arena, Munich: p. 65 top, 115
- Angewandte Solarenergie – ASE GmbH, Putzbrunn: 3.7
- Ano, Daici/Nacása & Partners Inc., Tokyo: 2.15, pp. 140–141
- Barnes, Richard, San Francisco: p. 8
- Bereuter, Adolf, Lauterach: pp. 63 top left and bottom left, 76–79
- Betts, Michael/view/artur, Cologne: p. 64 bottom left
- Bitter, Jan, Berlin: 1.36, p. 169
- Braun, Zooey/artur, Cologne: 1.18
- Bredt, Marcus, Berlin: 3.12
- Brunner, Arnold, Freiburg: p. 46
- Burt, Simon/Apex, Exminster: p. 113
- Cook, Peter/view/artur, Cologne: p. 112
- Davies, Richard, London: pp. 104–107, 109
- Denancé, Michel, Paris: p. 67 bottom right
- Esch, Hans-Georg, Hennef: 2.10
- Feiner, Ralph, Malans: p. 28
- Fink, Dietrich, TU Berlin: pp. 110 top and bottom, 111
- Fotoarchiv Hirmer Verlag, Munich: 1.32
- Hagemann, Ingo B., Aix-la-Chapelle: 3.9
- Halbe, Roland/artur, Cologne: 3.4, pp. 69 right, 190–193
- Hamm, Hubertus, Munich: p. 114
- Heinrich, Michael, Munich: 1.33
- Helfenstein, Heinrich, Zurich, pp. 74–75
- Hempel, Jörg, Aix-la-Chapelle: pp. 151–153, 155–157
- Hevia, José, Barcelona: 1.23
- Hirai, Hiroyuki, Tokyo: pp. 135–137
- Holzherr, Florian, Munich: 1.15, pp. 143, 147

- Hunter, Keith/arcblue.com: pp. 92–93
- Huthmacher, Werner, Berlin: pp. 61 bottom right, 63 bottom right, 87, 89, 91, 94–95, 97
- Janzer, Wolfram/artur, Cologne: p. 127
- Kaltenbach, Frank, Munich: 1.39, pp. 65 bottom, 120, 144, 149, 171–173
- Keller, Andreas, Altdorf: 3.10
- Kisling, Annette, Berlin: 2.14, p. 170
- Kletzsch, Sascha, Munich: pp. 102–103
- Koppelkamm, Stefan, Berlin: 1.7
- Korn, Moritz/artur, Cologne: pp. 162–163
- Krase Waltraud, Frankfurt: 2.13 right
- Krippner, Roland, Munich: 3.2
- Lang, Werner, Munich: 2.2, 2.11
- Leistner, Dieter/artur, Cologne: pp. 159–161
- Malagamba, Duccio, Barcelona: p. 119
- Marburg, Johannes, Berlin: 1.16, pp. 62, 66 left, 80–83, 85
- Meyer, Constantin, Cologne: 3.11
- Miguletz, Norbert, Frankfurt: pp. 61 top left, middle and bottom left, 70–73
- Mishima, Satoru, Tokyo: pp. 178, 181 top
- MM Video-Fotowerbung, Kaufungen / Josef Gartner GmbH, Gundelfingen: 2.13 left
- Müller, Alfred/IHK, Munich: 2.12
- Müller-Naumann, Stefan/artur, Cologne: pp. 128, 130 bottom, 131
- Nikolic, Robertino/artur, Cologne: p. 165
- Ott, Thomas, Mühltal: pp. 166–167
- Ouwerkerk, Erik-Jan, Berlin: p. 61 top right, 90
- Passoth, Jens, Berlin: 3.3
- Pictor Interntional: 1.43
- Richters, Christian, Münster: pp. 68 bottom left, 125, 139, 145–146, 182–185
- Schittich, Christian, Munich: 1.2, 1.4, 1.8, 1.13, 1.17, 1.21, 1.22, 1.25, 1.26, 1.27, 1.28, 1.31, 1.40, 1.42, 2.3, 2.4, 2.6, 2.7, pp. 67 bottom left, 121–124, 126, 148
- Shinkenchiku-sha, Tokyo: 1.30, 1.37, 1.38, pp. 134, 174–175, 177, 179, 180–181 bottom
- Spiluttini, Margherita, Vienna: 1.24, 1.35, pp. 64 bottom right, 132
- Suzuki, Hisao, Barcelona: p. 68 bottom right
- Takenaka Corporation, Tokyo: p. 66 right

- Walti, Ruedi, Basle: 1.19, pp. 186–189
- Warchol, Paul, New York: pp. 98–101
- Wiegelmann, Andrea, Munich: p. 67 top right
- Young, Nigel, Kingston-upon-Thames: 3.5, 3.6
- Zentrum für Sonnenenergie und Wasserstoff-Forschung, Baden-Württemberg: 3.8
- Zwerger, Klaus, Vienna: 1.3

from books and journals:

- Ackermann, Marion and Neumann, Dietrich (Ed): Leuchtende Bauten: Architektur der Nacht, Stuttgart 2006, p. 131: 1.41
- Daidalos, No. 66, 1997, p. 85: 1.6
- Gebhard, Helmut: Besser bauen im Alltag, Munich 1982, pp.8/9: 2.8, 2.9
- Piano, Renzo: Building Workshop, Volume 1, Stuttgart 1994, p. 3: 2.5
- Stephan, Regina (Ed.): Erich Mendelsohn, Gebaute Welten, Ostfildern-Ruit 1998, p. 95: 1.34
- Sullivan, Louis: The function of ornament, 1986, p. 69: 1.9; p. 93: 1.10

Articles and introductory b/w photos:

- p. 8; Dominus Winery, California, USA; Herzog & de Meuron, Basle
- p. 28; Teachers' Training College in Chur, Switzerland; Bearth + Deplazes, Chur
- p. 46; Office Building at the Main Station in Freiburg, Germany; Harter + Kanzler, Freiburg

Dust-jacket photo:
Prada Aoyama Centre in Tokyo
Architects: Herzog & de Meuron, Basle
Photo: Christian Richters, Münster